100 THINGS
BRUINS FANS
SHOULD KNOW & DO
BEFORE THEY DIE

Matt Kalman

TRIUMPH
BOOKS

Triumph Books and colophon are registered trademarks of Random House, Inc.

Library of Congress Cataloging-in-Publication Data

Kalman, Matt, 1975–

100 things Bruins fans should know & do before they die / Matt Kalman—2nd ed.

p. cm.

ISBN 978-1-60078-699-0

1. Boston Bruins (Hockey team)—History. 2. Boston Bruins (Hockey team)—Miscellanea. I. Title. II. Title: One hundred things Bruins fans should know and do before they die.

GV848.B6K35 2011

796.962'640974461—dc23

2011028478

This book is available in quantity at special discounts for your group or organization. For further information, contact:

Triumph Books
542 South Dearborn Street
Suite 750
Chicago, Illinois 60605
(312) 939-3330 | Fax (312) 663-3557
www.triumphbooks.com

Printed in U.S.A.
ISBN: 978-1-60078-699-0
Design by Patricia Frey
All photos courtesy of Getty Images unless otherwise specified

To my wife Amy, for always believing in me

Contents

Foreword by Mike Milbury ix

1 No. 4 Bobby Orr 1

2 Eddie Shore Hockey................................... 8

3 Bourque Carried on D Legacy 12

4 Father of the Bruins 16

5 Small Garden, Big Memories 20

6 Believe in the '11 Bruins 24

7 Mr. Bruin.. 29

8 Phil Esposito: The Babe Ruth of Hockey.............. 33

9 1969–1970: Big, Bad...and Champs 36

10 Ross Was the "Godfather" 39

11 Lack of Spending Sullies Sinden's Reputation........ 41

12 Chief 47

13 Taz 51

14 Bench Minor Leads to Major Collapse in '79.......... 54

15 Espo Enters... 57

16 The First Cup....................................... 60

17 ...Espo's Out 63

18 The Goal 66

19 Neely Was Nails Tough............................... 69

20 The Photo 73

21 "Cheesie" Was on the Money.......................... 75

22 Willie O'Ree: Hockey's Jackie Robinson.............. 78

23 Cup Mini-Drought Ends in '39 81

24 Cam Comes to Boston................................. 84

25 Dit 86

26 Bourque Makes Espo's Night 89

27 Starving for Stanley Since '72 91

28 Being a Bruin Means Being Big and Bad 96

29 "Lunch Pail A.C." Carried the Post-Orr Mantle 100

30 Cam Was the "Comeback Kid" 103

31 Mr. Zero 106

32 Chara Writes Own Tall Tales in Hub 108

33 Cowboy 112

34 Tiny 115

35 '72 Success Set the Standard 117

36 Jacobs 120

37 The Turk 126

38 Hitch 130

39 The Voice of the Bruins on TV 132

40 The Voice of the Bruins on the Radio 135

41 Grapes 139

42 Two Cups in Three Years 143

43 Dryden Did Them In in '71 144

44 Cash Earned All He Got 148

45 Everyone Loves Normand 151

46 Post-Orr, Park Won Them Over 153

47 Jinx? What Jinx? 156

48 Bruins Trust in the Bradley Boys 158

49 Turnaround Begins July 1, 2006 161

50 You Can't Sour the Kraut Line Legacy 165

51 The Uke Line 168

52 If You Hate Anyone, Hate the Habs 169

53 Nifty Was Truly Magic 174

54 Bourque Was the Star of Stars 176

55 Even Injury Couldn't Bring Bergeron Down 180

56 Sudden Death. 184

57 Gallery Gods Had the Bruins' Backs 186

58 Flaman Made You Keep Your Head Up 189

59 Milbury Made It the Hard Way 191

60 "Terrible Ted" Made Terrible Years Tolerable 194

61 Lockout Plan Set Franchise Back 198

62 Orr's Impact Sparked U.S. Hockey Growth 201

63 Vote for the Seventh Player. 203

64 Pie 205

65 Remembering Ace 208

66 Johnston Survived Last Full Season 211

67 Flyers Became Bigger and Badder in '74. 213

68 Offensive D-Men Owe It to Orr 216

69 "Jumbo Joe" Just Couldn't Measure Up to History. 219

70 Horton Hears the "Woos!" 223

71 Punching Their Way into Fans' Hearts. 226

72 Thomas Terrific 229

73 '53 B's Slew Goliath-Like Wings 233

74 Kluzak Over Bellows 236

75 Julien Joins Champions Club 239

76 Orr Ends Up in Chicago 241

77 Bourque Finished atop the Mountain. 244

78 Bruins Slip on Couple Oil Slicks 247

79 Uniform Timeline. 250

80 Pluses and Minuses to O'Connell's Stints 253

81 Chiarelli's Five-Year Plan. 256

82 Savard's Star Dimmed by Concussions 259

83 Gorton's Great Climb. 261

84 McNab Made Esposito's Area His Own 264

85 Bruins Just Missed Getting Jack 267

86 Fantastic Finish at Fenway 269

87 Gretzky's Shadow 273

88 Sweet Success for Sweeney 275

89 Ulf Leads List of Who to Hate. 277

90 Kasper Kept Cam on the Bench. 279

91 Hear Rene Rancourt Sing Both Anthems 282

92 Read about Plimpton in Goal. 285

93 Photos by Babineau 287

94 Boston Guys Have Basked in the Spotlight 290

95 Attend a Providence Bruins Game 292

96 Meet Me at Bobby Orr. 294

97 Visit Matthews Arena. 296

98 Watch *Rescue Me*. 298

99 Go Green Like Ference. 301

100 Bruins Benefit from Camping Kids 304

Acknowledgments. 307

Sources 309

Foreword

Hockey is a game for aficionados. It's not for everyone, but for those who embrace it, the sport is a passion. Nowhere in the United States is it more loved than in Boston.

And nowhere in the world are there more passionate and knowledgeable hockey fans than in Boston.

I grew up in this city. I saw the Boston Patriots come into this sports world. Trust me, they were not immediately embraced. I went to Celtics games with my brother when you could slink into a near courtside seat despite Bill Russell's run of championships. And, yes, there was always the Sox. The awful, dreadful Sox, who somehow managed to capture the attention of Bostonians but still, until recently, quite frankly, sucked.

And then there was the Bruins. From the beginning, they were embraced by all of the city. Gritty, like the city itself, but with an appeal to even the Brahmins, the Bruins were a jacket-and-tie crowd in the old Garden's loge. Hey, the Madison Square Garden Club was a place to be seen. But in the upper deck, there was always room for the average guy. And if you knew the right usher from Southie, the price of admission was overlooked.

Why? How did this sport adhere itself to the soul of Boston? Well, we're tough. And it used to be cold enough to skate on the multiplicity of ponds in the area by November before global warming was an issue. And all you needed was a pair of skates, a stick, and, if you were lucky, an orange to quench your thirst. The love came from this common bond of playing an unsupervised sport—a sport played outside without rules, without parents, and without restriction. If you could skate, you could play. No questions asked.

And with all of this in mind, Matt Kalman has tried to capture some of the personalities that have captured our hockey minds.

These characters are quirky, courageous, kind, creative, and bold. We love them for these qualities. More importantly, they capture our past and encapsulate our character.

Shore, Orr, Bourque, Neely, Middleton…all unique. And all the same. Hockey players. If you don't know their stories, read on. It will give you an insight into the hearts of athletes and into the guts of Boston.

"Da Broons!" Gotta love 'em. Thanks, Matt, for passing on the torch.

—Mike Milbury

No. 4 Bobby Orr

Bostonians are indoctrinated with the story of Paul Revere's ride and John F. Kennedy's ascension to the presidency from childhood on.

But in the hockey-mad Hub, the tale of how the Bruins found and signed Bobby Orr, and then went from NHL laughingstock to two-time Stanley Cup victors, might be even more important. Of course, the story could've easily just been a footnote in history had Orr not staged 10 of the most remarkable seasons by anyone in hockey history while wearing the black and gold of Boston's team.

Former Bruins coach Don Cherry has said that the way to tell that Orr is the greatest player of all time is to think about what would result if a team of five Orrs battled squads of five Wayne Gretzkys or five Gordie Howes. "The Orrs would win hands down," he said, because of their ability to play stifling defense and control the entirety of the rink.

Orr won the Calder Trophy in 1966–1967, won the Norris Trophy eight straight seasons following that inaugural campaign, and captured the Hart Trophy three times. He led the league in plus/minus six times and was an amazing plus-597 for his career. He became the first defenseman to win the Art Ross Trophy as the league's leading scorer in 1969–1970 and then the last to do it in 1974–1975. No blueliner, obviously, captured it in between.

It's almost impossible to put into words how Orr managed to revolutionize the game and save a franchise.

"His was the platinum combination of skating gifts, breakaway speed, devastating acceleration, and a powerful stride," wrote Michael Ulmer in the *Hockey News*.

*Hall of Fame defenseman Bobby Orr on the ice at Boston Garden during a
game in February 1975, his last full season in the NHL and his last as a Bruin.*
Photo courtesy of AP Images

"I think Bobby Orr is the greatest player who's ever laced a pair
of skates on," said former Bruins and Flyers player Joe Watson. "I
know the game has changed considerably today, but you know he
revolutionized the game. He could control all the ice surface. You
talk about Wayne Gretzky and [Mario] Lemieux and these other

players. They're great players, but they controlled the ice from center ice in. He controlled the whole ice surface. If he could be the leading scorer in the National Hockey League for point total three [two] different times, I think, in his career, that says a lot about the person. As a defenseman, it's unheard of."

At the time the Bruins discovered Orr, it was unheard of for the Boston-based franchise to sign such a player in the heart of Toronto territory with Detroit scout Bucko McDonald coaching the 12-year-old prodigy. The days before the amateur draft were also the days that the Canadian franchises in particular received all the glory and the best prospects.

Scout Wren Blair, who would be instrumental in delivering Orr to Boston, was the one who suggested the Bruins' brass take a trip to Gananoque to watch Doug Higgins and Rick Eaton play against a team from Parry Sound in spring 1961. Boston was desperately attempting to revamp its farm system, which hadn't produced a legit NHL star in years. The Parry Sound club wasn't known to possess any prospects, that is until Blair and six other members of the Bruins' front office saw a diminutive No. 2 do things they hadn't seen someone that young do before. The Bruins' observers sat separately to avoid influencing each other's opinions until Blair went over to general manager Lynn Patrick to discuss the player they would find out later was named Robert Gordon Orr.

"What a find he was," said Bruins legend Milt Schmidt, who was on the trip in his role as assistant GM. "He was only 12 years old at that time, and you could tell at that particular time that he was, by far and away, one of the best prospects ever in the NHL."

Blair found out Orr was not signed by anyone, so he was at the Orr house the very next day to begin the process of securing him for Boston. Imagine a college coach like Jack Parker or Jerry York doing everything under the sun—without the rules of NCAA limiting their actions—to sign the best player in the nation. That's what it was like for Blair as he tried to get Orr signed for a Bruins junior club when the defenseman turned 14. That didn't make him Boston property yet, but at least it gave the Bruins the inside track.

Blair's work on the ground lured Orr to play for the Oshawa Generals for $10,000 Canadian. Well, he also promised to stucco the Orr house and buy the family a new car, but he got the deal done. And the Bruins needed it. They were in the midst of eight straight years (including Orr's rookie campaign) without a playoff berth and had little hope for success on the horizon. Orr became a national sensation in Canada, and the anticipation for his arrival before Boston was like a million Christmas Eves. *McLean's* magazine in Canada ran a cover photo of Orr along with the story "How hockey's hottest 16-year-old is groomed for stardom—has Boston captured the NHL's next superstar?"

After setting all kinds of junior hockey records, Orr set out to sign with Boston in 1966. Following difficult negotiations between Bruins GM Hap Emms and agent Alan Eagleson (in the days when agents were frowned upon), Orr signed with the Bruins for a reported $40,000 a season for two years. Previously, rookies had been limited to no more than $8,000.

Boston's teams, great and awful, were always led by a blue-chip defenseman, from Eddie Shore in the Cup-winning years to Ted Green in the lean years of the '60s. No one could really have predicted that the Bruins would now be led by the ultimate blue-chip backliner.

Orr recorded an assist in his first NHL game but was leveled by the great Howe while watching a pass he made.

"I think he was trying to give me a reminder: 'Kid, you've got to keep your head up in this game,'" Orr said.

That was a lesson Orr took to heart. He kept his head up and for the next 10 seasons made opponents hang their heads in frustration. The Bruins improved from sixth place to third place in Orr's second year. And they began to be the team everyone would call the "Big, Bad Bruins" because of their ability to intimidate and their undying desire to defend each other. Even Orr would drop the gloves when pushed to the brink.

The next two springs they were back in the playoffs, and then came the magical 1969–1970 season. Orr led the league in scoring with an unfathomable 120 points. The lasting sight of that season is the Bruins' star defenseman flying through the air after beating Glenn Hall with the Cup-winning goal that put Boston back on top of the NHL for the first time since 1941. It didn't look like anything could knock Orr and his club off its perch.

"The beauty of Orr was that the Bruins defenseman simply had no weakness. None. Nada!" hockey broadcaster and writer Stan Fischler once wrote. "He could do anything the best forwards could do—and then some—and the numbers underline the point. On defense, he was nonpareil."

Shore had been a beast with Boston. Flash Hollett, Red Kelly, and Doug Harvey had all made a mark by adding some offense from the defense position. But no one had ever done the things Orr did. In the years between his scoring titles, he finished second three times and third once in the race for the Ross Trophy. And each year he did it with his knees one season of rigor worse, breaking down to the point that his career would end prematurely at just 31 years of age.

"He was two steps ahead of anyone," Bruins teammate and fellow defenseman Brad Park once said in George Plimpton's book *Open Net*. "And even after all his knee injuries, he was one step ahead. No one like him. Players like [Gilbert] Perreault and [Guy] Lafleur are exciting to watch, but they can't control a game like Orr did."

A Montreal Canadiens upset of Boston in the first round of the '71 playoffs—Orr produced 139 points and a plus-124 rating that season—prevented a dynasty, but the Bruins rebounded with another Cup in '72. Orr scored the game-winner and set up a second goal in the clinching win at New York.

Along the way, Orr was more than just a great player. He was the perfect face of the franchise, with his blond locks blowing back as he sped down the ice, and his maneuvers more awe-inspiring than that of any athlete, matinee idol, or rock star. The Bruins, led by Orr, became a box-office sensation and must-see television.

"From 1969 through 1972, the rating [on Channel 38] for regular-season games, regardless of the opposition, was 25. That meant one in four Boston TV homes would be watching—about a million people," legendary Bruins play-by-play voice Fred Cusick wrote in his autobiography. "All New England was clamoring to see Bobby Orr, so Channel 38 was the beneficiary of expanded cable coverage. When Orr was on TV3, it would cause a 25 percent decline in viewers of the three network affiliates."

Every parent wanted their kid to grow up to be like Orr. It wasn't just his talents and his endorsements that charmed everyone. No one played the game with more class and sportsmanship. Orr definitely led the league is least-boisterous goal celebration, even when he'd turned five defenders into human pylons.

"If you look at every goal he scored, it was almost as if he would be saying under his breath, 'Sorry, guys, I really didn't mean to embarrass you like that,'" said Cherry.

Although he never wore the captain's "C," Orr was a de facto captain, as well. The best player in the game, in any generation, can't help but be the one others look up to.

"Having Bobby Orr was just icing on the cake. He was a tremendous leader," said Derek Sanderson. "He believed in his teammates, he believed in where he was going and how he was getting there. He thought about it all the time, every day. He was an unbelievable influence."

Boston reached the Cup Finals again in '74, when the Philadelphia Flyers decided to take it to Orr rather than sit back and marvel at his exploits. He still put up solid numbers, but the Flyers won in six games. A blueprint for stopping Orr was now drawn up. Of course, Orr burned those plans with a scoring title in '75, his last full NHL season.

Orr's second contract with the Bruins had been signed in 1967 for three years and reportedly paid him somewhere between $300,000 and $400,000. His third and final Boston salary was, according to Eagleson, the "highest in the history of hockey and one of the highest in the history of professional hockey."

When that last deal expired in 1976, the Bruins were going through an ownership change. Eagleson had built up a ridiculous amount of clout as head of the players' union and an agent to the stars, and had figured out ways to take actions that were cloaked in secrecy and benefitted him most. The story goes that despite question marks about Orr's knees (he played just 10 games in 1975–1976), the new owners offered Orr a deal that included a stake in the Bruins. Whether the league would've allowed someone to be a player/owner, we'll never know. And whether Orr would've accepted will also be a mystery. Eagleson, it's widely believed, never told Orr about the offer and instead delivered Orr's services to the Chicago Blackhawks. Although Orr only played 26 games over his last two seasons, his loss crushed New England. The new owners, led by Jeremy Jacobs, would never live down the fact that they let the great Bobby Orr leave town. The season-ticket waiting list became a blank sheet. Only general manager Harry Sinden's shrewd maneuvering to bring in Park and others kept Boston at a championship level in the second half of the decade.

Park, Ray Bourque, Zdeno Chara…they've all pulled on Bruins sweaters and tried to be the next Orr. But there will never be another Bobby Orr. The Bruins benefitted from the one and only. Boston got to see him do the unthinkable on a daily basis and pull its franchise from the doldrums. The legend still gets passed on from fathers to sons. If there was a Boston sports Mount Rushmore, no one could push Orr off the mountain.

"They've had in Boston three or four of the greatest players to ever play their sports—Ted Williams and Larry Bird, and Bobby," said Sinden.

2 Eddie Shore Hockey

"Yeah, sure old-time hockey! Like Eddie Shore. Yeah."
—*The Hanson Brothers*

The phrase "Eddie Shore hockey" became a rallying cry in the Paul Newman flick *Slap Shot* from back in 1977 the way "wax on, wax off" drives *The Karate Kid*.

More than 30 years since the release of the film that detailed a season with the Charlestown Chiefs, and more than 60 years since Eddie Shore retired from professional hockey, players who pull on a black-and-gold Bruins sweater are still expected to strive to play the game the way Eddie Shore did.

From Milt Schmidt to Johnny Bucyk to Bobby Orr, Phil Esposito, and Terry O'Reilly to Cam Neely and Don Sweeney to Milan Lucic and Zdeno Chara, every player who's forged a perfect balance between skill and physicality has been trying to replicate the essence of No. 2.

Shore marked his territory as the toughest player around during his first training camp with the Bruins in 1926. Owner Charles Adams acquired Shore and six other players for $50,000 (a steep sum for the time) from the disbanded Western Hockey League. By then, Shore had already earned his nickname the "Edmonton Express," but an incident during a Bruins scrimmage would quickly establish Shore as a force on the East Coast.

As legendary hockey writer Stan Fischler recounts, both Shore and veteran Bill Coutu exchanged punches before a truce was seemingly reached. Then Coutu lined up Shore for what would be a "pulverizing bodycheck" that amazingly didn't budge Shore.

The "Edmonton Express" Eddie Shore set the standard for toughness as well as skill on the ice as a four-time Hart Trophy winner who played with the Bruins from 1926 to 1940 (seen here in 1934 in New York).

However, Shore soon realized his ear was bloody and hanging loose. Several physicians told Shore the ear had to be amputated until he finally found one who gave him a prognosis that was music to his ear (pun intended).

9

"Eddie instructed the physician just how he wanted the job done," wrote Fischler, "almost like a customer telling the barber how to part his hair."

Shore racked up 130 penalty minutes as a rookie and followed that up with a then-record 165 PIM as an NHL sophomore. The "Big, Bad Bruins" were still 40 years away from hitting the ice in the Hub, but Shore had already planted the seeds for hard-nosed, physical hockey becoming a hallmark of Bruins hockey for the Orr-era teams and beyond. And Boston fans ate it up faster than they downed their beer on St. Patrick's Day.

Shore-Bailey Incident Made Its Mark

As can be the case with many players who combine skill and speed with grit and physicality, sometimes a line can be crossed. Eddie Shore crossed that line on December 12, 1933, after he was tripped by King Clancy of the archrival Toronto Maple Leafs. An incensed Shore took off to find the next Leafs player he could find, and unfortunately for "Ace" Bailey, he was that man. Shore used his stick to whack Bailey's legs out from under him and sent the Leafs' player into a backward somersault. Bailey hit his head and suffered a fractured skull in two places. Shore was then knocked out by a punch from Red Horner, but the Bruins' defenseman got off easy compared to Bailey's ordeal. Over the next 10 days, Bailey had to undergo two brain surgeries. Shore was suspended for 16 games—the longest punishment ever at the time—and actually took a vacation to Bermuda.

Shore's career was back on track the next season (although some say he wasn't his snarly self for almost a year), but Bailey never played again. In a sign that all's fair in love and hockey, however, the two defused any fears of lingering animosity or violence in the stands when they shook hands prior to the second of two benefit games for Bailey (this one held in Toronto).

"What could have been an incident that would've irrevocably harmed the sport became a milestone but not a gravestone," explained New England Sports Museum curator Richard Johnson.

In another twist to this tale of forgiveness, Shore started wearing a protective helmet designed by general manager Art Ross when his suspension was over. It would be decades before helmets would become a regular fixture on players' heads, but Shore was one of the first to make a statement that being tough and safe weren't mutually exclusive characteristics.

"Shore was both the Babe Ruth and the Ty Cobb of hockey," explained New England Sports Museum curator Richard Johnson. "He was the gate attraction, as well as this manic, riveting competitor who just would seemingly do anything to win."

The Bruins exaggerated Shore's role as a villain of the NHL, including playing "Hail to the Chief" when Shore took the ice moments after the rest of his teammates. He would wear a cape, and a valet would come out to take the accessory away when it was game time. Needless to say, this didn't play well with his opponents any more than Shore's bone-jarring hits or his quickly developing offensive game. Even some teammates found getting along with Shore impossible. When Babe Siebert, a longtime Bruins rival with the Montreal Maroons, joined forces with Shore in Boston in 1934, the two defensemen never spoke. However, they formed possibly the best shutdown defense pair in the league.

"It was like trying to fight through barbed wire to get to the Boston goal when those two were on the ice," former Maroons and Bruins player Herb Cain once said.

Shore's style of play often caused him to bleed (an estimated 80 cuts requiring 978 stitches), lose teeth, and even break ribs, his collarbone, and hip. At least one incident left him motionless on the ice while the Bruins' physicians feared his death. Injury, however, rarely kept him from playing a full 60 minutes.

He was as hard-nosed at the negotiating table as he was on the ice. He frequently held out (including to start the 1938–1939 Cup season) and often demanded double the league's stated salary limit of $7,500 for one season.

And, of course, opponents hardly had an answer for Shore's play. It was virtually impossible to knock him down or take the puck away because of a crouch in his skating stride.

"He was a powerhouse of a hockey player, awesome," said Hall of Famer King Clancy. "He was a hard man to hit because he had that weaving style of skating."

Shore won the Hart Trophy as league MVP four times and was an NHL First Team All-Star seven times (the league didn't start picking All-Stars until 1930–1931). A lengthy suspension resulting from the famous "Ace" Bailey incident in December 1933 cost Shore a spot on the All-Star team, but he earned a berth again the next year. When he finally started to slow down with just three goals and one assist in 19 games in 1936–1937 (he missed time with a broken vertebrae), Shore bounced back the next year at the age of 35 to win the Hart and an All-Star selection.

Obviously, the fledgling Bruins franchise needed every ounce of blood Shore gave for the cause. He led the Bruins to their first Stanley Cup title in 1928–1929 in just their fifth season of existence. And then in what amounted to his swan song in black and gold, he contributed to the Bruins winning a second Cup in spring 1939.

The next season Shore purchased the Springfield franchise in the American Hockey League with the intention of playing for both the Indians and the Bruins. Bruins general manager Art Ross was against this idea from the start, and after some business posturing by both sides, Shore was finally traded to the New York Americans in January 1940.

Eddie Shore the man and player were gone from Boston, but "Eddie Shore" as a style of hockey would live on for generations.

3 Bourque Carried on D Legacy

Some players might have crumbled under the pressure of being a defenseman drafted high by the Bruins and being asked to carry the mantle that once belonged to the legendary Eddie Shore and Bobby Orr.

But not the unflappable Ray Bourque.

"Well, I never thought about being the heir apparent," said Bourque, almost a decade into retirement and owning a North End restaurant named Tresca. "I just wanted to come and play as well as I could. I thought I'd do okay. Looking back at my whole career, I never thought I would do as well. I was pretty confident coming in that I'd have a good chance to make the team. I had a really great camp that first year and had a great season."

So great, in fact, that Bourque's 65 points were more than Orr has registered as a first-year player. Bourque not only showed signs the Bruins would again boast the league's No. 1 defenseman on their back end for years to come, he proved general manager Harry Sinden and his staff shrewd for trading away goaltender Ron Grahame to Los Angeles for the eighth pick in the 1979 NHL Entry Draft.

"It's impossible for any of you to have seen a better 18-year-old defenseman than Bourque," said Sinden.

Bourque was the Bruins' mainstay on defense for 20-plus seasons starting with that Calder Trophy–winning campaign. Through an unprecedented combination of dedication and work ethic—he was famous for his 365-day workout routine—Bourque proved as durable and reliable as they come. Logging more than 30 minutes of ice time a night, battling the biggest and strongest opposing snipers, and sometimes carrying teams that weren't quite contender-caliber, Bourque seemingly never faltered.

Named captain of the Bruins before the 1988–1989 season, Bourque's overall approach to the game rubbed off on numerous teammates.

"His exemplary work ethic, his passion for the game…he was the type of guy who'd play 30 minutes a night, and coach would have an optional practice [the next day], and Ray would be there in the optional," recalled former teammate Steve Kasper. "The thing that I think was the success of the Bruins at the time, certainly from the time I joined the team to the time I left, was that the best players were always the hardest-working players."

Bruins Hall of Fame goaltender Gerry Cheevers coached Bourque in the blueliner's first few NHL seasons.

"If everyone was like him, coaches wouldn't have any problems," said Cheevers.

Although he didn't limit his leadership to the defense corps, players like Garry Galley, Gord Kluzak, Glen Wesley, Don Sweeney, and Hal Gill benefited most from skating alongside Bourque and then being able to pick his brain after a game or practice. As Sweeney explained years later, getting the puck into Bourque's hands was "never a bad play for a young player." Bourque had soaked in tons of knowledge from Brad Park when the two were Boston teammates, so he just saw it as paying the favor forward.

Bourque's tutelage paid off, as the Bruins' defense was able to hold up its end of the bargain in relation to the deep forward corps and a few solid goaltending tandems that led Boston to two Stanley Cup Finals appearances (in 1988 and 1990) and a few trips to the Cup semifinals ('83, '91, and '92). By the time the Bruins ran into the eventual-Cup-champion Penguins in those two conference finals series in the early 1990s, Bourque was into his thirties but hadn't lost a step.

"That's amazing. He was playing 30 minutes a night, and to be that consistent every night.... I remember the playoff series in '91, by the end of the series—we were playing against that team, they weren't that deep on D—Ray played 30, 35 minutes a game," recalled former Penguins and eventual Bruins forward Mark Recchi. "And physically, that was our job, every time he had the puck, to hit him. He just kept going and kept going. This was the semifinals, he'd already played 95 games and 30, 35 minutes a night, he still was.... It was just amazing how strong he was and how great a player he was."

Amazingly, it took Bourque seven seasons to win the Norris Trophy as the league's best defenseman. He was runner-up twice before he won the first of five in 1987. He was also runner-up four more times, including his NHL swan song of 2000–2001 (he turned 40 in December of that season with Colorado).

It might've been difficult to get recognition over defensemen like Denis Potvin, Paul Coffey, Chris Chelios, and Rod Langway over the years, but when Bourque was in his prime, many considered him in a totally separate category—the debate that included Wayne Gretzky and Mario Lemieux for best overall player in the game.

"I've never seen a better all-around player than Ray," remarked Bruins goaltender Andy Moog in 1990. "Paul [Coffey] could carry a game, but Ray can carry a game and never touch the puck, like when he's killing a penalty. Even considering Wayne [Gretzky], Ray's the most complete player in the game."

Bourque passed Johnny Bucyk for the Bruins' all-time scoring lead in February 1997, more than 30 years after the "Chief" had passed Milt Schmidt. Bourque finished with 1,506 points in black and gold. His 1,111 assists, 1,518 games played, and 161 playoff points are also the standard for Bruins players. Unfortunately for the Bruins and their fans, Bourque had to go elsewhere to win his Cup. In the most painful decision of his career, he requested and was granted a trade in 2000. The next season Bourque returned for one last try at the Cup and was instrumental in the Avalanche's seven-game defeat of New Jersey. He retired not long after the victory and was inducted into the Hockey Hall of Fame in 2004.

Even if he won his lone Cup in another uniform, and even if he never consciously tried to stack himself up against Shore and Orr, the other defensive icons of Bruins history, Bourque shattered everyone's expectations for him and chiseled his name onto the Bruins' Mount Rushmore of defensemen with the skill, dedication, and class that became synonymous with his name.

"You do your thing, things go well, and you just try to establish yourself as a solid NHL player. I stayed consistent and kept putting up good numbers," he said. "And the comparisons that first year, because I did put up some numbers, were unavoidable—the questions about Bobby and being the next one. I'd say, 'If I'm just doing my job and just become half the player that Bobby Orr was, I'd be a really good player.'

"So I never tried to be somebody else—just played my game and looked for perfection in terms of my own game, and that allowed me to be consistent throughout my whole career."

4 Father of the Bruins

Is it ironic that the Bruins exist because their original owner and founder Charles F. Adams journeyed north to Montreal to witness the Stanley Cup Finals in 1924 between Calgary and the Canadiens and decided that he wanted the excitement of pro hockey for Boston?

Or maybe a better adjective would be *appropriate*. After all, it didn't take long after the birth of the Bruins for Montreal to become the franchise's bitter rival—the hatred between the two teams has lasted more than 80 years since the Bruins' inception.

Pro hockey would've probably found its way into the Boston sports scene sooner rather than later because of the region's passion for the game. But Adams made sure the wait didn't last long and the love affair between the Bruins and the region got an early start.

Adams, a native of Vermont, earned a degree from Jenney Business College after making a reputation as a hard-working teenager as a chore boy at a corner grocery store and then as a log-purchaser for his father's sawmill. He showed a true knack for business while working for his uncle's Smith and Adams wholesale grocery business and then at the New England Maple Syrup Company after he decided to move to Cambridge, Massachusetts. He then moved on to the banking and brokerage firm of Fitzgerald,

Hubbard & Company and then John T. Connor Company. It was at John T. Connor that he rose to the presidency of what became known as the First National Store chain, or Finast.

Adams' store chain wasn't his only passion. At times he owned the Suffolk Downs horse racing track and the Boston Braves baseball club. As for watching sports, Adams, like thousands of Bostonians, loved to take in amateur hockey games at Boston Arena. When a scandal involving some amateur players taking pay for their play broke, however, Adams soured on the sport a bit.

Then he had his epiphany about pro hockey. Adams returned from the '24 Cup Finals and reportedly told his business associates, "Those pros in the NHL can really play this game. I'm determined to get a team for Boston."

The ball started rolling at the NHL Governors meeting February 9, 1924, as two franchises were granted to businessman Thomas Duggan with the intention of having them both be based in the U.S. Adams purchased the franchise from Duggan for $15,000, and at an NHL meeting on October 12, 1924, at the Windsor Hotel in Montreal (there's that city again), Adams applied for Boston to become an NHL city. On November 1 Boston was admitted into the NHL. The Boston franchise would play its first NHL game December 1 against the Montreal Maroons at Boston Arena. After the selection of the nickname Bruins to go along with the brown-and-yellow color scheme, Adams hired hockey star Art Ross as coach and manager, the franchise was off and skating.

"It was a natural that the Bruins would be the first American NHL team because it was a hockey-rich area and continues to be," said Richard Johnson, curator of the New England Sports Museum.

Adams and the Bruins must've wondered how easy life in the NHL was going to be when the team defeated the Maroons 2–1. Fred "Smokey" Harris scored the first goal in Bruins' history, and Carson Cooper registered the game-winner in the triumph.

However, the Bruins soon got a lesson about life at the game's highest level, as they dropped the next 11 games. With a team made up mostly of castoffs from the Canadian Northwest League, Boston finished sixth in the six-team league with a record of 6–24–0. Some players, like Jimmy Herberts (10th in scoring with 24 points), established themselves, while others faded away. Goaltender Norman "Hec" Fowler couldn't take a liking to Boston and bailed out after appearing in just seven games. Charles Stewart happily gave up his dentistry practice to tend goal, earning five wins and posting a 3.08 goals-against average.

The slow start aside, Adams was confident he had made the right decision in bringing pro hockey to the Hub. He was encouraged by his team winning three of its last five outings and by the enthusiasm of the fan base for the sport. As John J. Hallahan of the *Boston Globe* wrote at the time, "Owner Adams, although losing money, believes that he did as well as could be expected under the conditions. He says that in another year he will give Boston a team that will be in the thickest of the fight, and expresses appreciation to the fans that supported the team."

Over the next several years, Adams put his money where his mouth was. First he put up $50,000 to purchase seven players from the disbanded Western Hockey League in the 1926 off-season. Although his fellow owners cried foul over the deal, Adams only traded off two of the players and kept the other quintet to form the foundation of a championship-caliber club. Most famously among that group Adams retained was the great Eddie Shore. With the snarling defenseman anchoring the back end, the Bruins became a Cup contender—they reached the Finals for the first time in 1927 and then won the Cup in 1929.

That 1928–1929 season also witnessed the opening of the Boston Garden. Adams had grown tired of paying rent to the Boston Arena and also thought his team could draw more than that building could hold. Adams paid Tex Rickard $500,000 for a five-year

A Name to Bear

When the Boston NHL franchise was born, there were no questions about what its color scheme would be. Owner Charles Adams' First National Stores were known for their brown-and-gold scheme, so obviously his team would take on the same hues. Heck, Adams loved brown so much it was written that, in addition to his 50 stores, he also owned four thoroughbreds and some cows, pigs, and hens—all the color brown. The Bruins didn't switch to black, gold, and white until the 1937–1938 season. (Theories about the color change are many, including a need to have a better contrast for photos to Adams' son, Weston, wanting to change the Bruins' luck.)

But naming the team was a little trickier. Adams stated that the name "should preferably be related to an untamed animal whose name was synonymous with size, strength, agility, ferocity, and cunning, and in the color brown category." A contest was held, but none of the suggested nicknames from the masses really won over Adams or manager/coach Art Ross. As luck would have it, Ross' secretary, Bessie Moss, suggested Bruins, which appealed to both men. No surprise, the Bruins, who were born because of Adams' excitement about pro hockey after attending a game in Montreal, were named by a transplanted Montreal native.

Adams really identified with the bruin. His employees presented him with a pair of cubs early in the 1926 season, and a stuffed bear that is now on display at the New England Sports Museum took up residence in Adams' office for most of his stint as the club's president.

Players obviously have affection for the team mascot, as well. A bear head has decorated a wall of the dressing room in both the old Garden and the current TD Garden for decades. Rumor has it that players used to rub it for good luck. And after hat tricks, the bear head (which folklore says was caught by Bruins legend Johnny Bucyk), usually finds itself wearing one of the hats the fans have thrown on the ice.

lease at the new Boston Madison Square Garden, which was built in about a year over North Station. Later the "Madison Square" would be dropped and, of course, the "r" in Gah-den would also become long forgotten among the Boston faithful.

Adams held the presidency of the club until the conclusion of the 1936 season, when his son, Weston W. Adams Sr., took over. During his time at the helm, Charles Adams' passion for the game never waned. After a 3–2 loss to the New York Americans in 1931, Adams filed a protest with the NHL because of what he called "a dull spectacle for the hockey fans in Boston." Of course, Adams had a hard time accepting that some teams didn't have an Eddie Shore to always keep spectators on the edge of their seats.

The Bruins won the Cup twice more—1939 and 1941—in Adams' lifetime. He passed away in 1947. Following his death, he was inducted into both the Hockey Hall of Fame and the Canadian Sports Hall of Fame. The Adams family held control of the Bruins until 1951, when Boston Garden Arena Corporation purchased a 60 percent interest and Weston Adams resigned as president. Adams did return as president from '64 to '69, and his son, Weston Jr., took over from '69 to '75. But the Adams family was completely out of the Bruins' business when Sportsystems Corporation of Buffalo purchased the team and the Garden in 1975.

For Charles Adams, a burning desire lit in Montreal glowed with glory in Boston for years. George C. Carrens of the long-defunct *Boston Daily Record* probably said it best when he wrote, "Everything Charley Adams tackled turned to gold—groceries, hockey, baseball, racing, finance."

5 Small Garden, Big Memories

"Architecture is destiny."
—*New England Sports Museum curator Richard Johnson*

The esteemed historian of Boston sports quoted above might not be the only one to have made such a statement, but there couldn't be a more appropriate proverb to explain why the Boston Garden was the perfect home for the Bruins and how the Bruins went about formulating their philosophy for producing winning hockey.

The Garden ice surface measured just 191 feet by 83 feet—nine feet shorter and two feet thinner than a regulation rink (which is now standard in all 30 NHL buildings). With home-rink dimensions like that, there was no better way for the Bruins to play than with a large dose of physicality and intimidation. To make that strategy work, you needed big players. In the 1920s, '30s, and '40s, Boston built its teams around Dit Clapper, Eddie Shore, Johnny Crawford, and Ray Getliffe. The result was three Stanley Cup triumphs.

When it came time to rebuild in the late 1960s—a reworking that led to two more Cup titles in '70 and '72—Phil Esposito, Ken Hodge, and Wayne Cashman combined with other "Big, Bad Bruins" to complement Bobby Orr, who at 6', 197 pounds could hold his own, as well.

"The idea was that no one would shove you around in the Boston Garden," said Harry Sinden, the coach of the 1970 team and the architect of every Bruins team from 1972 through the end of the century. "The rink was small, the building was so intimate and close, it kind of was a great fit. And we could win with it. Not so much initiating it all the time, but everybody knew that we wouldn't be intimidated."

The popularity of the Bruins while playing at the old Boston Arena (now still standing on the campus of Northeastern University as Matthews Arena) required original owner Charles Adams to seek out a new, larger home for his club. After four years in the old barn, the Bruins moved into the new Boston Madison Square Garden in 1928. It was built by Tex Rickard for $10 million over the North Station train stop and was a great venue for boxing and eventually basketball, but most of all NHL hockey.

Right off the bat, the Bruins' spirited play inspired a boisterous reaction from the Garden faithful. And with such close proximity of the seats to the playing surface—with stands built almost straight up along the side and end zones, and balconies that hung over the ice—the so-called "seventh man" was almost actually in the action.

"I think I speak for anyone who ever played in the Garden, whether you were on the Bruins or any other team for that matter, the Garden was a special place to play," said Lyndon Byers, a nine-year Bruins tough guy in the '80s. "If you were the enemy, you hated it because everybody seemed to get run into all the time. And if you were playing for the Bruins—Bruins fans are phenomenal, they're ferocious, they're passionate, and all of that comes through when they're hanging over that second balcony and it's almost like you can reach up and high five them."

The Bruins lost their first Garden game 1–0 to the Montreal Canadiens on a goal by Sylvio Mantha against Cecil "Tiny" Thompson. The following spring, however, they made their inaugural season in the Garden even more memorable by capturing the Cup.

Boston enjoyed an overwhelming home-ice advantage almost all the time. They went 23–1–0 at home during the 1929–1930 season and 17–1–5 the next season. Over two seasons, ending in November 1976, Boston rolled at a 27–0–5 clip at the Garden ice.

If there was a league stat for home-ice noise, the Bruins would have dominated it.

"In a thundering game like a playoff game or a Canadiens game, when the Bruins would score a goal, there was an acoustical structure that, when that goal was scored, the eruption of noise just thundered down off the glass," said Bob Snow, a hockey writer and former longtime season-ticket holder. "It used to take me five, six days before I could hear again because it was so exciting down there."

The players felt the noise as much as the fans.

"The Celtics played Detroit, it was the fifth game in the Garden. And I went to that game, and it was loud," Hall of Fame forward Cam Neely recalled. "I'm like, *Oh my God, I can't believe how loud this is.* And that same year, we played Montreal in the playoffs. And a friend turned to me and he said to me, 'Are you kidding me?' He said, 'This doesn't compare to what it was like for your game the other night.' Now, when you're down there, you know it's loud. But it really put things in perspective of what it would be like to sit in the stands."

Fans weren't the only ones close to the action. Broadcasters were able to really get a feel for the play from their booth.

"The Garden was a wonderful place," explained Bruins legendary radio voice Bob Wilson. "We were hanging off the balcony. We were almost part of the game we were so close to the action. None of the new buildings can create that."

The Garden endured its share of weird occurrences over the years. The vibrations from the train station sometimes wreaked havoc on the ice. In 1935 the ice-making machine at the Garden actually broke. Without much in the way of temperature control, the Garden could fill with fog on hot spring and summer days. And most famously the blown transformer during the 1988 Cup Finals caused a blackout that forced the suspension of Game 4 and the shift of the series back to Edmonton for the Oilers' championship-clinching win.

On the ice wasn't the only place players would interact with fans. The building's unusual layout forced the players to walk through the concourse to get back to the dressing room.

"People were smoking on the concourse, and you're walking through there," said Neely. "They ended up putting up a curtain, but you're walking through the concourse. The fans would be there, in between periods, you'd get the buzz.... You'd hear it [if it was a bad night]."

On some of those bad nights, Bruins center Peter McNab had a Garden trick to help him pass the night. Sometimes benched for lackluster play, McNab found "a nice couple sitting there, and they'd give me peanuts through a hole in the glass."

The Boston Garden was a glorious venue until it was left behind. All the renovations in the world and additions of luxury suites couldn't keep it as a viable home for the Bruins if the club was going to compete financially with the rest of the NHL.

The Bruins closed the old Garden September 26, 1995, after an exhibition win over Montreal. Legions of Bruins greats from the past were celebrated during the postgame's "Last Hurrah" ceremonies. There wasn't a dry eye in the house. And no matter what they name the new building or any other future facilities, there will never be another Boston Garden.

Believe in the '11 Bruins

It took a lot of skill, speed, toughness, and strategy for the Bruins to win the 2011 Stanley Cup championship.

But most of all it took an enormous amount of belief.

The entire organization believed that a team built around the same core that became just the third squad in NHL history to blow a 3–0 lead in a best-of-seven series just one year earlier could win four rounds in the playoffs.

Everyone associated with the Bruins believed that after losing three Game 7s the previous three seasons, the 2011 squad could win not just one or two series finales but three Game 7s and become the first team in NHL history to do so in the process.

And a belief that they could overcome 0–2 series deficits in both the first round against the archrival Montreal Canadiens and then in the Stanley Cup Finals against the Presidents' Trophy–winning Vancouver Canucks powered the Bruins on their drive to end a 39-year championship drought.

If any team was living proof that what doesn't kill you makes your stronger, it was the 2010–11 Boston Bruins.

"I think it helped us tremendously," said Bruins general manager Peter Chiarelli days after his team won Game 7 in Vancouver. "To go through those experiences firsthand, to see the pain and experience the pain, and see the pain on the players, to know that they have the character in the first place…so I was really confident that we were going to grow on that. I know it's easy to say in hindsight now, but you know there was something that, with the core that we kept following last year's series loss, we knew that they would grow on that. And we made sure it was a priority, we addressed it from Day One of training camp and in all of our activities. If you go through history, recent history, there's always those teams that end up winning. There's a year, there's an experience that they grow from and we just happened to have two successive years that we were able to springboard off of."

Yes, the loss to the Philadelphia Flyers wasn't the first postseason disappointment during Chiarelli's tenure as GM. The first major fall came in 2009, when the Bruins were the top seed and lost to the sixth-seeded Carolina Hurricanes in seven games.

All that bitterness now just looks in hindsight like the early ingredients in Chiarelli's championship recipe. That recipe also included combining head coach Claude Julien and his staff with a team that was talented up the middle with Patrice Bergeron and David Krejci at center, an All-World defenseman in Zdeno Chara, and a record-breaking goaltender in Tim Thomas between the pipes. Along the way, the Bruins added complementary parts like future Hall of Fame forward Mark Recchi, workhorse defenseman Dennis Seidenberg, and sniper Nathan Horton.

During the Bruins' solid regular season—which featured them winning the Northeast Division crown and the third seed in the Eastern Conference with a 46–25–11 record—Chiarelli added forwards Chris Kelly and Rich Peverley and defenseman Tomas Kaberle to make up for the loss of star center Marc Savard to injury and to make certain the Bruins wouldn't be shorthanded should a calamity strike again.

"You do different things and when you learn more about your team and you learn more about the experiences you've been through, and we talk about players going through adversity, coaches go through adversity too, and they learn from those situations. But there's certain things you can control and some you can't," explained Julien. "And I really felt we were undermanned last year against Philly. You can say what you want, but when you, and I know we blew a 3–0 lead, but when you lose the players that you lost [Krejci was injured in Game 3 vs. the Flyers], you've seen that we've beat teams this year that had just a few injuries and couldn't overcome those things. So you understand that, and that's something that coaches can't always control, but the one thing we were able to control this year is the fact that we had some depth and we felt we had the right players in our locker room and whenever somebody went down, we were able to move somebody else in and did a decent job."

There were different heroes every night, including young forward Milan Lucic (the primary assist on both of Horton's overtime game-winners in the Montreal series), rookie Tyler Seguin (two goals against Tampa Bay in Game 2 of the conference finals in just his second playoff appearance), and defenseman Andrew Ference (three playoff goals matched his regular-season total).

And there was the magical play of Thomas in goal. Following up on a regular season that featured him setting a single-season record for save percentage (.938) and also leading the league in goals-against average (2.00)—numbers that earned Thomas his second Vezina Trophy in three years—Thomas actually bettered his statistics in the Bruins' 25 playoff games. He ended the Cup championship run with a .940 save percentage and 1.98 GAA. He set records for saves in a Cup Finals (238) and an entire postseason (798) on his way to the Conn Smythe Trophy as playoff MVP.

"I've got to tell you," said Bruins president Cam Neely after the Cup triumph. "He elevated his game, especially in the Stanley Cup. He was so calm and composed. He took it to another level, and it was really fun to watch him play."

If the Bruins needed more than past adversity to inspire them, Recchi provided another element to spur them on. Before the playoffs even started, the 43-year-old veteran announced that if the Bruins won the Cup, he would retire. As well-liked as any player that's ever pulled on a Bruins sweater, Recchi's teammates wanted to send him out on top.

"I don't know if it was to rally them," said Recchi. "But I knew that if we won there's no way I'd be able to train hard enough to be ready for September."

Well, Recchi was able to end any thoughts of training for another season after the final horn sounded on the Bruins' 4–0 win over the Canucks on June 15, 2011, at Rogers Arena.

It was hard to believe the Bruins had reached the pinnacle of the sport when you looked back at how the postseason had started. Against the Canadiens, who held a 24–8 all-time playoff series record over the Bruins, Boston fell behind two games to none on home ice. No Bruins team had ever overcome a 2–0 deficit to win a best-of-seven series.

Behind the play of Thomas, some timely goals, a "save" by winger Michael Ryder, and those two overtime scores by Horton, Boston got by Montreal. Up next was a second-round rematch with Philadelphia.

After a rout and an overtime win on enemy ice, the Bruins returned home and grabbed another 3–0 series lead on the Flyers. This time, however, they closed things out in Game 4. Ironically, Krejci, whose injury had cost the Bruins dearly a year earlier, thrived in the series with four goals, including the Game 2 winner, and nine points in the four games.

"It's nice that we're not going to have to answer any more of those questions," said Lucic about erasing the memories of the 0–3 collapse. "I think we learned a lot from that experience last year."

The Tampa Bay Lightning proved to be a stiffer test than the Flyers. The Lightning won Game 1 at TD Garden and later forced Game 7 with a home victory in Game 6. Again it was Horton who provided the offense with the lone goal, a third-period-score, in a 1–0 victory that clinched Boston's first Cup Finals berth since 1990. Horton became the first player in NHL history to score two Game 7 game-winners in the same postseason.

After carrying the NHL's best record in the regular season into the playoffs, the Canucks needed the same 18 games as the Bruins to advance to the Finals. Once there, Vancouver was heavily favored and looked ready to make it a short series with a pair of one-goal wins on home ice.

However, back home the Bruins erupted. Partially inspired by Horton's season-ending concussion suffered at the hands of a high hit from Canucks defenseman Aaron Rome (who was suspended for the rest of the series) in Game 3, the Bruins outscored the Canucks 12–1 in Games 3 and 4 before losing Game 5 in Vancouver 1–0. The TD Garden proved fruitful again for the Bruins with a 5–2 victory to stave off elimination two nights later.

Playing a Game 7 for the third time, the Bruins ended talk about their inability to win a big game. But they hadn't yet ended the 39-year drought. With 5:23 left in the first period, Bergeron—the Bruins' longest-tenured player—scored the first of his two goals on the night, and the Bruins were on their way to the title.

"We're a [team that spends to the salary-cap ceiling] and we built this team to win, but I can't say I'm not surprised," Chiarelli said. "It's such a long two months and we had our ups and downs. That series was a tough series, but we came back."

Spending to the cap and playing their best, the Bruins ended the longest wait for a Cup title in franchise history. And they made believers out of everyone.

7 Mr. Bruin

There are a number of ways to quantify what Milt Schmidt has meant to the Bruins' franchise since he first signed with the team in 1935 all the way through now.

The best number of his career: four. As in, four times he has had his name engraved on the Stanley Cup as a member of the Black and Gold. Twice as a player and twice as general manager, Schmidt ascended to the top of the hockey world—no one else in Bruins history can claim that feat.

"To think that as a skinny kid—when I signed my first pro contract I was about 147 pounds and 18 years old—and then the All-Star teams, the MVP trophy, the Hockey Hall of Fame, and to have been associated with all the great players who you read about like Dit Clapper, Tiny Thompson, and Eddie Shore and all the awards I have received and now this," Schmidt once said. "My life certainly has been wonderful."

And to think that the Bruins almost didn't benefit from Schmidt's talent and determination on the ice or acumen behind the bench and in the front office. Bruins manager Art Ross actually had to be convinced by Schmidt's junior teammates and fellow Kitchener, Ontario, natives Bobby Bauer and Woody Dumart to sign the skinny teenager. By the 1937–1938 season, Schmidt, Bauer, and Dumart formed the line combination they had started earlier with the Providence Reds farm club—the trio that would be known forever as the "Kraut Line."

The Krauts helped lead the Bruins to the Stanley Cup in 1939 and 1941. In 1940 Schmidt led the league in scoring, and Dumart and Bauer finished second and third, respectively. The Krauts lived together in Brookline, Massachusetts, and pushed each other on and off the ice. They even negotiated their contracts together to make sure no one made more or less than the other two players.

Dumart was the defensive stopper of the line and the best corner man in the trio. Bauer was known for his gentlemanly play (he won the Lady Byng Trophy three times) and stickhandling. Schmidt was the engine that made the line go, with his offensive abilities and his sheer grit. Carrying on a tradition that Eddie Shore started a decade earlier—and maybe took too far—Schmidt was a not-so-big but "bad" (in a positive way) Bruin.

"Milt possessed a fearlessness that often was translated into hand-to-hand combat with his foe," longtime hockey writer Stan Fischler once penned.

Schmidt staged legendary battles with "Black Jack" Stewart of Detroit, Montreal's Elmer Lach, Toronto's Ted Kennedy, and Detroit's Sid Abel. He dropped the gloves when necessary, but most of the flare-ups were just good, clean hockey. The star center wasn't immune from the rugged play of Montreal's Maurice "Rocket" Richard, who once removed some of Schmidt's teeth with some stick work.

"A lot of guys went into the corner thinking he was just wiry," teammate Pat Egan once said, "and they landed flat on their ass."

The *Hockey News*, which named Schmidt one of its top 50 all-time players in 1997, once described Schmidt's desire by writing that "he considered it a source of pride that he was the first into the corner at both ends of the rink."

With Schmidt and his linemates entering their primes in the early '40s, it looked as though nothing would stop the Krauts from dominating the NHL for the rest of the decade. However, with WWII raging overseas, all three Krauts volunteered for the Royal

Canadian Air Force. They departed after a spectacular 8–1 win over Montreal in February 1942. They didn't return until the 1945–1946 season.

But even time away from professional hockey didn't derail Schmidt and the Krauts. In his second season back, 1946–1947, Schmidt produced a career-high 62 points. Four years later he put up 61 more points. In fact, all the Krauts put up better numbers after their return from the service. The only thing that ended their reign was Bauer's early retirement in 1947.

Schmidt's style of play brought the Bruins glory and earned him 575 points in 776 games. He earned the MVP in 1951. The

Milt Schmidt (15) grew up and played hockey with Bobby Bauer (17) and Woody Dumart (14) before they became the Boston Bruins' famed Kraut Line. The three pose in the locker room prior to their last game in February 1942 before joining the Royal Canadian Air Force to fight in World War II.

stats and honors, however, all came at a physical cost. Over the years Schmidt battled through arm, hip, shoulder, jaw, chest, and knee injuries in addition to a litany of cuts and bruises. After 23 games of the 1954–1955 season, Schmidt's knees just wouldn't allow him to keep playing. So, naturally, he just took over as coach.

Unfortunately, after a fast start, Schmidt's coaching career didn't quite bring the glory of his playing days.

"The first [full] three years that I coached, we went to the Stanley Cup Finals twice, and I thought, *Oh, what an easy job this is,*" he recalled. "But I found out in a hurry that it was the worst job in hockey. I admire anybody who's coaching today. You have to have a lot of patience. And you have to have togetherness, you have to be able to talk to your own players as though they're your own son."

Schmidt served two stints as coach during the dismal early '60s for the Bruins organization. After the '66 season, he was saved with a bump up to the front office. He served as assistant GM under Hap Emms and then took the head job in 1967. Schmidt couldn't have taken over soon enough. While some of Emms' moves were questionable at best, one of Schmidt's first maneuvers turned out to be one of the greatest swindles in NHL history.

On May 15 Schmidt traded defenseman Gilles Marotte, forward Pit Martin, and goaltender Jack Norris to Chicago for forwards Phil Esposito, Ken Hodge, and Fred Stanfield. Esposito blossomed into the league's most prolific scorer of his time, and all three players became cornerstones of the "Big, Bad Bruins" teams that would win two Stanley Cups in the early '70s.

Schmidt left for a brief stint in the front office and on the bench with the Washington Capitals but soon returned to manage the Boston Garden Club for many years before going into full retirement.

"Out of the three jobs I had—player, coach, GM—playing was the best. At that time, if you didn't feel very well, you got knocked on your rear end, so be it. All of your thoughts and your nervousness went different ways, and you didn't have to think about what was going to happen to another 18 guys that you had to look after all the time [as coach and GM]," Schmidt once explained.

There have been plenty of times over the last several decades that the Bruins wished Milt Schmidt were still playing. He had a combination of talent, smarts, and grit that he might as well be held up as the franchise's poster child.

Or he can just forever be known as Mr. Bruin.

Phil Esposito: The Babe Ruth of Hockey

If success were only as simple to achieve as Phil Esposito and Harry Sinden made it seem.

Upon being acquired from Chicago in one of the most—if not *the* most—lopsided trades in NHL history in 1967, Esposito reported to the Bruins and was instantly empowered by head coach Sinden. "He saw something in me that I didn't even know I had: my scoring potential," Esposito wrote about Sinden. "I knew I had hands, as they say, and I had developed the snapshot from watching Bobby Hull when I played in Chicago.

"He said, 'I'm going to make you a scorer.'"

Had Sinden's words carried the same magical powers with every other player he coached, or later acquired as general manager years later, as they did with Esposito, the Bruins probably wouldn't have enough room in their trophy case for all the Stanley Cups they would have won. After all, Esposito finished his career, which also included stints with the Blackhawks and New York Rangers, with 717 goals and 1,590 points in 1,282 games. He retired as the second-leading scorer in NHL history behind only Gordie Howe.

The Bruins had gone eight seasons without tasting the playoffs prior to Esposito's arrival. Even the ascension of Bobby Orr to the NHL didn't help Boston get into the playoffs in 1966–1967. Much to the Bruins' delight, Esposito couldn't get along with Chicago head coach Billy Reay, and the Blackhawks wanted to deal Hull's set-up man. General manager Milt Schmidt stepped up and made the deal that made the Bruins into a powerhouse for the better part of the next decade.

"I knew that Espo was a great goal-scorer and a good play-maker," Schmidt recalled. "He wasn't the fastest man in the world, but he was something that we needed—somebody who can score and somebody who could make plays. I just was in favor of Espo right away."

In working out a new contract with the Bruins after his first season with Boston, Esposito set the bar for his success way higher than anyone thought he could go. He wanted $10,000 plus $2,000 for 25 goals because he could make $12,000 driving a truck. Schmidt offered bonuses of $500 for 20 goals and $1,000 for 25 and 30, and Esposito countered by asking for $2,000 for 35, 40, and 50.

"Whatever you want," Esposito remembered Schmidt saying.

"Bobby Hull always told me, 'Reach for the stars,'" recalled Esposito. "And I ended up that year getting every stinking bonus he could give me. And I wound up making about $13,000 or $14,000. I had 49 goals."

That 49-goal season was part of a 126-point campaign, shattering the previous single-season record of 97 points. Esposito earned a new nickname.

"I got the tag the 'Babe Ruth of Hockey' for two reasons," he wrote in his autobiography. "They said I was built like him, and I was the first to hit 100 points, like the Babe was the first to hit 60 home runs."

Unlike the Babe, who hit his 60 home runs at 32, Esposito surpassed 100 points in a season at just 26 with his prime ahead of him. In 1969–1970 he totaled 43 goals and 99 points in the regular season and then helped catapult the Bruins to their first Stanley Cup title since 1941 with 27 points (13 goals) in 14 playoff games. In the Bruins' second Cup season of the decade, he racked up 24 points (9 goals) in 15 1972 postseason games. Cars throughout New England were decorated with bumper stickers that read: "Jesus Saves—Espo scores on the rebound."

If Orr owned the length of the ice, Esposito's territory was the slot.

"People would say, 'He's a garbage collector.' Well, I scored a lot of goals in front of the net because I positioned myself properly, and I'm proud of it," Esposito wrote.

The two Cup-winning years were sandwiched around his greatest individual year and one of the best season-long performances ever. In 1970–1971 Esposito scored a then-NHL-record 76—yes, 76—goals as part of a 152-point season. Of course, that season—which featured four 100-plus-point scorers and 10 20-plus-goal scorers in Bruins sweaters—was derailed in the postseason by rookie goaltender Ken Dryden and the hated Montreal Canadiens. Esposito found the back of the net three times and totaled 10 points in that seven-game series, but it wasn't enough to get the Bruins to overcome the Habs.

"There were some who charged Phil was more interested in his own point total than the welfare of the team," Don Cherry, who coached Esposito a few years later, once explained. "I never felt this way. I honestly think that Phil figured he was doing the best for the club by playing three- and four-minute shifts instead of coming off the ice sooner. Maybe he was right. He won a lot of scoring championships and he also played on two Stanley Cup winners."

Esposito led the league in scoring five out of six seasons through 1973–1974 and finished the next season with a not-too-shabby 127 points. Injuries to Orr, defections of key players from the title teams to the WHA, and other factors kept the Bruins from winning the Cup again. And by fall of 1975, Sinden, now the GM, decided to shake up his organization by dealing Esposito to the New York Rangers in a multiplayer trade that turned star defenseman Brad Park into a Bruins backliner.

Esposito still remembers Cherry, in "the ugliest pajamas you ever saw," coming to his Vancouver hotel room with Orr to tell him about the deal. Esposito had turned down a no-trade clause when negotiating his last contract with Sinden. And now he was dealt not only out of Boston, but to one of his all-time archrivals. It took years for Esposito to forgive the Bruins, and he still claims to have a bit of a grudge against Sinden for both the deal and the way he was informed. In 1987 the Bruins finally retired Esposito's number in a memorable ceremony featuring Ray Bourque relinquishing the number in a surprise move.

No one should've worn the number that once belonged to the "Babe Ruth of Hockey" after Esposito but, considering Boston's history with the Babe, maybe it was understandable. Nonetheless, there was no curse associated with Esposito—just goals, points, and two Cups.

1969–1970: Big, Bad...and Champs

It's one thing to be "big and bad" and enjoy some regular-season success. It's a whole other thing to be "big and bad" and champions.

In 1969–1970 the "Big, Bad Bruins" of Bobby Orr and Phil Esposito made sure that Boston's Stanley Cup drought dating back to 1941 ended and that the catchy nickname for the club would mean much more than just another titleless era in the team's history.

Some might say the 1970 championship season started a spring earlier, when the Bruins—in the playoffs for the second straight year—dropped a heartbreaking six-game Cup semifinal series to Montreal on Jean Beliveau's overtime goal. Little did anyone know that one year after that dramatic disappointment, the Bruins would spark a celebration in similar fashion.

"That '68–'69 season was a very important season for us," Orr once said. "We learned a lot. They say about losing, you can learn a lot from losing. And we learned a lot from losing."

The rebuilding of the Bruins, starting with the signing of Orr and continuing with the acquisition of Esposito and Ken Hodge, was complete. All that was left for the '70 Bruins to do was to put it all together and turn regular-season success into postseason glory.

Boston's season started somewhat ominously with key defenseman Ted Green getting seriously injured by St. Louis' Wayne Maki in a preseason game in Ottawa. Green, his face contorted by the retaliatory blow of Maki's stick, required two surgeries to stave off death because of a fractured skull. The Bruins were obviously shaken up by the incident. Without Green for the season, however, others picked up the slack, and the Bruins managed to march on with a rallying cry of "winning one for Teddy."

Orr and Esposito finished 1-2 in the NHL in scoring, and the team enjoyed a 17-game home undefeated streak. Esposito led the top line with Hodge and Wayne Cashman on his wings. Two more dangerous lines followed that group onto the ice, with Johnny Bucyk centering "Pie" McKenzie and Fred Stanfield, and Derek Sanderson centering Ed Westfall and Wayne Carleton (after he was acquired in December). On defense, Orr led the charge with Dallas Smith, Don Awrey, and Rick Smith. In the net, Gerry Cheevers and Eddie Johnston formed a perfect tandem.

Boston finished second to Chicago in the East Division, despite its overflowing talent. That didn't matter, however, once the playoffs started. After splitting the first four games of their Cup quarterfinal series with the New York Rangers, the Bruins then embarked on a history-making run that featured a still-team-record 10 straight wins until the Cup was theirs.

Boston disposed of the Rangers in six games and then wiped out the Blackhawks in four straight. The expansion St. Louis Blues were then the next victim on the list.

"We knew if we played to our potential, and they played to theirs, the game would have been over in the first period," St. Louis goaltender Glenn Hall once said about Game 4 of that Cup Finals series with Boston leading the series 3–0. "I apologize for not feeling badly that they beat us, but I don't. Geez, their coach must have been saying to them in the dressing room, 'Look at their lineup and look at ours—what are we doing in overtime with these guys?'"

The Bruins had outscored the Blues 16–4 in the first three games. But there they were in overtime, tied at 3–3 in the fourth game. The steaming hot Boston Garden was dying for a party and an end to the club's Cup drought. The potential championship years that were ripped away by WWII, the seasons ended by power-houses from Detroit and Montreal in the '50s, the doldrums of the pre-Orr early '60s, could all be erased with just one goal.

It took Orr just 40 seconds of the extra session to cash in on a give-and-go with Derek Sanderson. It was Orr's only goal of the series. The iconic image of that goal, captured by photographer Ray Lussier, became a representation for everything great about hockey. But most important, it clinched Orr and the "Big, Bad Bruins" a place in history. What the Red Sox had failed to do in '67, what the Patriots wouldn't do for another few decades, and what the Celtics wouldn't achieve again for a few more years (they would go titleless from '70 until '74), the Bruins accomplished for the city of Boston.

"It was special. We hadn't won the Cup in all those years," Orr said. "Growing up in Canada, lying in bed at night, that was something I'd dreamed about. There I was, following Chief [Bucyk] around the ice with him hoisting the Cup over his head. It was cool."

The next day, an estimated 140,000 showed up for the Cup parade in Boston. The party continued. The players rode in convertibles all the way to City Hall Plaza. Green, who had made it to the clinching game as an observer, rode along with his teammates. The Stanley Cup was Boston's, the "Big, Bad Bruins" era had been legitimized, and hockey owned the Hub for years to come.

10 Ross Was the "Godfather"

Original Bruins owner Charles Adams was the father of the franchise. Art Ross, Adams' handpicked coach and manager, was the "Godfather" of the organization.

Everything the Bruins were in their first 30 years of existence, they owed to Ross' acumen. "Ross was a creative executive steeped to his neck in hockey knowledge," longtime hockey writer and broadcaster Stan Fischler once wrote.

Ross was a great player of his era before he went into refereeing and then managing/coaching. When Adams needed someone to run the first-born U.S.-based NHL squad, he did all he could to secure Ross' services. Maybe Ross' physical features played a part in that, as well.

"He was a real Bruin," said former Bruins defenseman Fernie Flaman about Ross. "As a matter of fact, he looked like one. He had a real gruff look on his face. I don't think I ever saw him smile."

Ross might not have had the capacity to show joy, but he must have felt some during his successful 30-year stint as the club's manager (which included three stints as coach). The Bruins won the Stanley Cup three times under Ross' watch, starting with the 1929 Cup. That team really started to come together after the Adams' purchase of the legendary Eddie Shore and other players from the disbanding Western Hockey League, a move instigated by Ross in 1926. That Ross had a childhood relationship with the league's organizers, Frank and Lester Patrick, certainly came in handy when it came time for the Bruins to acquire the best defenseman of that era.

The who's who list of Bruins greats of that era were all signed and developed by Ross, including goaltender Frank Brimsek; the Kraut Line trio of Milt Schmidt, Bobby Bauer, and Woody Dumart; "Dit" Clapper; and Bill Cowley. Ross astutely made his moves and ran the business for Adams. A famous story told by Schmidt recounts how, when trying to get more money than Ross was offering, Schmidt went to the manager's office. Upon hearing Schmidt's request, Ross left the room to go talk to Adams. When he returned, Ross explained that he had fought for Schmidt but couldn't get a penny more out of the owner. Schmidt stopped by the owner's office on his way out to thank him for the contract, only to find out the owner was not in.

Amazingly, Ross was able to accomplish all he did for the Bruins while also thinking of ways to improve the sport and help the league. He donated the trophy that was originally presented to the league's outstanding player and later became the award for the league's leading scorer. He redesigned the puck in the early 1940s so that it had beveled sides and would no longer cause such vicious cuts with its sharp corners. The double-half-moon-shaped net with much-improved nylon mesh was also a Ross design. The checkered red line that would show up better on black-and-white television, the early prototype of a skater's helmet, and the idea to pull the goalie for an extra skater in the closing seconds of close games—also thought up by Ross.

Along the way he also found time to keep a rivalry burning with Toronto's Conn Smythe, who held up his end of the bargain to create some of the funniest moments in the early history of the NHL. The feud reportedly started when Ross conned Smythe into purchasing a player who was nowhere near worth what Smythe paid. Over the years they came to blows once, Smythe purchased an ad in the Boston papers to taunt the slumping Bruins, and he once sent King Clancy to Ross with a bouquet of flowers featuring a snarky message in the card.

Ross made sure the Bruins were set for the future without him by hiring Lynn Patrick as coach and then grooming him to be the next general manager. That kept the Bruins competitive during the '50s. Even when retired, Ross still stopped by the Bruins' offices to lend advice to Patrick and anyone with ears.

Adams brought NHL hockey to Boston, and the throngs of fans fell in love with Shore and his teammates. Ross' orchestration in the team's early maneuverings were what made sure the Boston Bruins would survive as one of the storied franchises of the National Hockey League.

11 Lack of Spending Sullies Sinden's Reputation

"I watch over it as though it were even better than my own. I'm not the guy who's about to give the store away."
—GM Harry Sinden, on owner Jeremy Jacobs' money

It's a bit ironic. The man who left the organization over a $5,000 dispute after coaching the Bruins to the Stanley Cup in 1970 returned to the club as general manager and, for more than 30 years, built a reputation as a "penny-pincher."

That's not just something former players and league observers have branded Harry Sinden with. It's also a term used in his bio on the Hockey Hall of Fame website. Sinden laughs at the idea that even the Hall of Fame isn't above criticizing his way of running a team. Instead, he thinks he should be celebrated for his method. After all, had the other owners and managers followed his lead, there might not have been a season-cancelling lockout in 2004–2005.

"Certainly, just prior to the lockout, most of those Cups were bought. What happens is, if you're going to blow a lot of money like that, you can bring in players and have them fail," Sinden said when asked to explain why the Bruins always seemed to operate under their own salary cap despite the overflowing wealth of owner Jeremy Jacobs. "It's like the Red Sox and Yankees can do. You can pay them big money and have them fail and try someone else. If you're trying to make a business work, you can't do that. So you pass on a lot of players. And also, I felt that you could win in this league even without having the best players. And you can do it; teams have. Tampa Bay [in '04].

"And then if we could win and be in the bottom third of the payroll, then it might influence everybody and stop the madness that led us to shut this entire league down. There's only one reason it shut down, and I'm happy to say I didn't have any part in that."

But *he* also hasn't played a part in bringing a Stanley Cup back to Boston since he mentored Bobby Orr, Phil Esposito, and the "Big, Bad Bruins" of 1970 to a title. The victory was the culmination of what the Bruins had been building ever since Sinden and Orr arrived in the Hub in 1966–1967. However, it wasn't enough for the Bruins to offer Sinden any more than a $5,000 raise on his $17,000 salary. He left for a $40,000 job with Stirling-Homex, a company that sold prefabricated housing. Sinden was going to support his wife and children the best he could and wasn't going to be low-balled.

He returned to coach Canada during the 1972 Summit Series and turned down a few offers from NHL clubs before the Bruins came calling again. Fresh off winning their second Cup in three years, Boston hired Sinden as general manager to replace the promoted Milt Schmidt. If there was one thing Sinden provided the Bruins from that point on, it was loyalty. Of course, that wasn't the only thing. His trade track record leans heavier toward the positive side than that of most general managers, especially considering the uncharacteristic length of his tenure. Aided by assistant GM Tom Johnson and an astute staff of scouts like Bart Bradley, Gary Darling, Jim Morrison, Bob Tindall, and others, Sinden was able to keep the Bruins in the championship mix without dropping to the bottom for the better part of 20 years.

"I always thought that, as he always said, the greatest talent any general manager can have, a gift, is to be able to tell who can play and who can't," said Nate Greenberg, longtime Bruins public relations guru and then-assistant to Sinden. "The rest is important, but that's the most important—who can play and who can't.

"[We] had a group of guys that could do that and do it well."

Not too many managers would've had the courage to ship the popular superstar Esposito out of town for anyone, let alone Bruins-hating New York Rangers defenseman Brad Park. But Sinden knew there was a need to make sure the Bruins were covered in case Orr couldn't return due to injury or, heaven forbid, left the organization (Sinden was removed from the negotiations to prevent Orr's departure). A glowing report from Bradley on Park convinced Sinden to make the deal.

Bruins fans know the list of Sinden's lopsided deals in the club's favor by heart by now. He shipped Ken Hodge to get Rick Middleton, and dealt Barry Pederson for Cam Neely, and Brad McCrimmon to add Vezina Trophy winner Pete Peeters. He acquired a first-round pick for Ron Grahame and then drafted Ray Bourque. Sure, there were some duds along the way. But the wins outweighed the losses right up through the early '90s, as far as Sinden's trades. With a track record like that, you'd think Sinden would've been more eager to swing in-season deals to bolster his club for the stretch run and a possible annexing of the Cup. Unfortunately for many, those trades were few and far between.

"It's hard to know. It really is," said Middleton when asked if the Bruins might've won a Cup if Sinden had done more to mortgage some future for the here and now. "You look at it…the only thing I remember him doing, and it was when we started the [1984–1985 season 2–4–0], he got Charlie Simmer. The only time I can remember, he went out and spent a draft pick because we were so lousy, not because we needed that one missing link. Those years of coming so close with Montreal, losing two straight Finals and then a [semifinal], why not just keep going with that team and add to it instead of subtracting? It just seemed that we always took two steps back to take one step forward. If we were really that bad and things didn't work out, he would then add to it because we couldn't be that bad. So let's spend a few more dollars or draft picks so we're not horrible because we've got to be competitive. The fans won't come if we're not competitive. So we always seemed to have competitive teams; we never took that step."

Mike Milbury was Sinden's assistant for a couple years after coaching the Bruins to the Cup Finals in 1990. He understands where his former boss was coming from.

"I think Harry gets a really bad rap in this town. There have been very few general managers more successful. And the fact that he didn't win [a Cup], it's tough," said the former defenseman. "But he made a lot of money for the Jacobs family. That's his job. I don't see why that should be held against him. I don't even know what guys were made available at what time he could've picked up. I know when I was coaching, we picked up Brian Propp along the way. It wasn't like he didn't ever pick up guys in the stretch run to help things out."

In the '90s the relationship between spending money and winning became tighter in all professional leagues, including the NHL. Sinden and the Bruins, however, stuck to their guns. The philosophy was to have five $2 million players rather than one $10 million superstar. You might be able to succeed under that mantra if you continue to draft well and make one-sided trades in your favor. However, the Bruins began burning first-round picks on the likes of Rob Cimetta, Evgeni Ryabchikov, and Dmitri Kvartalnov. Sinden's touch with trades also loosened, as evidenced by the deals of Andy Moog to Dallas for Jon Casey and Gary Galley to Philadelphia for Gord Murphy. Making life more difficult was the role salary was playing in these deals (Galley believed a rich arbitration victory hastened his departure). After Sinden's acquisition of Kevin Stevens and Shawn McEachern for Glen Murray and Bryan Smolinski in 1995 was proven a poor decision, mostly by Stevens' inability to live up to his hefty contract, Sinden actually admitted he made that trade for more than just hockey reasons.

"You thought it was a good deal, all the media thought it was a good deal," he told the *Boston Globe*. "And we thought it was good—not great, but good. Everyone in the hockey world thought it was a good deal. So if I had Stevens to do over again, I would probably do it. At the time, though, I thought it was a bad deal; I didn't think it was that great, and I especially didn't think he was worth $3.5 million. You people didn't know it, though, because you thought we had a prize. I didn't like it, but I thought, *I'll make it to satisfy the people who say we aren't willing to spend the money.* And that was stupid on my part."

Maybe the Bruins could've made up for their deficiencies by being more active in free agency. But that wouldn't have been a guarantee ever, as Galley once explained.

"Guys around the league are worried to go there," said the defenseman. "You hear them say that it might not be the place to go. And before, hey, guys loved to go there. It just seems now the mystique is over, the old Garden's gone. It's a new building and a new team, and from a player's perspective, no one wants that kind of turmoil all the time."

The Bruins' move from Boston Garden to the new building on Causeway Street was accompanied by the requisite steep increase in ticket and concession prices. But the product on the ice didn't live up to the money. Instead of championship banners, fans were treated to contract holdouts—like those of Jason Allison and Anson Carter—and vicious arbitration hearings. Even the great Bourque was subjected to a hearing. Sinden actually made history in 1999, when he walked away from the contract of Dmitri Khristich rather than pay his team's leading scorer what an arbiter had awarded him.

Bruins games were no longer guaranteed sellouts, and venom from disgruntled fans flew at both Sinden and Jacobs—with Sinden bearing the brunt because of Jacobs' absentee ownership approach up until the early 2000s.

When prospect Joe Juneau threatened to go play in Switzerland if he didn't receive a one-way contract from the Bruins before he'd even worn an NHL sweater, Sinden's response was, "Well, I hope he learns to yodel." That was good for a laugh. Unfortunately, it was always Sinden's way or the highway, and that inflexibility took its toll.

The Bruins were bad enough in 1997 to earn the first pick in the draft that June, and after a couple brief playoff runs in '98 and '99, they missed the postseason two straight years for the first time since the 1960s. In 1999 they ranked 20th in the 28-team league in terms of payroll.

That year Michael Felger of the *Boston Herald* summed up Sinden best when he wrote, "Harry Sinden's lack of popularity is beyond dispute. He is reviled and vilified, held largely responsible for the Bruins' 27-year Stanley Cup drought. But even Sinden's harshest critics must admit: few can consistently get more out of less. When he has his fastball, Sinden is a very able general manager."

Sinden officially relinquished the GM title to assistant Mike O'Connell in 2000 with an all-time record as GM of 1,170–763–301. He remained as the Bruins' president until 2006, when Peter Chiarelli's hiring as GM ushered in a new era in Bruins hockey.

"It's been a delightful, wonderful relationship," Jacobs said after Sinden was given the title of senior adviser to the owner.

Obviously, the man who benefitted most from Sinden's management style would throw roses at his feet. Bruins fans and some former players would be less complimentary because they're left to wonder what might've been had Boston spent a little more here or added another player there. The Cup drought might not have reached 39 years prior to 2011.

Nonetheless, two-thirds of Sinden's stint running things featured a run of success that almost any franchise would pay a fortune to enjoy for as little as a quarter of the time—even if the Bruins wouldn't be willing to spend that same fortune for it.

Chief

For more than 50 years, the Bruins' theme song might as well have been "Hail to the Chief."

After all, the franchise relied on Johnny Bucyk for 21 seasons as a player, and then as an assistant coach and radio broadcaster. For the longest time now, the Bruins have leaned on Bucyk for his expertise as the team's road services coordinator.

When the "Big, Bad Bruins" of the early 1970s needed to slow down a puck-carrier with a vicious hip check or break a team's will with a clutch goal, Bucyk was there. As amazing as his numbers were as a player, you'd be hard-pressed to find a travel coordinator who could get an NHL team door to door, Atlanta to Buffalo, in just three hours, 27 minutes, as Bucyk did early in the 2009–2010 season.

"I love it here. I love the organization, they've been very good to me," Bucyk said of the team he never left after he was traded from Detroit on June 10, 1957. "I've had a good career, and not too many people can say they've worked for any job for that long. But I enjoy it. I like the atmosphere around Boston, the fans are great, my family's all here, and everybody's here to enjoy it. So we'll stay."

Johnny Bucyk skates around New York's Madison Square Garden with the Stanley Cup on May 1, 1972, after the Bruins defeated the New York Rangers 3–0 in Game 6 of the Stanley Cup Finals. Photo courtesy of AP Images

When the Bruins swapped future Hall of Fame goaltender Terry Sawchuk to Detroit for Bucyk, they couldn't have predicted what "Chief" would mean to the organization. No other person in Bruins history can claim to have had three nights in his honor. The first came in spring 1968, when a serious back ailment led some to believe Bucyk might call it a career at 32. The Bruins presented Bucyk with a car, his teammates chipped in to buy him a boat, the New York Rangers sent him some golf clubs, and the Chicago Blackhawks sent him a rifle. Had he retired after that season, Bucyk would have finished with a solid career featuring three top-10 finishes in goals and points and one trip to the Stanley Cup Finals in 1958. His four-season run reunited with fellow Ukrainian-Canadians and former Edmonton Flyers forwards Vic Stasiuk and Bronco Horvath—the "Uke Line" they were called—had carried on the tradition of Boston relying on trios like the Dynamite Line and the Kraut Line. The Uke Line was the first in NHL history to feature three 20-goal scorers in one season.

However, Bucyk had no intention of hanging up his skates. He was fitted for a back brace that he wore for the next 10 seasons, and the very next year he posted 66 points. After suffering through eight straight playoff-less seasons, 1960 through 1967, there was no way Bucyk was going to miss the "Big, Bad" years now that Bobby Orr and Phil Esposito had arrived and were hitting their stride. Bucyk was so determined to not miss anything, he started a streak of 418 consecutive games played in January 1969.

The Uke Line was a decade in the rearview mirror when Bucyk found a new home on left wing with center Fred Stanfield and John "Pie" McKenzie for parts of five seasons, including the Cup-winning years of 1970 and 1972. With Bucyk working the corners along with McKenzie, the Bruins had a solid second line to complement the high-scoring trio of Phil Esposito between Ken Hodge and Wayne Cashman. Bucyk produced seasons of 69, 116, and 83 points in 1970 through 1972 before McKenzie left the Bruins for the World Hockey Association.

Seemingly able to play with almost any pair of forwards and fight off any signs of aging, Bucyk remarkably put up an 83-point season in 1975–1976 at 40 years old and with the Bruins transitioning from the "Big, Bad" days to Don Cherry's "Lunch Pail A.C."

"I think the big thing was that I signed one year at a time," Bucyk said of his longevity. "I only had one multiyear contract in my whole career. I signed one year at a time, and if I didn't produce, I felt I wouldn't be back, so I had to produce."

No one would have accused Bucyk of not being as big and bad as the rest of his teammates. Former Bruins coach/general manager/president Harry Sinden once described being hit by Bucyk as "being hit by cement." Anyone who was victimized by one of his patented hip checks would second the notion. But that didn't stop Bucyk from winning the Lady Byng Trophy for gentlemanly play twice in the early '70s.

"It's a trophy that's given to the player who shows sportsmanship play without earning penalty minutes and combines it with great ability," Orr once said. "He deserved it. In fact, I thought Chief should have won it long before he did."

By the 1976–1977 season, Bucyk started to slow down, and he retired after registering just 18 points in 53 games the next season. That allowed the Bruins to hold another night in his honor, this time to retire his No. 9 at Boston Garden on March 13, 1980. He retired as the fourth-leading scorer in NHL history and in 1981 was inducted into the Hockey Hall of Fame.

Bucyk never stopped contributing to the team's cause. So in 2007 a third night was held in tribute to him—this time for 50 years of service to the club. Around the Bruins and TD Garden, everyone knows that if you hear "Hi, Chief"—a nickname given to Bucyk way back in junior hockey by Horvath because the left winger was "the guy who used to sneak into the corners and lead the attack to get the puck"—it means the reliable, professional legend of the game is in your presence. Life in Boston without Bucyk is hard to imagine, so don't be surprised if the club holds more nights to hail him down the road.

13 Taz

When Bruins coach Don Cherry's son, Tim, needed a kidney transplant, Terry O'Reilly was one of the first players to offer to donate blood.

On off days, O'Reilly was known to go antique shopping with Cherry, who still owns an aquarium he bought on one of their sprees. Kids and people who are less fortunate throughout New England have been touched by O'Reilly's kindness and willingness to give his time.

So I ask of you: are these the actions of the Tasmanian Devil?

Well, of course, O'Reilly's nickname—given to him by former teammate Phil Esposito in the '70s—was all about the bulky right winger's *on-ice* exploits, which were both a whirlwind and a pleasure to watch from the stands or the ice. "I always felt that if in my career a Stanley Cup wasn't going to be in the cards, then the hockey gods gave me the next best thing: I got to play with Terry O'Reilly," said former linemate Peter McNab. "Because he was an absolute...it was amazing to play with him. The way that he approached the game and how he played, and there was a fire that just never went out—whether it was practice or it was games."

He hated to talk about fighting, but O'Reilly never backed down from a challenge. Even once he was an established NHL star, O'Reilly would still drop the gloves in training camp.

"I would always say to him, 'Taz, why in training camp do you fight these guys that are never going to play?" recalled McNab. "And he would always say the same thing: 'Because when I was coming in, somebody fought me; somebody gave me a chance.'"

O'Reilly had been a goaltender until the age of 13, so when he got to the Bruins, he had only been skating as a forward for about seven years. His skating was a work-in-progress, but he didn't let that hinder him. Although he has said he regrets not getting formal skating lessons, he got better on his skates and learned to manipulate the puck with his feet when need be.

It should be no surprise that as one of five sons of a milkman, O'Reilly learned right away what hard work was all about. As a kid, he often had to aid his father on his route.

"We worked on the weekends with him. It wasn't a voluntary occupation," O'Reilly explained. "Friday night at the dinner table, he would look around and [point] and say, 'You are working with me tomorrow.' Whatever plans you had for Saturday, you just scrapped them and you were getting up at 4:00 AM."

O'Reilly established himself as a full-time NHL player in the 1972–1973 season, one year after the Bruins won their fifth and last Stanley Cup. For his first five seasons with the Bruins, O'Reilly posted modest point totals and enormous penalty-minute totals— endearing him to an entire legion of Bruins fans, including the famous Gallery Gods.

Then, amazingly, his penalty-minute amount kept increasing while his offensive output similarly increased. In 1977–1978 he led the Bruins with 90 points and 211 PIM. He became the first NHL player to finish in the top 10 in scoring and accumulate more than 200 PIM.

Of course, quantifying what O'Reilly meant to the Bruins is impossible.

"O'Reilly wasn't about the numbers. He was about the trying, caring, making the moment, every moment, matter," *Boston Globe*

Hall of Fame writer Kevin Paul Dupont once wrote. "To appreciate that, you had to see him play, game to game, shift to shift, the heart underneath that spoked-B as obvious as the number on his back."

Cherry had an up-close look at the best O'Reilly years. O'Reilly embodied what Cherry terms the "Lunch Pail A.C." teams of the late '70s that reached the Stanley Cup Finals twice and lost a Cup semifinal series in a seventh game now known as the "too-many-men game."

"You actually didn't coach him, you just opened the door and let him go," said Cherry. "That was one of the few guys that in my career I really had to let him go because that's the way he played. It'd be like putting a bridle on a horse. All the guys played the system, and Terry just played his system. But it was effective, so I let him go."

Injuries began to catch up with O'Reilly in the early '80s. He also endured a regrettable situation in the 1982 conference semifinals, when he took a swing at referee Andy van Hellemond in Game 7 of the series with Quebec. The Bruins were eliminated, and O'Reilly was suspended for the first 10 games of the next season.

"If I could take that back, I would take that back because there's no room in the game for someone who takes a swipe at an official," he said.

After playing 63 games in the 1984–1985 season to run his career regular-season total to 891, O'Reilly retired at 34 years old. Needless to say, that was a difficult moment in Bruins history.

"The immortal words of [Harry] Sinden: 'This is a day that I've dreaded a long time.' And he meant it," longtime assistant to the Bruins' president Nate Greenberg recalled his boss saying after O'Reilly called it quits. "There was no replacing what O'Reilly meant to the team. From a heart standpoint and a winning standpoint, he brought some things that very few guys could bring to a franchise.

"Every generation, you get one O'Reilly."

On and off the ice, there was only *one* O'Reilly.

14 Bench Minor Leads to Major Collapse in '79

"Six men on the ice. Sixty men on the ice. How many men on the ice? The story has become legend, the number swollen, in less than a decade, the highlight (lowlight) of the entire streak, stowed in the same sad Boston footlocker as the ground ball that rolled through Bill Buckner's legs and the home run that the Yankees' Bucky Dent hit into the screen on a fall afternoon.... Who loses a game, a series, because too many men are on the ice?"
—*Leigh Montville in a 1988* Sports Illustrated *article*

Even all these decades later, it's hard to fathom. The Bruins were 2:34 away from a trip to the 1979 Stanley Cup Finals when they were whistled for the most famous penalty in NHL playoff history. And they were still 1:14 away from a date with the New York Rangers, a team that finished just third in the Patrick Division with 91 points, when Canadien Guy Lafleur scored the tying goal that went down in infamy in Bruins lore.

After an end-to-end rush, Lafleur one-timed a slap shot from the right faceoff circle past goaltender Gilles Gilbert and inside the far post. People still ask Gilbert about the tying goal all the time.

"And I just reply: 'Did you ever stop a bullet?' I never did, and I never will," Gilbert explained years later.

Defenseman Brad Park was on the ice when the Bruins' dreams of closing out the win in regulation were shattered by Lafleur's shot.

"I call it a one-in-a-thousand shot," he recalls. "You could shot it a thousand times and to get it this far off the ice and this far inside the post, it's very hard."

Everyone who wore a Habs or Bruins jersey on May 10, 1979—most of whom were following the action from the outside—pretty much expected the winner that day to roll over the Blueshirts to the Cup parade. So Game 7 of the Cup semifinal series was a de facto championship game.

Maybe it would have been easier had the three-time Cup champion Canadiens just built a sweep off their series-opening two wins at home at the Montreal Forum and put the Bruins out of their misery without lifting the hopes of an entire region. Their dreams crushed so many times over the previous 30-plus years by the Habs, including in the previous two years' Cup Finals, Bruins fans probably could have accepted it if their team just served as another piece of road kill for the Montreal dynasty.

However, coach Don Cherry's "Lunch Pail A.C." team refused to let the hated Habs waltz down to Broadway. A pair of one-goal wins back at Boston Garden—capped by an overtime-winner by Jean Ratelle—and then a home-and-home split set the stage for a winner-take-all showdown. Hall of Fame Montreal writer Red Fisher remembered Rick Middleton playing "like a demon" that night. And Middleton helped the Bruins grab a 3–1 lead through two periods with a goal and two assists. After Montreal rallied to tie the game, Middleton again scored with 3:59 remaining on the clock with a shot "from almost behind the net" that went off Dryden's arm and in.

And then came the line change from hell. Don Marcotte had been double-shifting to shadow Lafleur. To this day, Cherry hasn't revealed the identity of the offending player—and some reports say there might have been two or three culprits. Linesman John D'Amico, maybe joking, later said, "I didn't want to call it after six or seven [players], but after nine I had to."

If the Bruins' players began to think the Montreal jinx was about to continue, their fans were even more distraught.

"When Lafleur scored to tie the game, it just seemed then that it was inevitable that the B's would eventually lose," said longtime Bruins season-ticket holder and author Kevin Vautour. "It's hard to explain the heartache I felt. I guess I was too young and did not understand that it was only a game, but I was upset."

It took just 9:33 of overtime for Yvon Lambert, a guy Bruins defenseman Mike Milbury had knocked out earlier in the game, to tap in Mario Tremblay's pass to the front of the net for the game-winner in a 5–4 victory.

After the game, Cherry took full blame for the gaffe, saying that he hadn't spelled out the assignments well enough and that the guys on the bench must have thought they heard him send them onto the ice. Cherry knows he'll never live that penalty down.

"Well, I'm still known for it, and I'm always going to be known for it. It was one of those unfortunate things," he said. "What really kills me on television is, there's too many men on the ice, and they always put the camera on the coach. Like the coach says, 'Listen, everybody jump on the ice and get too many men.'"

Whether it was Cherry's fault or not, it turned out to be his last act as coach of the Bruins. Cherry left after that season after an ongoing passive-aggressive battle with general manager Harry Sinden and his staff boiled over.

But Middleton knows that there's plenty of blame for too many men on the ice to go around.

"Ultimately, too many men on the ice is a player's fault," he said. "You've been doing it for your whole life, when a coach calls up the next line. Okay, Donnie Marcotte might've been double-shifting with Lafleur, but we played three series in three years against these guys. We knew how to do it. It was just something that happened in the heat of the game. They could've scored, they couldn't have scored, we could've won that game. It's just something that happened."

Not *just* something that happened but *another* thing that happened in the Canadiens' favor. And another thing that kept the Bruins' Cup drought alive. Nothing short of an end to that drought can erase the agony of the too-many-men game for anyone associated with the Bruins.

Espo Enters...

It wasn't just Phil Esposito's scoreless six games in Chicago's 1967 Stanley Cup semifinals loss to Toronto that eventually got the bulky center dealt from the Blackhawks.

His mouth, often as big as his knack for scoring, helped pave the way to Boston.

"You guys are going to mess this whole thing up, you surely will, because you don't know what you're doing," Esposito remembered saying to Blackhawks general manager Tom Ivan and coach Bill Reay one night at a team reception after a few too many cocktails.

Luckily, the great Bobby Hull pulled Esposito away before he could put his foot any farther into his mouth. But the "Golden Jet" couldn't stop the Hawks from trading his linemate, who had helped him lead the NHL in goal-scoring in 1966–1967. Espo produced 61 points in that regular season. On May 15, 1967, Bruins general manager Milt Schmidt completed the deal that acquired Esposito, Ken Hodge, and Fred Stanfield for Boston in exchange for Gilles Marotte, Pit Martin, and Jack Norris. Not only is that deal considered the most lopsided in the history of both franchises involved, it's arguably the most lopsided in the history of the NHL.

"There was nothing wrong with him physically. But he couldn't get along with the coach, who was Billy Reay at the time," Schmidt recalled more than 40 years later. "He says he can't get along with him and he's disturbing the club, so we want to get rid of him."

"I knew that Espo was a great goal-scorer and a good play-maker," Schmidt continued. "He wasn't the fastest man in the world, but he was something that we needed—somebody who could score and somebody who could make plays. I just was in favor of Espo right away."

Esposito was leery about joining the Bruins after battling with the likes of Ted Green and Bobby Orr over the last couple seasons. Harry Sinden, who coached the Bruins to a sixth-place finish in the six-team league in his first season the year before, was excited about the deal.

"It should help us to get into the playoffs—we got something to build three lines around," Sinden said at the time.

Never mind the playoffs. As the leader of the Bruins' forwards on a team featuring Orr on the team's back end, Esposito helped the Bruins to two Stanley Cup titles—in 1970 and 1972—and recorded 459 goals and 1,012 points in black and gold until his trade to New York in 1975. That first season he no longer had to defer to Hull and scored 35 goals. The next three seasons he buried 49, 43, and a then-record 76 goals for the Bruins.

Had the deal just been a three-for-one affair, it still would've been a Bruins victory. However, the Bruins added two more keys to their Cup-winning puzzle with Hodge and Stanfield to make the trade a historic triumph for Boston. Hodge finished his nine seasons in Boston, spent mostly on Esposito's wing, with 289 goals. Stanfield chipped in with 135 goals of his own in six seasons on Causeway Street.

Now compare that to what the Hawks received from Boston. Pit Martin was a solid scoring winger for most of his 10-plus seasons in the Windy City. He reached 30 goals three times, including a career-high 32-goal season, and finished his 17-year career with 324 goals. Marotte, a defenseman, put up some decent

Originally a Chicago Blackhawk, center Phil Esposito blossomed after coming to Boston prior to the 1967–1968 season, becoming one of the top goal-scorers of all time and helping lead the Bruins to two Stanley Cups in 1970 and 1972.
Photo courtesy of AP Images

numbers from the back end but was a minus-player during his journeyman career. Norris was gone from the league after just three more seasons.

While the Hawks didn't fall off the map after the deal—they reached the Cup Finals in '71 and '73—they didn't bring home the coveted chalice the way the Bruins did in their two shots at it. Imagine if the Blackhawks had had Esposito, Hodge, and Stanfield to aid their cause.

Esposito became beloved in Boston not just because of his goal-scoring acumen but his gregarious, outspoken persona. The latter helped make him a steal for the Bruins.

16 The First Cup

Like a longtime boyfriend finally popping the question, the Bruins had to do something in 1928–1929 to forge an eternal bond with their fan base in just their fifth season of existence.

Two springs prior Boston fell to Ottawa in its first trip to the Stanley Cup Finals (two losses and two ties in the best-of-five series). The next season the Bruins failed to advance past the league semifinals. Finally, everything came together for the Bruins during season No. 5, and Lord Stanley made his first-ever visit to the Hub.

The Bruins set a franchise record that winter with 26 wins against just 13 losses and five ties en route to a second-straight American Division title. Their 89 goals, led by the league's seventh-leading scorer, Harry Oliver (17 goals, six assists), were the most ever by an American Division team. The promotion of Ralph "Cooney" Weiland from the minors allowed new player/coach Cy Denneny to put together what would become known as the "Dynamite Line"— completed by Aubrey "Dit" Clapper and Norm "Dutch" Gainor.

Gainor netted 14 goals, while Weiland potted 11 and Clapper nine. (Keep in mind that this was the last season forward passing wasn't allowed in the NHL.)

On defense, future Hall of Famer Eddie Shore and perennial star Lionel Hitchman were at their peak performance level. Shore even scored 12 goals from the back end.

And in net, the newcomer Cecil "Tiny" Thompson had supplanted the veteran Hal Winkler. Thompson started all 44 games and recorded 12 shutouts and a 1.15 goals-against average. No one was spared that season by Thompson, not even his brother Paul, who was a goaltender for the New York Rangers. In the first-ever matchup of sibling netminders, "Tiny" Thompson shut out the Rangers 2–0 with 33 saves on December 4, 1928. For the season, the Bruins only allowed 52 goals in 44 games.

If all the talent general manager Art Ross had assembled wasn't enough to buoy the Bruins to higher achievements, the club opened its new home, Boston Garden, on November 20, 1928. The team dropped a 1–0 decision to the Montreal Canadiens that evening, but Boston would get its revenge later in the playoffs.

A then-league-record 13-game (11–0–2) unbeaten streak that lasted until February 2, 1929, and an 11–1 drubbing of Chicago on March 12 were further proof of the Bruins' ability to dominate. But nothing would have mattered much if all Boston did was reach the

Shore's Championship-Caliber Drive

Talk about showing championship drive and determination. Eddie Shore, the man who put the Bruins franchise on the map with his all-around skilled play and hard-nosed style, didn't know in January 1929 that a few months later he'd be lifting the Stanley Cup. All he knew was that a traffic jam forced him to miss the team's overnight train to Montreal for a match with the Maroons, and he wasn't about to miss the game. Not an incoming snow storm nor a squeamish chauffer (on loan from a wealthy friend) nor a fall into a ditch by his friend's powerful vehicle (Shore used a hearse and a chain to pull it out) could keep Shore from getting to the Forum.

After making a late-afternoon arrival on January 3, 1929, Shore took an hour-long nap and showed up for the game with bags under his eyes. However, all he needed was the sight of the Maroons and the hostile crowd to get his blood pumping better than a gallon of black coffee. Shore scored the only goal in a 1–0 win to cap off his arduous journey.

As the story goes, the following exchange between coach Art Ross and Shore concluded the evening:

Ross: Nice game, Eddie. I'm sure glad you made it here.
Shore: Thanks, boss. It's a trip I'd like to forget.
Ross: Then I've got something that'll remind you of it. I'm fining you for missing the damn train in Boston.

playoffs, even the Cup Finals, again. Bringing the Cup home was the only goal.

The Canadiens, who accumulated 59 points and won the Canadian Division title, were the only team to finish ahead of Boston in the overall standings that season. For some reason that still remains shrouded in mystery, the Bruins and Montreal met in the first-round, best-of-five series. Montreal was led by impenetrable goaltender George Hainsworth (22 shutouts in 44 games) and scoring forward Howie Morenz (17–10–27 in 42 games). During the regular season, Boston had beaten the Habs once in four tries with one tie. In those two losses and tie, Boston failed to score against Hainsworth.

To say that Thompson answered the challenge of facing Hainsworth would be an understatement. The Bruins' puck-stopper recorded 1–0 shutouts in both Games 1 and 2 of the season (the first two postseason games ever played at Boston Garden) and then went into enemy territory for a 3–2 Game 3 win at Montreal Forum. Shore scored the winner in that game, and Hitchman reportedly played throughout the contest with "blood flowing from a huge gash in his head."

The only thing that stood in the way of the Bruins and the Cup were the New York Rangers, who had finished second in the American Division to Boston with 52 points. It was the first-ever Cup Finals featuring two American teams, but the Canadian-born Thompson turned the series into his own goaltending exhibition. He blanked New York 2–0 in the first game and finished the playoffs with a 0.60 GAA in five games.

Boston's two years of postseason failures came to an end on March 29, 1929. Bill Carson's goal with just 1:58 left in the game made sure Thompson's stellar goaltending stood up. The Bruins won Game 2 of the Finals 2–1 for a two-game sweep and the first Stanley Cup title in Boston history. Boston and hockey in the U.S. would feel the reverberations from the win for years to come.

"For an established American team to reach the top and to do it with the excellence that the Bruins did early on in the franchise's life was very significant," said longtime hockey writer Stan Fischler.

The Bruins, who had already been welcomed home like heroes after the triumph over Montreal, returned to the Hub with the Cup and were treated like the second coming. While team president and owner Charles Adams divvied up the $35,000 in bonus money for the players, the players in turn surprised their owner with a two-foot-high bronze bear that was imported from Russia. Ross received a new set of golf clubs.

"There has never been a professional team where there has been less bickering, fewer jealousies, and better spirit," said Ross. "All season long that has been the case."

Boston not only had professional hockey, it now was the home of championship hockey. A region and an NHL team tied the knot that magical season.

17 ...Espo's Out

As the son of longtime Western Canada-based Bruins scout Bart Bradley, future Bruins director of player personnel Scott Bradley and his brother often got to take off from school to go into the Boston dressing room when his dad's team was in town.

One such day was November 7, 1975, which also happened to be the day Boston general manager Harry Sinden dealt Phil Esposito and Carol Vadnais to the New York Rangers for Brad Park, Jean Ratelle, and Joe Zanussi. Needless to say, what Bradley witnessed from his heroes like Terry O'Reilly and Wayne Cashman that morning is permanently etched in his mind.

"We go into the rink, the Bruins are practicing at 10:30. We get there and [the trade has] just been announced. So as two kids, pre-teens, my dad said, 'Just stay out of the way; get in the corner,'" Bradley recalled. "There's [Don] Cherry and everybody. The scene, as being such a part of the Bruins as a kid, with Bobby Orr and Phil Esposito, it was watching grown men cry for the first time. O'Reilly and Bobby Orr, and Phil on the pay phone.... As a kid, it was really surreal."

The Bruins were just 5–5–2 at the time. The Rangers were 5–7–1. Both teams needed a spark.

"The circumstances for both teams were right," recalled Sinden. "We had the best two teams in the league—the Rangers and Boston—and we both started off really poorly. And I said to [Rangers GM Emile Francis], 'We ought to make a trade that counts and maybe both of us will get going.' And he said, 'Yeah.' And we talked a little bit and got around to his best player [being] Park, and mine was Espo because Bobby was hurt. And when you get a chance to do a defenseman for a forward, that'll help each team, those deals come together. When you trade a defenseman for another defenseman, it could end up a wash. It just came together."

For Park, a perennial All-Star blueliner, the deal meant going to a city he had skewered in his book *Play the Man* three years prior. Park, an often outspoken member of the Rangers, classified the Bruins as "a bunch of blood-thirsty animals" and accused them of such transgressions as padding their stats and taking sneaky punches. Nonetheless, Sinden made the deal for Park, who was informed of the deal early in the morning at the team hotel in Oakland.

"It [was] such a shock, especially to Boston. I mean, I used to have to get an FBI escort on and off the ice because of the fan mail I would get when I was with the Rangers," Park recalled. "Now I'm getting traded to this place? I didn't even know the names of the FBI guys, but I wanted to find them."

Park's decision to insult in print an opposing team that he would eventually join was unfortunate. Esposito's decision to not get a no-trade clause from Bruins general manager Harry Sinden was catastrophic. Esposito had spurned an offer to jump to the World Hockey Association, where a handful of Bruins players defected after the '72 Cup win, to re-sign with Boston for six years at $400,000. When Sinden offered the no-trade, Esposito turned it down because of all the things the two men had been through over the seasons.

"All I could think of was the million-dollar cash bonus I had turned down to go to Vancouver because I had wanted to stay in Boston," Esposito remembered about the day he was dealt to New York. "Me, I was more loyal than anyone, including Bobby Orr, only to have the fuckers fuck me like that.

"I still haven't forgotten Harry Sinden. We've talked, and I've tried to be friends, and I've laughed with him and had a few drinks, but I treat him like anybody else. There isn't that special feeling anymore."

The famous line from then-Bruins coach Don Cherry came after he and Orr made their way to Esposito's hotel room in Vancouver to make notification about the trade. Esposito told Cherry, "If you say New York, I'm going to jump out that window." Cherry reportedly turned to Orr and said, "Bobby, open that window."

Legend has it, Esposito's longtime friend and linemate Wayne Cashman threw a television set out the window into the parking lot and ordered 100 sandwiches from room service to stick the Bruins with the bill. Luckily, Esposito didn't jump out the window. But there were many in New England who wanted to follow him to New York. The trade wasn't well-received by the masses—both because of Esposito's popularity and the hatred for Park. The great writer D. Leo Monahan wrote, "My heart says it's terrible, my head says let's wait and see."

Park and Ratelle, however, turned out to be a great fit for Boston during its transition from the "Big, Bad Era" to "Lunch Pail A.C." under Cherry. The Bruins won their division and lost in the Cup semifinals that season, but reached the Finals each of the next two springs. In seven-plus seasons with the Bruins, Park was a rock on defense and even produced a 79-point season in 1977–1978. As it turned out, he arrived just in time because Orr would only play 10 more games with Boston before injuries ended his season and eventually his time with the Bruins. After finishing the 1975–1976 season with 90 points, Ratelle enjoyed years of 94, 84, 72, and 73 points for Boston.

The positive results of trading Esposito for Park and Ratelle were as strong as the negative emotions in the immediate aftermath of the deal. And Sinden had made sure the post-Orr Bruins would be competitive into the next decade.

 **The Goal**

It's not quite Babe Ruth calling his home-run shot against the Cubs in Game 3 of the 1932 World Series, because as far as we know Ruth's Yankees teammates weren't also boasting about hitting one out in that game.

But Game 4 of the 1970 Stanley Cup Finals, which the Bruins won to complete a sweep of St. Louis and end a 29-year championship drought for the club, is the closest to a "called shot" the franchise has in its history. To a man, the Bruins all knew they were going to score to end the series, even if they couldn't agree on who was going to find the back of the net. Of course, everyone should've known it was going to be Bobby Orr, the 120-point defenseman who would go on to set the standard for all future blueliners.

"You couldn't have written the script better. Bobby had to get that goal in overtime," center Derek Sanderson recalled about the conclusion of the Bruins' May 10, 1970, victory.

Phil Esposito recounted in his autobiography what the locker room chatter was like before the extra session:

> Derek said, "I'm getting the goal—me. Don't worry about it. I'll take care of it."
> "Okay, Derek," we said. "Sure."

Esposito's line and the Bruins' other two trios also clamored to get the first chance to score. Esposito, Ken Hodge, and Wayne Cashman had combined for 188 points in the regular season and had been just as effective in the playoffs. But coach Harry Sinden put Sanderson's line, the Bruins' top checking unit, on the ice to start the overtime because St. Louis countered with its top offensive threats—Red Berenson, Larry Keenan, and Tim Ecclestone. Orr and Don Awrey joined Sanderson, Wayne Carleton, and Ed Westfall on the ice.

"Overtime doesn't necessarily tell you which team played the better game or which team was the better of the two. I put Bobby out to start the overtime because it was very unlikely that the Blues would get a top-scoring chance with him out there," said Sinden.

Of course, there's no way Sinden would have dared to start any key stretch of a game without the indefatigable Orr in action. The Blues were well aware of Orr's everlasting presence but were still incapable of stopping him. When Sanderson shot wide of the goal, defenseman Jean-Guy Talbot then tried to work the puck up the wall to Keenan. But Orr pinched in from the point and dished the puck to Sanderson below the goal line to start the most famous give-and-go in hockey history.

"When Bobby gave it to me, it wasn't rocket science to realize he was going to the net," said Sanderson. "The key was getting it

Bobby Orr is tripped and starts to go flying a split second after scoring the Stanley Cup–winning goal in the 1970 Finals against the St. Louis Blues.

back to him because there was no one at the point. I had to make sure to get the puck over the one St. Louis stick and onto Bobby's. I was behind the net; it was a three-foot pass, and I'd have killed him if he missed it."

Westfall also knew that Orr was headed toward the St. Louis goal. "When Bobby rushed up the ice, you covered for him—that's how we did it back then," said Westfall. "I was covering Orr's ass— covering the point where he should have been. As a matter of fact, I think I should have had an assist on the play."

We all know how the play ended. Orr snuck Sanderson's pass past Glenn Hall just 40 seconds into overtime. And then, propelled by Noel Picard's defending stick, Orr made like Superman with his arms out—soaring into history.

"I'd like to tell you that I put the puck up on its edge, I saw his legs open, and I shot it between his legs," Orr admitted. "But I just put it on net. And because Glenn was moving across, his legs opened up, and I put the puck between his legs."

What might have happened had Orr not kept the puck away from Keenan? Well, a review of the play shows that Berenson is clearly off to the races. But that was the magic of Orr. He always made sure opponents would be left wondering "what if?"

"Even if Bobby didn't get the puck, and St. Louis had a break-away, it was always worth the chance for him to pinch, because maybe one in 50 times he wouldn't get the puck or get back in time," said Sinden. "He was a fantastic, powerful skater. He was so much better than everyone, and it was almost certain that we'd win the overtime if he was on the ice."

There might have been more to Orr's ability to seemingly fly after the goal than just Picard's stick and simple physics. After all, an entire region, a whole generation, of frustrated Bruins fans all released a spontaneous dose of jubilation at once. Perhaps that put a little more air under Orr.

The goal not only made sure the "Big, Bad Bruins" would be remembered as a triumphant participant in NHL history, but also provided Ray Lussier with one of the greatest photographs in all of sports.

19 Neely Was Nails Tough

Could it be that Cam Neely has a soft side?

Throughout his career, he accumulated a list of Hollywood A-list performers—including Michael J. Fox, Woody Harrelson, Denis

Leary, and Glenn Close—as friends. "Most of my Hollywood friends are blue-collar," Neely says now.

Then there's the Neely Foundation, with its mission statement to be "dedicated to helping patients and families deal with cancer."

"The best part about Cam, he's a better human being than hockey player," former teammate Lyndon Byers once told author Rob Simpson. "He takes care of his family, he takes care of his friends, and he takes care of strangers."

Of course, when he played in the NHL—from 1983 to 1996, including 10 seasons with the Bruins—"taking care of" had a much different meaning, as in Neely would flatten, mash, and pummel any opponent who needed "taking care of." And he did it all while scoring 395 goals (344 as a Bruin) and racking up 694 points. You want to talk about the Big, Bad Bruins? More than a decade after they were dissembled, Neely embodied everything those teams of the early 1970s stood for after he landed in Boston, along with a first-round pick, in a lopsided trade that sent Barry Pederson to Vancouver.

"It was actually told to me on a number of occasions that the way I played, I could've played in any era here," Neely recalled one day taking a break from his duties as the team's vice president. "Which, quite frankly, was a nice thing to hear. But that was one of the things I heard a lot when I first got here."

Perhaps no player in the history of the game was a better combination of skill and physicality.

"For 10 seasons here in Boston [1986 to 1996], a decade that now seems to have been played at fast-forward speed, Neely shaped a career as the game's most feared scorer, hitter, fighter," Hall of Fame hockey writer Kevin Paul Dupont wrote upon Neely's induction into the Hockey Hall of Fame in 2005. "He may not have been the most prolific point-getter—his time, after all, coincided with the heydays of Wayne Gretzky and Mario Lemieux—but the unique concoction of his talents—his strength, his shot, his speed,

Vice president and former Bruins star Cam Neely brings the puck up the ice during the Boston Bruins Legends Classic before the Winter Classic at Fenway Park on January 2, 2010. Photo courtesy of AP Images

and above all, his rage—made Neely the game's most cantankerous commodity at right wing."

And the Boston fans, of course, loved it. They loved him so much, they twice voted Neely the Seventh Player Award for surpassing expectations in a season. They learned to hate Ulf Samuelsson as though the Pittsburgh defenseman had injured a member of their family—his several questionable hits on Neely in the '91 Wales Conference Finals began Neely's career-ending battle with serious injuries. And they packed the house at the "new"

Garden in January 2004 to watch his No. 8 get lifted to the rafters—the 10th retired number in Bruins history.

All it took for Neely to blossom was a trade from Vancouver, where he was buried on the depth chart before he was dealt on his 21st birthday. The blue-collar crowds of Boston, plus the tiny ice surface at Boston Garden provided a perfect breeding ground for Neely to blaze a trail as a new kind of player. He was so different, observers had to come up with a new way to classify him.

"He became the quintessential power forward. In fact, they coined that expression because of Cam Neely," said longtime hockey writer and broadcaster Stan Fischler.

"He *invented* superstar power forward. He was it," Byers explained. "He's by himself; he's on a plateau by himself. It's pretty simple."

With 36, 42, and 37 goals in his first three seasons with the Bruins, Neely was just getting started. He erupted for 55 in the 1989–1990 season, which ended with the Bruins falling in the Stanley Cup Finals, and then added 51 the next season. Of course, the '91 the postseason featured a matchup with Pittsburgh and Samuelsson. Neely's thigh injury—as a result of Samuelsson's "cheap shot"—led to a rare condition where muscle turned to bone. In dealing with that, Neely soon started to have problems with his left knee and eventually his hip. He only played 22 games over two seasons before his near-miraculous 50-goal-in-49-game comeback season of 1993–1994.

After an injury to his right knee ended that magical season, Neely returned for two more seasons. When a 1998 comeback attempt proved to him his hip wouldn't hold up to the NHL grind, he called it a career. Neither Boston, nor the NHL, has really seen anything like Neely in his prime since.

"It's a very, very difficult thing to find a player who played quite as physical as he did and found time to score all those goals," said former Bruins general manager Harry Sinden.

As for those Hollywood connections that have led him to parts in movies like *Dumb and Dumber* and *Stuck on You* and television shows like *Rescue Me*, Leary isn't buying the notion that Neely's actor friends are in his class toughness-wise.

"Speaking for myself, and a few of the other guys, I don't think we're anywhere near as rugged as hockey players," Leary said.

There are legions of hockey players who could say the same thing about how their ruggedness compares to what Neely displayed as the biggest, baddest Bruin of his era.

20 The Photo

A graduate of the Franklin Institute of Photography in Boston, Ray Lussier was working for the *Boston Record American* in the spring of 1970 as a general assignment photographer. Little did Lussier know that on an unbearably hot day inside Boston Garden, Bobby Orr would provide the subject for one of the greatest sports photos in history.

"I've signed that picture so many times…but it's still great," said Glenn Hall, the St. Louis goaltender victimized by Orr for the Cup-winning goal historically captured by Lussier from a corner of the west end of the Garden. "When I played at the All-Star Game in Boston [in 1971], every fan had a copy, and I got my dollar for every autograph."

The photo did more than just put dollars in Hall's pockets. It made Lussier, one of three *Record American* photographers on duty that day, a household name, especially among photography enthusiasts. It made it easy to decorate any bar room, pool hall, or sports memorabilia store in New England, as any place in those categories that doesn't have The Photo hanging obviously doesn't belong in

Boston. And it became a NHL marketing tool, with its perfect depiction of the grace and "super powers" of Orr combining with the exuberance of triumph in sport from both the players and fans.

"It was sort of a de facto hieroglyphic for hockey," said New England Sports Museum curator Richard Johnson. "It's hard to think of a single still picture, in any sport, that captures the essence of the sport better than that. You have the greatest player scoring the most dramatic goal. Now, okay, they swept the Blues, so it wasn't like a walk-off home run in the seventh game. It wasn't Bill Mazeroski. But it was Robert Gordon Orr at the height of his powers, bringing a Stanley Cup to a city that hadn't seen one in 29 years, at home on Mother's Day before a national television audience so that people were watching this across the country. It's the picture that launched a hundred hockey rinks; that inspired kids to play hockey."

Lussier, who tragically passed away in 1991 at just 59 years old, needed a little bit of luck to get the photo that would eventually hang in the Hockey Hall of Fame. Positioned in the east end of the Garden on May 10, 1970, Lussier made his way west just before overtime because he figured the Bruins would quickly go for the kill. He found a stool vacated by another photographer (Lussier never identified the man in future tellings of the story) who had gone to quench his thirst in the heat that was well above 90 degrees inside and out. Just 40 seconds later, Orr and Derek Sanderson worked the most dramatic give-and-go in hockey history, and Lussier snapped away.

He raced back to the office ahead of the other photographers who had to stick around to shoot the celebration. He showed the contact sheet to his boss, who helped edge Lussier toward a date with immortality.

"That one right there!" sports editor Sam Cohen reportedly bellowed while pointing to the historic shot. "Print it. Big!"

Several photographers took similar shots of the goal, but Lussier's photo was the first one everybody saw. Years later, that shot was voted by more than 400 writers and broadcasters as the MasterCard Greatest Moment in NHL history.

"There have been more spectacular goals scored in this league," Orr said after that vote. "I'm not sure they've been caught like this [on film]. The way this was caught, it was overtime, it was Mother's Day. I was thrilled to have been able to score the goal, but growing up in Canada, the dream was to play hockey in the NHL and be on a Stanley Cup–winning team.

"When I see [the picture], I think about Chief [John Bucyk] carrying the Cup around. I think about the celebration and having my father there. I look back at 10 years of wonderful times. I remember Teddy Green, and that was the year he was hurt, he was standing on the bench with tears coming down. You start thinking about the characters you had on the team, and we had some characters. That's what I think about. We had a close, fun group."

Maybe the same karma that allowed the Bruins to find Orr all those years before the goal in Parry Sound, Ontario, also smiled on Lussier that afternoon at Boston Garden. Whatever the forces at work were, The Photo made sure that The Goal would be remembered forever.

21 "Cheesie" Was on the Money

There's no goaltender in Bruins history you'd pick to start one game that you absolutely needed to win other than Gerry Cheevers.

Call him a "big-game" goaltender or a "money" netminder, but no matter what moniker you give him, it better involve winning.

"To me, you lose as many as you win," said Cheevers, a 1985 Hockey Hall of Fame inductee and the Bruins' third all-time leader in victories. "Some people say, 'Well, you were a money goalie.'

Well, I lost some semifinals and finals, too. Fortunately, they remember the ones you won. If you can't play in a Stanley Cup game, if you can't perform, you shouldn't be in this business."

The Bruins drafted "Cheesie" away from Toronto in 1965. With Boston's Oklahoma City farm club, he impressed coach Harry Sinden enough to later leap frog Bernie Parent on the depth chart when Eddie Johnston suffered an injury. Later that decade, the Bruins were wise enough to protect Cheevers and Eddie Johnston in the expansion draft. Although Parent went on to his own Hall of Fame career, the Bruins' remaining goaltending duo made sure that a couple of the most dynamic offensive teams ever would have enough puck-stopping to win the Stanley Cup in 1970 and 1972.

Cheevers won 229 regular-season games and 53 playoff games in black and gold. His 24–0–8 stretch of the 1971–1972 season is still an NHL record for longest unbeaten streak. All the while, he did it with almost a split personality. Off the ice, Cheevers was unaffected by any hype surrounding the games. The great Leigh Montville once wrote in the *Boston Globe*, "Gerry Cheevers was a visible rendering of the pilot's calm voice as the aircraft hit just a little bit of turbulence over Schenectady."

His famous white mask covered in black notches where pucks hit him in the face over the years was a direct product of Cheevers' sense of humor and disregard for how dangerous his position could be. A cigar and the Daily Racing Form were everyday ornaments in Cheevers' mouth and hands right up until game time, regardless of the magnitude of the contest.

"Cheevers' idea is that it's only a game. He's not going to make himself sick over it," one-time Bruins coach Don Cherry told author George Plimpton. "He'll just do the best he can. If it's not good enough, the next time he'll do better. The fact is, you've got to leave your bad games out on the ice."

The bad games were few and far between, whether Cheevers was playing behind Bobby Orr and the "Big, Bad" teams of the early '70s or Cherry's "Lunch Pail A.C." squads during the latter part of the decade. Mostly he was successful because when he stepped between the pipes, that laid-back persona became a stranger. No one was as intense and feisty as Cheevers, who would often use his stick to ward off would-be crease-crashers and venture well out of the net to cut off the shooters' angles and even handle and clear the puck.

"Gerry gets burned sometimes, but not as often as you think," longtime Bruins coach, general manager, and president Harry Sinden once said. "What seems like a gamble to you and me is not a gamble to him. He doesn't make a play unless the odds are with him."

Cherry once hit the jackpot in a pinch with Cheevers during the Bruins' run to the '79 Cup semifinals. Before Game 3 of the club's quarterfinal series with Pittsburgh, Cherry learned that goaltender Gilles Gilbert had broken out in hives. Cheevers, who had been told he wouldn't be starting after he had won the first two games of the series, had already washed down two hot dogs with a soda. But that didn't stop him from going out on short notice and beating the Penguins 2–1 with a performance Cherry called Cheevers' best of his career.

"Gerry Cheevers is one of the top-notch goalies of all time," said defenseman Gary Doak, who was also Cheevers' roommate. "When the game was on the line, Gerry played as good as any goalie that the Bruins have had over the last 50 years. He was a money goalie, and when the money was on the line, he played well."

Cheevers, like a number of his teammates and fellow NHL stars, chased the money to the WHA after the Bruins won the Cup in '72. He spent three and a half seasons with the Cleveland Crusaders, for whom he led the league in goals-against average (2.84) in 1972–1973. When he returned to the Bruins in the 1975–1976 season, he proved he hadn't missed a beat with a 7–0 shutout of Detroit on February 8. The Cheevers-Gilbert combination was the last line of defense for Bruins teams that reached the Cup Finals twice and semifinals once before the 1970s closed, but Boston never captured the Cup.

Cheevers retired after the 1979–1980 season and became the Bruins' coach his next season. Although he had to learn to adjust his approach to the game for each of his individual players, he was successful enough to lead the Bruins to four playoff berths and two Adams Division titles before he was fired in his fifth season.

Coaches can't control the result of the games the way a goaltender can. And with the pads and mask on, no one could turn a big game in his team's favor the way Gerry Cheevers could.

22 Willie O'Ree: Hockey's Jackie Robinson

The most amazing thing about Willie O'Ree's breaking of the color barrier in hockey may not just be that when he skated for the Bruins against Montreal on January 18, 1958, he became the first black NHL player. How about the reality that the presence of a black player in the Boston lineup hardly made a ripple?

"The fact that we beat the Canadiens 3–0 in the Forum—now that was big news," O'Ree recalled about the postgame focus of the media after that historic night.

It wasn't until a few days later that O'Ree found out he was the first black player in NHL history, and it wasn't until 1961, when he returned to the Bruins for a second NHL stint, that he was branded as the Jackie Robinson of hockey.

"It was the greatest thrill of my life. I'll always remember this day," O'Ree was quoted after that game.

Black players who have followed O'Ree to the NHL haven't let him forget that day. While it took 10 years for the next black player to skate in the league, there have been close to 20 black players in the league at a time in recent seasons. Greats like Hall of Fame goaltender Grant Fuhr and Calgary superstar Jarome Iginla have cited O'Ree as an inspiration.

Goaltender Kevin Weekes carved out an 11-year NHL career and often worked with O'Ree and the NHL diversity programs.

"With him being the first black player to play in this league, there were a lot of other players right around the same time, or even just before, who could've been the [first] players, too, but didn't have the opportunity. That's frustrating, especially in a place like North America," said Weekes. "But at the same time, that was a different point then than it is now. But again, it takes time, and it's evolution. And without him being the first, who knows if we'd be playing today?

"Any time somebody blazes a trail in a positive light, creates opportunities for others…and also, it's not just for us. I think it reflects well on the game as a whole because, in the end, we want to be a game that's accessible to everybody and everyone wants to play, be fans of, or be corporate partners of."

O'Ree, who had been recalled from the Quebec Aces of the QHL because of a rash of injuries with the Bruins, played just one more game in black and gold that 1957–1958 season. But he returned for a 43-game stint during the 1960–1961 campaign.

"I remember what type of a character he was. Willie was a lot of fun. He fit right in with our team, and both on and off the ice, we did everything together," said longtime Bruins captain Johnny Bucyk. "And Willie, he became part of it so quickly. We made no mistake, we just dragged him right with us, and we just had a ball."

O'Ree started playing hockey as a kid in his native Fredericton, New Brunswick, at the urging of his older brother Richard. Coincidentally, another early influence on O'Ree was Jackie Robinson. O'Ree recalled during a television appearance that when he was 14, his baseball team won the league championship and was

O'Ree Broke Color Line with One Good Eye

Not to downplay the abuse and ridicule Willie O'Ree had to take as the first black player in the NHL, but racial bias might've been the second-biggest challenge he had to face. You see, in O'Ree's last season of junior hockey, his teammate Kent Douglas took a slap shot that ricocheted off a stick and caught O'Ree in the right eye.

O'Ree still tells the tale of how Dr. Henderson proclaimed that the puck shattered the retina and O'Ree would never play hockey again. Of course, 45 NHL games, 21 pro seasons, and 450 pro goals later, Henderson was proven very wrong.

A left-hand shot playing on left wing, O'Ree couldn't see out of his right eye, so he had to turn his head around to see the puck with his left eye. He kept the handicap hidden for pretty much his whole career, although he believes the Bruins might have found out at some point in his second stint. But he still managed to blaze two trails as the first black NHLer and perhaps the first blind one.

rewarded with a trip to New York City. At Ebbets Field to attend a Brooklyn Dodgers game, O'Ree's team got to meet Robinson. They talked about baseball, and O'Ree mentioned that he was also a hockey player. Robinson was a little surprised to hear there were black kids playing hockey, but his message was clear, regardless of what O'Ree and his teammates wanted to do with their futures: anything could be accomplished if you put your mind to it.

O'Ree's goal was to make the NHL, and he did. Along the way, he faced the same backlash in hockey Robinson had in baseball. Racial slurs from the fans and opposing players tried O'Ree's resolve. However, turning the other cheek the way Robinson did wouldn't work in hockey.

"I had to stand up and gain the respect of not only the players on the opposition, but the fans," he said.

There were highlights and lowlights during O'Ree's second stint with Boston. On January 1, 1961, he scored the game-winner against Montreal. However, one night he was pushed over the edge emotionally when he was butt-ended by Eric Nesterenko of Chicago.

A bench-clearing brawl ensued, and both players were ejected. O'Ree retreated to the dressing room, and coach Milt Schmidt wouldn't let O'Ree go back out to the bench for fear of his safety. O'Ree recalled sitting in the dark and contemplating his future in hockey.

"If I'm going to leave the league, I'm going to leave the league because I don't have the skills to play anymore," he remembered thinking. "I'm not going to leave the league because somebody's trying to run me out of the league. And if I have to fight, I'm going to fight."

O'Ree's pro career, which lasted more than 20 years, featured 45 NHL games with four goals and 10 assists. His impact on the game is still felt today in his role with the NHL, for whom he does dozens of clinics every year.

Although he's not in the Hockey Hall of Fame (a travesty indeed), O'Ree has been honored in recent years with induction in the New Brunswick Sports Hall of Fame and the San Diego Hall of Champions. His hometown of Fredericton named a new sports complex after him. And in 2008 he received the Order of Canada, one of Canada's highest civilian honors. It recognizes a lifetime of outstanding achievement, dedication to community, and service to the nation.

It might've taken O'Ree a while to get his due, but he's finally received all the recognition he deserves.

23 Cup Mini-Drought Ends in '39

The stretch between the Bruins' first Stanley Cup win in 1929 and their second in 1939 can hardly be called a drought, especially considering the Cupless decades the franchise would suffer through generations later.

However, with Eddie Shore, "Dit" Clapper, Cooney Weiland, and others in their primes for the better part of the '30s, and the arrival and formation of the Kraut Line in 1937–1938, owner Charles Adams, manager/coach Art Ross, and the Boston fan base must've been wondering what it was going to take to bring the Cup to the Hub again. As it turned out, everything prior had just been building toward a thorough domination of the NHL by the Bruins.

Boston finished in first place five times between Cup seasons but only reached one Finals. In 1937–1938 a 30–11–7 regular season went down the drain when Toronto swept Boston out of the Cup semifinals in three straight.

While that defeat might not have fully convinced Ross to make a major change, he had been plotting his unpopular (at the time) decision to move veteran goaltender Cecil "Tiny" Thompson out and replace him with up-and-comer Frank Brimsek. The Bruins certainly didn't look like they needed a change when they woke up November 28, 1938, with a 5–1–1 record. However, Ross still traded his four-time Vezina Trophy–winning goaltender to Detroit for Norm Smith and cash, and then Brimsek was promoted from the Providence Reds for good.

"The team took it pretty badly," Schmidt said about the trade of the Bruins' first Cup-winning goaltender. "Dit Clapper was Tiny's roommate, and he was ready to quit. We just couldn't understand Mr. Ross replacing a sure thing with a rookie."

The Bruins' players and fans, who were equally miffed by the deal, soon found out why Ross had made the move. After losing his first game that season, Brimsek pitched shutouts in six of his next seven to earn the nickname "Mr. Zero." He went on to win the Calder and Vezina Trophy that season.

Of course, he had plenty of help preventing goals. The Bruins allowed a miniscule 76 goals that year, compared to the second-stingiest team (the New York Rangers with 105). Shore, Clapper (who moved from wing the season before), Flash Hollett, Jack Crawford, and Jack Portland proved a suffocating corps of D-men.

"In fact, our defense was so strong we used to do something that would be suicidal in later years," Ross once explained. "I used to order my forwards to play outside when back-checking against the opposing wings. In other words, instead of driving the play to the outside, which is normal, I had them driving it inside, *toward* the goal and not away from it. That way my forwards could be looking at their defensemen at all times and be ready for a pass or loose puck. You had to have a great defense to play like that, and we had it. They were the best team I ever saw in my life."

Just as astounding, those Bruins led the league with 156 goals scored led by Roy Conacher's 26. Bill Cowley's 42-point season led an overall balanced Boston offensive attack. Cowley centered Charlie Sands and Ray Getliffe during the regular season, a trio that was complemented well by the Kraut trio of Milt Schmidt, Bobby Bauer, and Woody Dumart.

After running away with first place in the seven-team NHL, the Bruins opened the playoffs against the second-place Rangers. Ross had already made some alterations to his lines, with Cowley now centering Conacher and Mel Hill. That decision, and the subsequent advice Ross gave Cowley to look for Hill in key situations because the defense would be keying on the more prolific Cowley and Conacher, helped get the Bruins back into the Cup Finals after a seven-game triumph over New York. Hill clinched the series with a goal eight minutes into the third overtime of Game 7—"Sudden Death's" third overtime winner (all set up by Cowley) of the series.

In the Finals the Bruins exacted revenge on Toronto by winning three straight after dropping Game 2. Changes were in store with Weiland retiring from playing and taking over the coaching reins from Ross. But the most important fact was the Cup was back in Boston after a decade away.

The Bruins had no idea that two years later they would capture the Cup one more time. Nor did they know that a much more painful drought loomed on the horizon after that victory. All they knew was that they were the kings of the NHL, and it looked like they had the makings of a dynasty.

Cam Comes to Boston

It's hard to believe that hulking Hall of Famer Cam Neely could ever have been overshadowed.

However, after Bruins general manager Harry Sinden acquired the then-21-year-old right wing from Vancouver in exchange for Barry Pederson in 1986—a deal many say was Sinden's best ever—Boston also received the option to take the Canucks' first-round pick that June or the following summer. While the Bruins had four solid prospects on their list to select if available at No. 7, the potential to get the No. 1 pick in '87 and select junior sensation Pierre Turgeon also made headlines.

By the time Boston opted to exercise their right to commandeer Vancouver's 1987 pick, and settled for the third overall pick (which became defenseman Glen Wesley), it was obvious Boston was about to win the deal going away, regardless of how Wesley or anyone the Bruins picked in the Canucks' spot panned out.

In his first season with Boston, Neely increased his goal total of 14 from his last season in Vancouver to 36 during a 72-point campaign in black and gold. By the time injuries shortened his career, Neely accumulated 395 goals in 13 seasons. In 2005 he was elected to the Hockey Hall of Fame.

"I wasn't playing as much as I wanted to," said Neely the day of the trade, "and I didn't do as well as I thought I would. I was really looking forward to the season, but I didn't get the ice time I thought I would. This is a great break for me. I'm coming to a team and to a division where there is a lot of physical hockey, and I should be able to get in a lot of hits. I'm not the most skilled player in the game, but I work at the game."

Neely, in his third NHL season in 1985–1986, had been buried on the Vancouver depth chart behind Tony Tanti and Stan Smyl by Canucks head coach Tom Watt. Discussions between coach and player often involved Neely lobbying for more time and Watt assuring him that his time would come when he was more experienced. Luckily for the Bruins, Neely's talents weren't hidden by the lack of playing time in the eyes of head scout Bart Bradley.

"People talk about Todd Bertuzzi being a power forward now," the late Bradley told the *Boston Globe* before Neely's HHOF induction. "Bertuzzi is big, and he can more or less bully his way to pucks. But Cam just beat guys with big checks—crushed 'em—and then he had the hands to make plays, and the big shot, too. You just don't see that."

A perfect storm of maneuverings in June 1986 set up Sinden to swing the historic deal. Pederson was a free agent with compensation who planned to test the open market. In covering themselves before the loss of Pederson, the Bruins had signed Vancouver free agent center Thomas Gradin (without compensation). Then the Canucks came up with an offer for Pederson that Sinden deemed would equal or exceed the compensation the Bruins would have received—either two first-round picks or a first-round pick and Vancouver's fifth player—if someone lured away Pederson. Of course, Sinden had the assuring reports from Bradley and scouting director Gary Darling that Neely was a rugged diamond in the rough.

Vancouver acquired the 25-year-old Pederson to provide better playmaking, and he lived up to his billing with two 70-plus-point seasons. However, his production severely dropped off after that. Meanwhile, Wesley justified his high status from the draft by becoming a mainstay on the Boston back end for seven seasons and eventually logging more than 1,400 regular-season NHL contests during the second half of his career with Hartford/Carolina. If Wesley's production made the deal lopsided in Boston's favor, Neely's performance put the Bruins in a different universe from the Canucks in terms of the trade.

Sinden had called Neely an "Adams Division–type player" when the swap was made. What the GM received was a player who epitomized what Eddie Shore had started in the 1920s and the "Big, Bad Bruins" of the late '60s and early '70s had ingrained on every Boston fans' brain about what being a Bruin meant in terms of toughness, desire, and determination. Oh, and it didn't hurt that Neely scored more than 50 goals in a season three times.

Bradley summed it up best about a year before his death.

"Gotta be the best trade I was ever a part of," he explained. "[Terry] O'Reilly had called it quits, and we needed that physical presence, a fighter. We were figuring Cam for maybe 25 to 30 goals a year, and we wanted that toughness in the lineup to replace Terry. We got the toughness and a whole lot more goals than we figured."

25 Dit

You might think that with a name like Aubrey "Dit" Clapper—what a fun name to say—a person would grow ornery over a lot of years of carrying that moniker. A name like that could be the object of ridicule and a source of embarrassment.

But Clapper's career with the Bruins was highlighted by two things—tons of on-ice success as a forward and a defenseman, and gentlemanly play that earned him respect among his contemporaries and from people around the NHL for decades after he left the league.

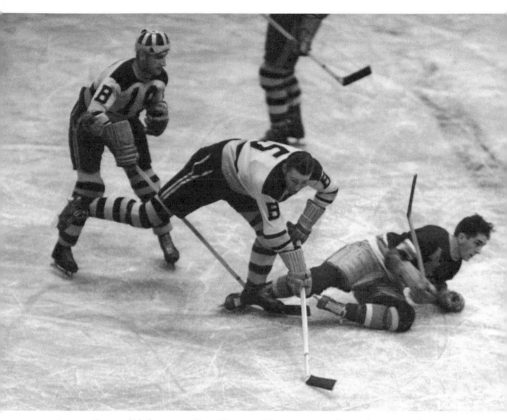

Bruins forward/defenseman Dit Clapper (5) tries to get the puck against the New York Rangers during a game in the 1930s at Madison Square Garden. Clapper played 20 seasons with the Bruins, from 1927 to 1947.

At 6'2", 200 pounds, Clapper played with the power expected of a man that size. He earned NHL Second Team All-Star accolades as a forward in 1931 and 1935, and then from the blue line was a First Team All-Star three times and a Second Team All-Star once—the only player to be voted an NHL All-Star at forward and defense.

Yet he did it all with such grace that even punching a referee didn't draw Clapper a ban. In 1937 Clapper struck referee Clarence Campbell, who would go on to become president of the NHL, while Campbell was breaking up a tussle. At the recommendation of Campbell, however, Clapper received just a $100 fine and a stern talking-to.

"I was talking loud when I should have been throwing them into the penalty box," Campbell was quoted after he shifted blame away from Clapper in his report to the league president Frank Calder.

Even the great Maurice Richard was touched by Clapper's sportsmanship. Early in the career of "the Rocket," Clapper made sure to let the injury-prone Richard know that skating with his head down was a no-no. Clapper reportedly wrapped his arms around Richard and told him, "Keep your head up in this league, kid."

A defenseman during his amateur hockey days, Clapper was shifted to forward by Bruins general manager Art Ross to start an NHL career that would become the first to last 20 years. Clapper scored his first NHL goal just 10 seconds into his first shift and didn't stop producing for two decades. In just his third season, he poured in 41 goals in 44 games as part of the Dynamite Line with Cooney Weiland and Norman "Dutch" Gainor. That trio helped lead the Bruins to their first Stanley Cup title in 1929.

After 10 seasons, 167 goals, and numerous accolades as a right winger, Clapper moved back to defense to first aid Eddie Shore and then replace the living legend. For the next 10 seasons, Clapper carried on the tradition Shore had started of defensemen excelling in all aspects of the game, including on offense. Clapper's 61 goals and 130 assists as a defenseman were Bruins records that stood for a quarter century until the great Bobby Orr surpassed them. Clapper, the Bruins' captain for six seasons, also starred on two more Cup-winning teams (in '39 and '41), making him the only player in Bruins' history to win three Stanley Cup titles in black and gold.

In the late '40s Clapper briefly served as a player/coach and then just head coach for the Bruins. But his gentlemanly ways proved to be a detriment to his ability to coach.

"Being a coach is a lousy job," he said. "I couldn't abuse these players. They're my friends."

Clapper's brief coaching stint did nothing to sully his reputation. A nickname that started because Clapper's little sister couldn't pronounce his middle name, Vic, became synonymous with hockey greatness. It wound up on a plaque in the Hockey Hall of Fame in 1947, when Clapper was the first living player inducted into the hallowed museum.

Bourque Makes Espo's Night

Like a giant-sized game of "telephone," a story over decades can get exaggerated, altered, and more convoluted than the simple original tale.

Longtime Bruins public relations master and senior assistant to the president Nate Greenberg, long since retired from the club, wants to once and for all put to rest any variations on the story of the decision to have Ray Bourque give up No. 7 and switch to No. 77 so that Phil Esposito's sweater number could truly be retired December 3, 1987.

"Nobody, including Bourque, knew about it until the day before," Greenberg said. "I've heard more stories about this player or this agent or whatever. And it was very last-minute, like the day before."

"I can remember like it was yesterday, we were playing in Hartford the night before the ceremony," he continued. "And we had the discussion. It was Tom Johnson and Harry [Sinden] and I, and we're driving down to Hartford and talked about asking Bourque to give up his number—which, of course, he was happy to do."

The decision made mostly by Sinden and then-Bruins coach Terry O'Reilly, and the willingness of Bourque to honor history, set the stage for one of the most emotional nights in Boston Garden history.

"It was unbelievable. And when he took [the No. 7 sweater] off, if you could read my lips, I went, 'What are you doing?' And he looked at me and said, 'This is yours, big boy, and it's always been yours, and it never should've been anybody else's.' I'll tell you, he got me," said Esposito.

Oddly enough, Bourque wore No. 29 during his first NHL training camp in 1979. But when the season opened, No. 7 was hanging in his stall. A number of his teammates told him to ignore any heckling he might receive due to wearing Esposito's number, and that's just what Bourque did at the outset of his Hall of Fame career. Hard feelings between Esposito and Sinden following the trade that sent the superstar center to New York in 1975, plus an allergy to retiring numbers on the part of Garden president Paul Mooney, had postponed Esposito getting his proper due since his retirement as a player in 1981. However, Bourque wearing the number paid better tribute to the club's single-season point leader than when the team gave the number to Sean Shanahan and Bill Bennett prior to Bourque.

Over the years, Bourque offered numerous times to give up the number. But even the day before the Garden ceremony, no one knew what would unfold. Getting dressed for the ceremony, Bourque made sure to pile on the sweaters in a separate room so no one would notice. And then came the presentation. After Bourque was introduced by master of ceremonies and Bruins radio voice Bob Wilson, the Bruins' star skated up to Esposito and handed him the No. 7 sweater. Then Bourque pulled off his own No. 7 sweater and revealed his new No. 77. "When I took off No. 7, it was the first time I ever saw Phil Esposito speechless," Bourque has often said when recapping that evening.

A banner, or even two banners, honoring Esposito and Bourque as legendary No. 7s in Bruins history might not have looked that odd in the Garden rafters. But there's no doubt that having Esposito's 7 and Bourque's 77—the Bruins retired Bourque's digits October 4, 2001—truly honors them as individual pillars of Bruins greatness.

And the night Bourque made his noble gesture is still talked about everywhere he goes.

"One of the special moments," Bourque said, "is when a fan tells me, 'That was great, I was at that game.'"

27 Starving for Stanley Since '72

Prior to 2011, the Bruins actually had the second-longest Stanley Cup drought among beloved Original Six franchises. Only Toronto had waited longer to win sports' most-famous trophy after Chicago won its title in 2010. It just felt like the Bruins had been waiting since the dawn of time for their title because of everything the franchise went through before ending its drought.

"It's hard to win; it's hard to win," said Mike Milbury, a player, coach, and assistant general manager with the Bruins for more than a decade in the post-1972 portion of the team's history. "What was it, 28 seasons without a missed playoff? That's pretty impressive."

Actually, the Bruins qualified for the postseason 29 straight years before missing the tournament in 1997. And then they were back in during the playoffs in '98 and '99. To some, Boston's run of success at participating in the playoffs made the lack of a championship tougher to bear. There's no doubt, a long-suffering, loyal fan base had its collective morale beaten down and its hopes crushed time and again.

Detailing every reason for the Bruins' inability to win a Cup would probably take a book of its own. So, if it's not too painful to read, we can hit some of the highlights—or lowlights, as the case may be.

Without question, the Bruins' best single-season squads were the victim of some poor timing as far as the peaking of other franchises. The late 1970s Montreal Canadiens, early '80s New York Islanders, and mid- to late '80s Edmonton Oilers were bona fide dynasties that maybe no one would have beaten.

"Obviously, I look at timing from our perspective," said Hall of Famer Cam Neely, echoing the sentiment of a number of his teammates. "When I was playing, the two years that we lost to Pittsburgh in the conference finals ['91 and '92], they ended up playing Chicago or Minnesota. Which it's a little different team than playing Edmonton. I feel like if we got by Pittsburgh, maybe we had a better shot at winning than playing Edmonton. So timing has something to do with it, too."

Unfortunate timing hasn't been relegated to just the identity of the opposition. Costly penalties might've held the Bruins back, as longtime general manager/president Harry Sinden said, "We were kind of a victim of our own reputation in the playoffs so often." And then there was the penalty that had nothing to do with the Bruins' "Big, Bad" reputation. Late in Game 7 of the Cup semifinal series with Montreal in '79, Boston got mixed up trying to shadow Guy Lafleur, and the whistle blow that was heard 'round New England sent the Canadiens on the power play. After the tying goal and the winning goal (in overtime) followed, the Bruins were denied a berth in the Cup Finals against the very beatable New York Rangers.

"For that time, in that era, I would say there was nothing that compared to that too-many-men-on-the-ice situation," said former

Bruins assistant to the president Nate Greenberg, calling that game the most heartbreaking in Bruins history. "Even though that was the Stanley Cup semifinals, that was really the finals. They had the Rangers after that. The Rangers were not that good of a team. It was really felt that the winner of Boston-Montreal would win the Stanley Cup. And to think that you could lose in such an unbelievably bizarre way…it's still incredible to me."

The arrival of the World Hockey Association with enough money to lure away four key contributors to the '72 Cup team obviously set Boston back in its quest for its own dynasty. Ken Dryden and Bernie Parent certainly had a say in the Bruins' fate when they heated up and "stood on their head" in goal against Boston. And then there was the parade of injuries. Every franchise in every sport suffers its share of career-altering or career-ending injuries to star or promising players. The Bruins' list of those short-circuited by ailments, however, seems particularly long and cruel.

Of course, you start with Bobby Orr, who battled through his knee injuries to get the Bruins to the '74 Finals and then fought through 80 games in 1974–1975 but then played just 10 more games in black and gold. Orr then played just 26 games over two seasons for Chicago before retiring at 31. Neely's various ailments, which he overcame to score 50 goals in 49 games in 1994–1995, forced him from the game at the same age as Orr.

At least Boston was treated to some tremendous prime years of marveling at Orr and Neely. The what-might-have-been group in Bruins history is even longer. In fall 1982 up-and-coming left winger Normand Leveille, Boston's first-round pick in '81, was discovered to have a defective blood vessel since birth. It ruptured one night during a game against Vancouver, although doctors said even the slightest thing like a sneeze could've triggered the complication. Surgery saved his life but left him disabled at 19 and unable to ever play hockey again.

"That was more a human tragedy than it is a hockey tragedy. Nonetheless, Normand Leveille was going to really be a good player," said New England Sports Museum curator Richard Johnson.

Gord Kluzak, who Boston selected first overall in 1982, was limited to just 299 regular-season games and missed two full seasons due to knee injuries. Had he stayed healthy, Kluzak, according to Johnson, was "going to be our Larry Robinson," comparing Boston's blueliner to Montreal's star defenseman.

Before he was traded for Neely, Barry Pederson was slowed by a tumor in his arm. Jonathan Girard might've become another stud defenseman for Boston in the early 2000s had he not suffered career-ending injuries in a car accident. Too often, the Bruins have been forced to dream of a player's star potential rather than getting to benefit from it.

Finally, some of the Bruins' shortcomings in the championship pursuit were self-inflicted. It's a volatile topic that seemingly gets fans' dander up and puts Sinden and longtime owner Jeremy Jacobs in full defense mode. Throughout the drought, and particularly from the 1990s up until the post-lockout salary cap was adopted, the Bruins were hesitant to spend much money on individuals. Many have said that Boston always spent enough, made just enough player additions, to make the playoffs. But when it came time to really go for the championship, financial decisions ruled the day. No player could ever guarantee the Bruins a Cup victory, so it was better to play it safe and protect the bottom line.

"Harry Sinden can spend whatever it takes to put that team out there," Jacobs told the *Boston Globe* in '97 when pressed on whether Sinden was free to spend on marquee free agents. "But it's been proven in hockey that you can't buy a team. Well, you can buy a team, but you can't buy a winner. I mean, look at Edmonton and

Buffalo this year. They've beaten the shit out of us this year, they've kicked our ass, and look how cheap their payrolls are—all lower."

Sinden, who always took the heat for the club's actions, always said he spent Jacobs' money like it was more important than his own. He's still quick, some 37 years since the last Bruins championship, to point out that Cup-winning teams prior to the lockout—such as the '94 Rangers and the multi-time winners in Detroit and Colorado—were bought. And then the Rangers, with an astronomical payroll, missed the playoffs more often than not after their Cup and before the salary cap arrived. Sinden doesn't shy away from his pride in avoiding a potentially money-wasting strategy.

"What happens is, if you're going to blow a lot of money like that, you can bring in players and have them fail. It's like the Red Sox and Yankees can do. You can pay them big money and have them fail and try someone else," said Sinden one day in a break from his role as the owner's senior adviser in 2009. "If you're trying to make a business work, you can't do that. So you pass on a lot of players. And, also, I felt that you could win in this league even without having the best players. And you can do it; teams have. Tampa Bay [in '04]. And then if we could win and be in the bottom third of the payroll, then it might influence everybody and stop the madness that led us to shut this entire league down. There's only one reason it shut down, and I'm happy to say I didn't have any part in that."

Milbury benefitted from Sinden adding Brian Propp to Boston's push in '90. And 14 years later GM Mike O'Connell was able to add Sergei Gonchar and Michael Nylander at the trade deadline to try to put the Bruins over the top. None of the moves ended the drought. And those instances of trading a bit of the future (draft picks, prospects) for established, tide-turning stars were few and far between.

"Being good enough but not quite there—maybe a player or two might've made a difference," makes Neely's list—and those of many players from the last almost 40 years—of reasons for the drought.

The Bruins' Cupless stretch grew more painful in the 21st century because of the overwhelming success of the New England Patriots and Boston Red Sox, and the resurgence of the Boston Celtics. Once kings of the town, the Bruins are now a distant fourth in the sports pecking order of the Hub. The Leafs might have a similar sob story about their drought, but they didn't have to compete with the success of multiple teams in their own backyard at the same time.

Finally, in 2010–11, GM Peter Chiarelli and his staff found the formula for solving the Bruins' championship allergy and made sure that the drought didn't reach 40 years, never mind half a century. Boston was starving for a Stanley Cup title and the Bruins finally delivered one.

28 Being a Bruin Means Being Big and Bad

So you want to play for the Bruins?

If you want to wear the spoked "B" on your chest and call the building on Causeway Street your home rink, you have to live up to certain expectations. Casting a large shadow is a start. But even if you don't measure up to some of the giants of the NHL, you have to play as though you do. That means playing with the heart of a lion, with little fear and tons of determination. And then there's the other element, the physicality that not only makes opponents think twice before going to the net or into the corner, but brings the Boston faithful out of their seats.

When it comes down to it—even in a more-regulated NHL— to play for Boston's hockey franchise you have to be a "Big, Bad Bruin."

"For me, that's the way and pretty much the only way I know how to play. So I kind of fit that mold," said young forward Milan Lucic, who is Boston's most recent combination of skill, smarts, and grit to capture the hearts of the Bruins' fandom. "It's kind of lucky and fortunate that I ended up somewhere like that. It's definitely every time you put the jersey on you want to keep that legacy alive and try not to disappoint."

That legacy is most closely associated with the Bruins teams of the late '60s that went on to win two Stanley Cup championships in the early '70s. However, you could trace the "Big, Bad" persona all the way back to the early days of the franchise. From Eddie Shore through the years of Fernie Flaman and then Leo Labine, Leo Boivin, and Ted Green, the Bruins' most beloved players—in lean years and successful ones—were the ones that best found a way to use physicality to be the most effective player they could be.

"The prototypical Bruins player is one who plays with skill but occasionally will have blood on his jersey, preferably not his own," explained New England Sports Museum curator Richard Johnson.

Blood and guts were permanently established as ornaments of a perfect Bruins uniform, finally, in the late 1960s. The signing of Bobby Orr—and his emergence as the game's greatest force— meant that opponents at a loss for a way to stop the sport-changing defenseman would resort to violence. Then with the trade for Phil Esposito, Ken Hodge, and Fred Stanfield, general manager Milt Schmidt began to add the type of size that would make the opposition think twice before taking physical liberties with any Bruins player.

"The first thing I have to do is get two or three big forwards. I got to thinking of guys who played for the Bruins in the days when we were winning. I thought of Dit Clapper, Eddie Shore, Johnny Crawford, and Ray Getliffe," said Schmidt at the time. "At one time, you know, they used to say that if you could get through the door, you couldn't play for the Bruins."

The Boston Garden, with its rink 15 feet shorter than a regulation sheet, was the perfect stage for bigness and badness. Less space to escape meant more hits and more blows. But the Orr-led teams had a bond that went beyond ice and translated into an on-ice *Three Musketeers* attitude that pushed "Big, Bad" to a whole new level.

"We had a two-beer minimum," explained forward Derek Sanderson, who was the epitome of "Big, Bad" for the Cup-winning teams of '70 and '72. "Everybody had to go together. It didn't matter if you had your family in town or whatever you were doing, you had to show up with the guys and come for a couple beers."

The familial atmosphere that drinking policy forged made the Bruins' players look at each other as brothers. And brothers stand up for each other. The preseason of 1967 featured a few bench-clearing brawls that proved no one was going to pick on the Bruins, who were fighting to end almost a decade of playoff-less seasons.

Opponents took notice.

"The front office long ago made it clear they wanted a big, hitting team," defenseman Brad Park wrote in his book *Play the Man* long before he was traded from the New York Rangers to the Bruins. "Players who joined the Bruins underwent dramatic psychological changes. Take Ken Hodge. When he played for Chicago, he was a relatively peaceful skater whose primary aim was scoring. But as a Bruin he suddenly started picking fights all over the place."

Those in the other dressing room probably chose to focus on the Bruins' fights because they were helpless to stop Boston from scoring. The Cup-winning teams were twice as good at beating teams as they were at beating them up. While no Cup wins have followed since '72, the "Big, Bad" philosophy has been behind the team's most successful seasons in the more than three decades after that triumph.

From Terry O'Reilly to Cam Neely to Lucic—and including numerous players who skated alongside them—the fans have demanded, and the coaches and general managers have tried to provide, "Big, Bad" players and teams.

"It's important to keep some identity of what the organization has been about, even though the game has evolved and changed over the years," said Neely, who carved out a Hall of Fame career as a "Big, Bad" player and has dedicated his time as the club's VP and president to making sure the legacy lives on. "But I think that identity of coming to work hard and play hard and be hard to play against should still be part of the fabric of the teams."

The game has obviously changed since the days of Orr and Esposito, and even the days of O'Reilly and the years of Neely. It could be construed as unfair to hold up modern-day players to the same standard as those who were allowed so much leeway as far as physical play and fighting. Some guys, even an overwhelming talent like Joe Thornton, have melted under the heat of "Big, Bad" expectations. Bruins players of the 21st century, however, have translated the "Big, Bad" approach to suit the climate of the day, by working hard, finishing checks, and showing emotion whenever possible.

"It's all about playing hard," young winger Blake Wheeler said. "Not everyone plays the style of game that's associated with the Bruins of the '70s and the Cam Neely era, but it's more about playing hard out there and doing the little things well—the little things that probably go unnoticed on the score sheet that this organization prides itself on. It's made a lot of great players and a lot of great teams. If you play hard and do what's expected of you, you're going to be well-received within the team, the organization. Obviously, the fans respond to the fighters and the guys who are putting people into the boards, as they should. But it's expected that you go out and play hard every night."

The legacy of the "Big, Bad Bruins" certainly lives on.

29 "Lunch Pail A.C." Carried the Post-Orr Mantle

After losing in the first round of the 1975 playoffs to the Chicago Blackhawks, the Bruins needed a new identity. Some even thought they needed a new coach, as Don Cherry hadn't exactly proved himself worthy of leading the likes of Bobby Orr and Phil Esposito during his first NHL season behind the bench.

General manager Harry Sinden, however, decided to not change his coach. He opted to let Cherry do whatever it would take to turn the Bruins back into a championship-caliber club.

"We went out to have a few pops and some Chinese food— Harry loves Chinese food—and he said, 'You've got to find a way to make this team win or we're both going to get fired,'" Cherry recalled years after that '75 conversation. "He said, 'Do whatever you have to do. Turn the players against me if you have to.' Well, I took that to heart and I took it to the extreme. We were us against the world. We thought Harry was against us, we thought the league was against us, everyone was against us."

Orr would play only 10 more games with the Bruins because of injury, and Esposito would be traded after just 12 games in 1975–1976. It was time for the "Big, Bad Bruins" to give way to a new era—and the "Lunch Pail A.C." was born.

Terry O'Reilly, the poster child for the Bruins' teams of those late '70s Bruins teams because of his all-out effort every night, described the "Lunch Pail" moniker as representative of the Bruins being "good, hard-working, honest players." You couldn't find a more relentless, courageous, determined bunch of players in the entire NHL.

Boston Globe Hall of Fame writer Fran Rosa was responsible for dubbing Cherry's teams with their nickname.

"It seems to me I was talking to someone about them and said, 'They're like working stiffs—get up and go to work and then go home,'" the long-since-retired Rosa once recalled. "And they said, 'Like a lunch pail guy.' And I said, 'Yeah, just like that.' I added gang because they were a team, and they were very much a team. It's funny because some of the players, I don't remember who exactly, almost resented the fact that I called them that, because they thought it implied that they had no talent; that they were just a bunch of working stiffs. It wasn't true. They had talent on those Cherry teams; the nickname just described the work they did."

"Lunch Pail Gang" morphed into "Lunch Pail A.C."—meaning Athletic Club—depending on who was speaking or writing about the teams that were not only endearing to the Boston faithful but the top draw on the road, as well.

"We had such a good team, and a hard-working team, a team that cared, that even the errors of one guy never really stood out," said winger Rick Middleton. "They were always covered up by the successes of others. If one line had a bad game, the other lines usually picked it up. And not often did we ever really throw a stinker out there."

The epitome of the "Lunch Pail" teams might've been the likes of tough guy John Wensink and stay-at-home defenseman Mike Milbury, players who weren't given a chance at an NHL career until Cherry gave them an opportunity. Stan Jonathan, Bobby Schmautz, Wayne Cashman, and O'Reilly were others who over-achieved under Cherry's tutelage.

However, anyone who would suggest the team was just about toughness—one writer even claimed that defenseman Brad Park and goaltender Gerry Cheevers were Cherry's only traditional stars—

would be insulting some great skill players of that generation. Middleton, Jean Ratelle, and Peter McNab were some of the most talented players around. They were perennially among the league's leading scorers. In the 1977–1978 season Boston featured 11 players with 20 or more goals. You don't get that type of production just by working hard. It takes talent. And that talent, combined with the hardest work ethic in the league, carried Boston to two Stanley Cup Finals and one Cup semifinals.

Maybe that talent was overshadowed a bit by the other antics, whether it was O'Reilly bludgeoning a guy in a fight or Wensink challenging the Minnesota bench to step on the ice and fight him. The team's foray into the Madison Square Garden stands also did little to discourage the notion that there was some barbarism running through their veins. But in a sport that requires a high level of team work, the "Lunch Pail A.C." guys were a brotherhood who never let each other down. And that turned into winning hockey.

"There was nothing better in the history of hockey than sitting with those players after a game, on the road, in the locker room after a game," said McNab. "It could be the greatest moment of your life or the worst moment. If you didn't play well, it was the most humbling, embarrassing moment. On the other hand, you could sit there, and Wayne Cashman would come by, Terry O'Reilly would come by and say, 'Good game, Maxie.' You could not be higher."

The ultimate win eluded Cherry's teams, and "Lunch Pail A.C." was pretty much disbanded when Cherry was fired after the 1979 Cup semifinal series that featured the infamous too-many-men game. However, a franchise that could've sunk to the doldrums after the departure of Orr, arguably the greatest player ever, was able to march on thanks to Cherry and his band of blue-collar workers. "Lunch Pail A.C." proved to be the perfect follow-up to the "Big, Bad Bruins."

30 Cam Was the "Comeback Kid"

Cam Neely has appeared in enough movies over the years that he could easily play himself in a retelling of his 1993–1994 comeback season.

But the scenes' drama might be a tad over his head—he's so far done only comedies, after all—and might actually require a Russell Crowe or George Clooney to reenact the story. (How has this movie not been made yet?)

To think that Cam Neely played just 22 games over two seasons prior to the 1993–1994 campaign and then returned to score 50 goals in 49 games, maybe even Hollywood wouldn't buy the tale as realistic.

"You couldn't even write a script where that's how it would play out," Neely said.

Neely enjoyed seasons of 55 and 51 goals in the 1989–1990 and 1990–1991 seasons. In 1991 he helped lead the Bruins to the Wales Conference Finals, where they met the eventual Stanley Cup–champion Pittsburgh Penguins. It was in that series that Neely unfortunately ran into defenseman Ulf Samuelsson, who battered Neely with a couple questionable hits, including one to Neely's left thigh. To this day, when asked about Samuelsson, Neely explains that he has "no respect" for the way his arch nemesis played the game. The thigh injury ushered the end of Neely's NHL career a little closer, as he battled related knee and hip problems until the conclusion of his stint.

The next two seasons were filled with starts, stops, and lots and lots of rehabilitation for Neely, as he logged just nine games the following season and 13 the year after that. Despite his physical, all-out style, Neely had missed just a handful of games since joining the Bruins in a 1986 trade. But it looked like the Samuelsson hit might be the last memory of Neely at his Hall of Fame best on the ice. Of course, when your ultimate destination is the Hockey Hall of Fame, you don't go away that easily.

When the 1993–1994 season opened, no one knew how much Neely had left in the tank. Ironically, linemates Adam Oates and Joe Juneau also broke camp with questions about their knees. But the only knee everyone was talking about was Neely's left one. Bruins general manager Harry Sinden and assistant GM Mike Milbury took some of the pressure off Neely that fall by telling their star to play only when he felt capable. The odds were he wouldn't play back-to-back games and would at least be a presence on the ice, even if he couldn't be the same producer he was before the injury.

Neely played the first two games of the season and scored a goal in each. After missing three of the next four contests, he scored twice in Vancouver on October 19. He took one game off and then came back to score three goals in two games, including a spin-o-rama for his sixth of the season against Ottawa. Suddenly the Bruins and their fans were able to dream of big things for their beloved No. 8.

As if battling a knee injury wasn't enough for Neely to take, in late November he also had to deal with the death of his father to cancer. Neely, whose mother had passed away five years earlier also because of cancer, left the team for three games to attend to family matters.

"Throughout my ordeal with my knee, as much as it was hard not playing, my dad was going through something a hell of a lot worse," he said at the time. "To see his positive attitude, he never once complained about his situation. He always thought he was going to beat it. That certainly rubbed off on me and the rest of my family. I learned a lot from him the past six or seven years he was battling cancer."

Michael Neely's impact on his son continued to pay off. Cam Neely returned to the Bruins on November 30 and scored against Quebec. The soap opera unfolded the same way all season. Some nights, you didn't know if Neely was going to play until the Bruins hit the ice for warm-ups. Sometimes he'd surprise you by playing consecutive games, and sometimes he'd miss a couple in a row and leave you thinking he might not be back.

But he seemingly always came back and left your mouth ajar.

"Some goals he'd score, you'd just laugh. You'd be like, 'Is this really happening?' I don't remember him getting a lot of lucky goals either," longtime *Quincy Patriot Ledger* beat writer Mike Loftus said.

By late February, the drama had hit a fever pitch. Neely had a chance to score 50 goals in near-record time. Two shy of 50 on March 7, his 44th match of the season, Neely wowed the crowd with a pair of scores—including the milestone marker in typical Neely fashion, as he beat Washington goaltender Olaf Kolzig with a waist-high tip of a Dave Shaw shot from the point. Elation and hats (even though it wasn't a hat trick) bathed the ice after Neely became the second-fastest to 50 goals behind only fellow legend Wayne Gretzky and tying Mario Lemieux.

"I would say that Cam's year that he scored [50 goals] in many ways is comparable—because of the situations that both players faced—it was a Bobby Orr year in every dimension," said Richard Johnson, curator of the New England Sports Museum. "It's amazing. It's a Bobby Orr year. Not many players have Bobby Orr years except for Bobby Orr."

Neely went scoreless in his next five games, and then the cruelest of fates hit on March 19. Neely injured his right knee in a collision with Ken Daneyko, an ailment that—despite some rigorous rehab in an effort to return during the playoffs—ended the power forward's season. Neely played two more seasons before retiring.

Maybe that ending was a way to remind everyone that Neely's dream season was happening in real life. If it was fiction, it certainly would have ended more triumphantly than with surgery and a Masterton Trophy, which Neely won by vote of the league's hockey writers. Abridged or not, Neely's comeback of 1993–1994 was by far one of the top dramas in Bruins history.

 **Mr. Zero**

If you're at a speed-dating party or playing the horses, the last thing you want to be described as is "Mr. Zero."

In fact, a goal crease might be the only place one would want that tag. Legendary Bruins goalie Frank Brimsek, who became the first U.S.-born player inducted into the Hockey Hall of Fame in 1966 and led Boston to two Stanley Cup championships, had no qualms about the nickname he earned when he made a remarkable splash as an NHL rookie in December 1938.

And to understand how astonishing Brimsek's breakout performance was, you have to realize that no one—except maybe Bruins general manager Art Ross—thought anyone but Cecil "Tiny" Thompson would be tending goal for the Black and Gold that season and for the foreseeable future. The odds that a Minnesota-born kid who was signed sight-unseen by Ross would knock a four-time Vezina Trophy winner like Thompson from his perch were too lopsided to compute.

Ross, however, had been impressed with Brimsek's play with the Providence Reds of the American League. And the rookie made a strong case for full-time NHL employment earlier in the season while filling in for Thompson, who was out with an eye infection, for two games—both victories. Ross had a regular Tom Brady–

Drew Bledsoe dilemma on his hands some 70 years before the two New England Patriots quarterbacks would vie for the adoration of their fan base and management.

In late November Ross played his hand by dealing Thompson to Detroit and handing the reins of his team over to Brimsek. The son of Slovenian immigrant parents was suddenly carrying the fortunes of Boston's franchise in a league overwhelmingly dominated by Canadian-born players. Brimsek faced the challenge of not only replacing a future Hall of Famer but also a player so popular with the fans and his teammates that defenseman Dit Clapper actually demanded a trade.

The cynical fan base—in Boston? Really?—received plenty of fuel for its fire when Brimsek dropped the first game of his return to the big league's while Thompson won his Detroit debut. He also didn't help his cause by wearing an old pair of red hockey pants rather than the traditional gold, brown, and white Bruins uniform.

However, jeers turned to cheers—and disgruntled teammates like Clapper had a change of heart—over the next couple weeks. Brimsek earned his famous nickname with six—six!—shutouts in his next seven games and began his march toward hockey immortality.

In only his fifth game with the Bruins, Brimsek broke Thompson's previous team record for consecutive shutout time—a stretch that ended at 231 minutes, 54 seconds, which is still the Bruins' record. Brimsek's second streak came up just short of his new record at 220:24. The kid from Eveleth (Minn.) High School had everyone wondering, "Tiny who?"

"The kid had the fastest hands I ever saw—like lightning," Ross was quoted about Brimsek in 1938.

Brimsek earned the Calder Trophy and the Vezina Trophy with a 1.56 goals-against average and 10 shutouts in his rookie season. In leading the Bruins to their second Cup, he compiled a 1.25 GAA in 12 playoff games. In the Cup year of 1941 he registered a 2.04 GAA in 11 games played and followed that with a Vezina-winning season in 1942 (2.35 GAA in 47 games). That '42 season truly wrote his name in permanent ink in Bruins' folklore as he carried a team that lost the famous Kraut Line of Milt Schmidt, Bobby Bauer, and Woody Dumart to the Canadian Armed Forces to a playoff spot (and a semifinals defeat to Detroit).

The next season Brimsek followed his high-profile teammates into the Armed Forces by enlisting in the U.S. Coast Guard. While the NHL went on without "Mr. Zero" for two seasons, Brimsek served aboard a patrol boat in the Pacific.

When he returned stateside, Brimsek rejoined the Bruins for four seasons, but he was never the same. "Walking those decks for two years was hard on my feet," said Brimsek, who passed away in 1998. "My legs were never the same again after the war."

Brimsek was immortalized with induction in both the Hockey Hall of Fame and U.S Hockey Hall of Fame, and the award for the best high school senior goalie carries his name, as well. On the Bruins' all-time charts, only Thompson ranks above Brimsek in games played (444), minutes played (27,010), and wins (230). Of course, arguably, Brimsek trumps Thompson when it comes to nicknames. Legions of goaltenders to this day would beg for that moniker.

32 Chara Writes Own Tall Tales in Hub

There were people all through the ranks of his youth and junior hockey careers that told Zdeno Chara he was too tall, too slow, and just not good enough to play at the game's highest level.

After eight seasons as a complementary player, he signed a five-year, $37.5 million contract with the Bruins in July 2006. Chara struggled in his first season, and his critics told him he wasn't good enough to be a No. 1 defenseman and lacked the ability to be a leader, a captain, of a top NHL team.

Luckily for the Bruins, Chara has made a career out of proving everyone wrong. He got the ultimate last laugh when he led the Bruins to the 2011 Stanley Cup championship two years after he was awarded the Norris Trophy as the game's best defenseman. The Bruins earned their first playoff-series win in 10 years that same year, won another first-round series in 2010, and then earned the 16 wins necessary for the Cup in 2011. But never once did Chara decide he was done working hard and improving.

"Every year I try to prove that I can be better," said Chara. "Winning the Norris Trophy was a big statement, was a big thing, and I really enjoyed it very much. But now I want to prove that it wasn't just a fluke.... To be able to win trophies, you need to be able to play well as a team, be on top of every aspect of the game as a team.... I still want to win the Norris Trophy, but the main thing is I want to win the Stanley Cup and bring it back to Boston. Being named to an All-Star team is also great, but again it's only because you have so much support from your teammates."

From the time of Eddie Shore all the way through the Bobby Orr and Raymond Bourque years, the Bruins were always at their best when they dressed the game's best defenseman. After a few subpar years in the aftermath of Bourque's trade out of town, the Bruins knew they had to do something to replicate that formula. Chara had no problem taking on that challenge.

"It was one of the reasons I chose to go to Boston—so much legacy and so much history. Having players, obviously, like Bobby Orr and Raymond Bourque, Brian Leetch, such great players to have in a club's history, was a big motivation, a big challenge," he said some four seasons into his Bruins stint. "So it was something I looked forward to going into Boston."

Chara assessed his options, and weighed offers from a reported 20 other teams before deciding to become a Bruin. Boston had finished

*Zdeno Chara shoots against the Philadelphia Flyers in Game 1 of the 2010
Eastern Conference Semifinals at TD Garden, a 5–4 Bruins overtime win.
Chara was awarded the Norris Trophy as the NHL's best defenseman in 2009.*

second-to-last in the East prior to Chara's arrival, but he predicted
bigger and better things for the franchise now that he was on board.

"You have to have guys who are willing to sacrifice and pay the
price to win," he said the week he signed. "I just felt with the guys
we have, they will do that, guys who are willing to make that extra
effort. We want to create on this team that definition, to be the
hardest team to play against. We want to be a really hard-working
team and just outwork other teams. I think that's what we have
been missing here."

But how could Chara mold himself into the best in the business at his position and also lead his brethren in black and gold to

a higher plane? Obviously it would take more than a big contract, a big shot, and a "C" sewn on his sweater. Chara's reputation for pushing his enormous, sculpted body—at 6'9" he is the tallest player in NHL history—to the max preceded him to Boston. The tales of him riding ahead of the Tour de France stages and working out six or seven hours a day during the off-season (and *only* an hour or two after games) foreshadowed the type of player and leader he could become. It was with that work ethic that Chara first made his mark with the Bruins.

"His worth ethic and his focus is second to none," said long-time teammate Andrew Ference when asked about Chara's presence among the Bruins. "He's a personality that he expects a tremendous amount out of himself. I guess that's probably his biggest asset as far as never being satisfied and really demanding a lot of himself. He's hard on himself…but he'll never go into that shell of feeling sorry for himself. He'll just push harder and work harder until he gets it right. Especially for the young guys coming in, we're not all going to be able to lift the same kind of weight as he will, but you can kind of strive for that kind of production that he demands of himself."

The Bruins didn't improve in Chara's first season, and he seemed lost as the team's captain. But in his second season, Chara came to the realization that his salary and captaincy didn't mean he had to do everything himself. With that burden off his shoulders, Chara emerged as an All-Star on a playoff-bound team and then made the Norris Trophy part of his collection.

"There is so much behind the story of my making it to the NHL," he said after winning the Norris. "This is such a reward, not just for me but for all the people who believed in me and never gave up on me. I wasn't supposed to make it past juniors. I was cut from every team. To prove the other people wrong is such a satisfying feeling."

It's satisfying for Chara *and* for the Bruins.

33 Cowboy

Long before Phil Esposito and Adam Oates became point-producing machines in Bruins sweaters and Wayne Gretzky and Mario Lemieux changed the entire game of hockey with their unheard-of offensive eruptions, there was Bill Cowley.

While skating in the shadow of the Kraut Line of Milt Schmidt, Woody Dumart, and Bobby Bauer, Cowley made his case as the Bruins' No. 1 centerman by putting up record-setting numbers and capturing the league's most prestigious awards.

A two-time winner of the Hart Trophy as NHL MVP and the 1941 Art Ross Trophy winner as the league's leading scorer, "Cowboy" set as impressive a mark as any player could during the 1943–1944 season. His 71 points in just 36 games, for an average of 1.97 points per game, set a standard that wouldn't be surpassed until Gretzky compiled a then-unthinkable 2.65 points per contest (212 points in 80 games) in 1981–1982. To this day, only Gretzky and Lemieux have averaged more points per game in a single season than Cowley.

"Two points a game over an 80-game schedule, that would be amazing. I never thought I'd see the day when a player would do that. I always thought that would be impossible," Cowley, whose '44 season is still the Bruins' standard, explained after his record was shattered by "the Great One."

Imagine what Cowley could have accomplished that season had Toronto's Jackie McLean not sent the Bruins' forward crashing into the boards in early January—a collision that separated Cowley's shoulder. A second injury, this time to his knee after a mid-February return, also cost Cowley a shot at the record for total points, which frequent linemate Herb Cain actually set that season (and held for seven years) with 82.

Of course, Cowley's pride in his points-per-game record wasn't as important as winning—he skated for the Bruins' Stanley Cup champion squads in '39 and '41—and teamwork. Mel "Sudden Death" Hill might have garnered most of the headlines for his three overtime goals in the 1939 NHL semifinals against New York, but it was Cowley who made each of the passes that led to those historic goals. Cowley took coach Art Ross' advice and looked for an open

Oates Was Always Assisting

While he never managed to match Bill Cowley, Bobby Orr, or Phil Esposito in the points-per-game department during his six seasons with the Bruins, 5'11", 190-pound center Adam Oates carried on the Cowley tradition in black and gold.

Sixth all-time in NHL history with 1,079 assists, Oates ranks ninth on the Bruins' career helper charts. His 97 assists in 1992–1993 (he averaged 1.69 points per game that season)—the most ever by a Bruins forward (and second overall only to Orr)—are made even more amazing when you factor in star power forward Cam Neely's absence for all but 13 games of that campaign.

Oates was Neely's primary set-up man during the winger's amazing 50-goals-in-49-games season of 1993–1994, which made Neely Oates' second career 50-goal linemate (Brett Hull was the first and Peter Bondra followed). While he finished his stint in the Hub third all-time to Orr and Esposito at 1.36 points per contest, he didn't limit his assistance to the rink. After a loss in Denver on February 18, 1997, he finally boiled over because of his team's losing ways in the post-Neely era. In a postgame tirade, he offered some suggestions to management.

"What they should do is trade a couple of us and rebuild instead of coming in after a first period and telling us to stay wide. Get some [expletive] players! That's the answer," Oates was quoted by the *Boston Globe* after he also ripped into general manager Harry Sinden and the Bruins' overall lack of a plan.

On March 1 Oates' wish was granted when he, Rick Tocchet, and goaltender Bill Ranford were shipped to Washington for a package highlighted by future Bruins captain Jason Allison, who actually enjoyed two seasons of better than a point per game in a Bruins sweater. The Bruins' streak of 29 straight years in the playoffs ended that spring.

Hill when the Rangers were keying on the Bruins' center and line-mate Roy Conacher.

The 5'10", 165-pound center's playmaking abilities during and after the Cup-winning years flourished. It has been said that Cowley "made more wings than Boeing," as seemingly every player fortunate enough to skate alongside him—including short-time "Three Gun Line" colleagues Conacher and Ed Wiseman—enjoyed a boost to their offensive totals.

"He would stickhandle down the ice and zero in on an oppos-ing defenseman," teammate Flash Hollett once said. "He wasn't fast on his feet, but that puck was glued to his stick. Somehow he seemed to freeze the defenseman in one spot.... Nobody passed any better than Cowley. He was a pleasure to watch when he made those beautiful passes."

Maybe the only thing that matched Cowley's offensive prowess was his morality. The year before he set the point-per-game mark, Cowley cost himself a chance at statistical glory and financial gain with an off-ice gesture that has probably never been matched.

The story goes that Cowley, who already held the NHL single-season record for assists, with 45, refused to accept an assist credited to him in a January 16 game against New York. In that game, Bruin Art Jackson was awarded a goal when a Rangers player threw his stick to prevent a score. Cowley was given the assist, but he made the unheard of move of writing to NHL president Red Dutton to set the record straight. "The official scorer has credited me with an assist, for having made the play that put Jackson in a scoring posi-tion," Cowley reportedly wrote. "I feel that this assist was not justified, owing to the fact that Jackson did not actually score the goal.... Therefore, may I ask that you eliminate the assist credited to me from your next official scoring summary?"

Dutton fulfilled Cowley's request, which wound up costing the player big time. Cowley only matched his record of 45 assists in a season, which cost him a monetary bonus in addition to the milestone. He came up one point shy to Chicago's Doug Bentley in the race for the Art Ross and finished his career with 548 points in 549 games, ever so close to retiring as a point-per-game player.

No doubt, Cowboy Cowley wished he could've lassoed at least one more point along the way. But he still set the bar for the greats who followed en route to a place in the Hall of Fame and Bruins history.

34 Tiny

A nickname that started out as accurate soon became ironic both because neither Cecil Thompson's stature nor his accomplishments in a Boston Bruins sweater were "Tiny."

Thompson had picked up the nickname playing hockey as a youth with mostly older boys in Western Canada. By the time he started to make his name playing amateur hockey in the early '20s with the Calgary Monarch Juniors, Pacific Grain Seniors, and Bellevue Bulldogs, he'd reached his consistent career playing size of 5'10", 180 pounds—above average for men, and goaltenders, of the time.

To this day, Thompson still maintains the top spot on the Bruins' all-time career list for shutouts (74), games played (468), minutes played (29,948), and—most important—victories (252).

Stardom, however, wasn't handed to Thompson when he joined the Bruins after three impressive seasons with Minnesota of the American Hockey Association. At his first training camp in 1928, Thompson had to beat out the popular Hal Winkler for the starting goaltender position. Winkler had earned 20 wins and a 1.51 goals-against average the season before while leading Boston to an American Division title.

Any pain that came with the decision to go with Thompson over Winker was relieved that fateful season, as Thompson recorded 12 shutouts and a 1.15 goals-against average. Thompson played in all 44 games and logged 2,710 minutes of action during a 26–13–5 regular season. February of that season featured a then-record 13-game unbeaten streak (11–0–2) for the Bruins, who repeated as American Division champs by five points over the New York Rangers.

Fortunately for the Bruins, playoff pressure did nothing to alter the 25-year-old rookie Thompson's performance. In an opening-round three-game sweep of the Montreal Canadiens, Thompson recorded two shutouts and allowed just two goals. And then he followed that up with just one goal allowed in a two-game sweep of the Rangers in the Stanley Cup Finals.

After the 1929–1930 season, the NHL permitted forward passing in the attack zone for the first time. Anyone who thought the rule change would render Thompson ineffective was sorely mistaken. Thompson won the Vezina Trophy four times (1929–1930, 1932–1933, 1935–1936, and 1937–1938) for lowest goals-against average and was also a First Team All-Star twice (1935–1936 and 1937–1938). Boston finished first in its division five more times with Thompson between the pipes, although another Cup win proved elusive.

In pursuit of another Cup, Thompson suffered maybe his bitterest defeat on April 3, 1933, at Maple Leaf Gardens in Toronto during the Cup semifinals. With the best-of-five series knotted at two games apiece, Thompson and Toronto's Lorne Chabot staged a goaltender duel for the ages. When the dust settled, Thompson received a standing ovation from the road crowd as he skated off in defeat after Ken Doraty beat him for the game's lone goal at 4:46 of the sixth overtime—which at the time set a record for longest overtime postseason game. Unofficially, Thompson was credited with stopping 112—yes, 112—Toronto shots. Chabot earned the win with a measly 89 saves.

Thompson, who also made his mark by becoming the first goaltender in NHL history to record an assist (in 1936), never missed a game between the 1932–1933 and 1937–1938 seasons. But he only played in one Cup Finals after that '29 season (in '30), and by the time the Bruins won the Cup again, their first superstar goaltender was plying his trade in Detroit.

General manager Art Ross, incensed by a three-game sweep at the hands of the Maple Leafs in '38, became convinced that the Bruins would be better off with up-and-comer Frank Brimsek between the pipes. Despite Thompson's 30–11–7 record and 1.80 GA in 1937–1938 and a strong start the next season, Ross dealt Thompson to the Red Wings on November 27, 1938, for Norm Smith and cash.

The choice of Brimsek over Thompson, like the one to go with Thompson instead of Winkler a decade earlier, proved prophetic, as the Bruins would win their second Cup in the spring of '39. Brimsek carried the mantle well, but Tiny Thompson had set the bar for all Bruins goaltenders with his giant decade in the crease.

35 '72 Success Set the Standard

Bruins great Ken Hodge explained what being part of the 1971–1972 Stanley Cup–winning Boston team meant to him prior to 2011 like this: "I think it means more today [than back then]. This is not a slap at the current Bruins…basically, they haven't won since. So there's a little bittersweetness there.… You're part of history."

That's right. For what seemed like a lifetime, the '72 Bruins stood as the last team to bring the Cup back to the Hub. What looked like the birth of a Bruins dynasty—two Cup wins in three years—turned out to be the start of a lengthy drought. Defections to the WHA, injuries, and the emergence of dynasties in other locales are all factors that have kept Boston from finishing atop the NHL for nearly four decades.

That the '72 team held the distinction as the last Bruins club to capture the Cup added to the importance of that club's spot in franchise history. It was also that team that had to erase every bad memory of the spring before, when the defending-Cup-champion Bruins suffered one of the worst playoff upsets ever against Montreal in '71.

"We went into that season obviously upset from the year before," Bobby Orr said. "We had one goal, and that was to be the champions again."

Boston's six-game victory over the New York Rangers in May 1972 proved that the "Big, Bad Bruins" were more than just a one-year wonder.

"The mood was one of determination," Tom Johnson, the Bruins' coach that season, once said about the Game 6 win. "I couldn't imagine them not winning that game."

That determination might not have shown up every night during the regular season—Derek Sanderson once admitted the team had "difficulty getting up for games against Buffalo and Vancouver"—but talent almost always won the day for the Bruins en route to 54 wins, including a league-record 26 on the road. They overcame the loss of Ken Hodge to injury for 20 games and made a key swap to acquire Carol Vadnais from California along the way.

Bobby Orr won his third straight Hart Trophy and fifth consecutive Norris Trophy. Phil Esposito repeated as the Art Ross Trophy winner. Gerry Cheevers set an NHL record with a 32-game

(24–0–8) unbeaten string (broken only when Johnson gave Orr and Esposito a night off).

However, the previous spring the Bruins had learned from Ken Dryden and the less-prolific Canadiens how quickly regular-season accolades could be deemed meaningless by postseason failure. Right off the bat in the '72 playoffs, the Bruins faced a stiff test from Toronto. After easily disposing of the Maple Leafs 5–0 in Game 1, the Bruins dropped Game 2 and had to squeak out wins in the next three games to advance. After that rout in the first game, the Bruins only outscored the Leafs 13–10.

It would have taken a rash of cockiness and maybe an actual team-wide rash to slow the Bruins' mowing down of the Blues in four straight in the next series. But a classic matchup with the Rangers was next. New York had finished second to the Bruins in the regular season.

Boston raced out to a 5–1 lead—that's right, the same lead they held in Game 2 against Montreal in '71 before they let the Habs get back into the series—in Game 1. Like déjà vu, the Rangers scored four unanswered goals to tie the score. Were it not for the heroics of Mike Walton setting up "Ace" Bailey for the winning goal with 2:16 left in regulation, the '72 Bruins might have repeated history with an enormous collapse. Instead, they marched toward history.

Despite a left knee that would require surgery in June, Orr was at his apex against the Rangers throughout the series. He scored two goals in the Game 4 win that put Boston on the brink of the title. After the Bruins lost Game 5 at home, they then went to Madison Square Garden intent on not having to make a return trip home empty-handed.

While Wayne Cashman scored twice, and Cheevers made 33 saves in the 3–0 shutout, Orr was again the brightest star on the New York ice sheet. He put the Bruins in front with a goal 11:18 in and then set up Cashman's first score 5:10 into the third.

"He just did it. He carried the team on his back," said Esposito of Orr.

Orr finished with five goals and 19 assists in the postseason and earned his second Conn Smythe Trophy as playoff MVP. The Bruins needed every one of those points with Esposito failing to score a goal in the six-game Finals.

A party back home awaited the Bruins after that victory. Little did they know that they had set the standard every proceeding Bruins team would be measured against for 39 years.

Jacobs

Could it really be that Bruins legendary defenseman Eddie Shore set the tone for Jeremy Jacobs' questionable decision to be an absentee owner for the majority of his more than 35-year possession of the Bruins?

According to Jeremy Jacobs' son, Bruins principal Charlie Jacobs, the Hall of Fame defenseman made a mark on the family as coach of the Buffalo Bisons of the American Hockey League in 1942–1943.

"Eddie would get mad…because my grandfather [Bisons owner Louie Jacobs] would come down, and after the games he would say, 'Great game, guys.' And this was just after Eddie had been in there giving them the business," explained the younger Jacobs. "So Eddie told my grandfather, 'Louie, I don't want you around the players.' So my dad really stuck to that philosophy. And save for the first game of the year's 'How you doing?' talk in the locker room, that's been the approach. Although that's changed a little bit recently. But for a long time, probably 30 years, that's the way it was."

Shore was certainly a great player and the Bruins' first superstar, but he wasn't the best at public relations. Sportsystems Corporation of Buffalo (later renamed Delaware North Companies, Inc.)—the business created by brothers Louis, Marvin, and Charles Jacobs in 1926—purchased the Bruins and Boston Garden in 1975 from Storer Broadcasting for $10 million. Unfortunately, one of the company's first orders of business was to re-sign free agent defenseman Bobby Orr. The man many believe to be the greatest player had won his second career league scoring title in 1974–1975, led Boston to two Cup victories at the start of the decade, and reinvigorated a franchise that suffered a string of futility in the early to mid-'60s that hasn't been matched.

A long and grueling negotiation process between Orr's agent, Alan Eagleson, and lawyers for Sportsystems didn't get the deal done. Famously, Orr was offered a substantial stake in the Bruins as part of his compensation and, as the accepted story goes, Eagleson never even told Orr of that offer. While the new owners might've given retaining Orr their best shot, his departure for Chicago (where he played only 26 more NHL games) at the time looked like a failure on their part. An ownership group that starts out its reign with one of the worst public-relations fiascos in franchise history probably should do more to put a positive face on the franchise than hideout and rule with a long arm from Buffalo, New York.

Over the next 35-plus years, Jacobs has been maligned for what players and fans have perceived as a philosophy that prizes profit over winning. As general manager and president of the Bruins over the entirety of the Jacobs' ownership until 2006, Harry Sinden reiterated for years that he was never put on a budget by Jacobs and he made all the decisions in relation to trades and free-agent signings. That admission made Sinden as vilified as Jacobs, but ultimately Jacobs has taken the most heat because the sports fans of Boston expect a commitment from the concessions magnate. And they're particularly bitter that their team owners choose not to live in the Hub.

The belt-tightening of the '90s—as salaries around professional sports began their steady climb to astronomic levels unthinkable in the previous decades of NHL history—turned the steady flow of vitriolic complaints turned all the way up. The Bruins moved from the old Boston Garden to the state-of-the-art FleetCenter right next door mid-decade. To his great credit, Jacobs built the new building for $160 million of almost all his own company's money (some public money was used for infrastructure).

But fans and players weren't impressed by the new concession stands and their inflated prices, nor did they care for the spacious luxury suites that helped maximize income. They wanted a winner. All observers could see was that while ticket prices went up, star players left or were alienated by vicious salary battles and win totals decreased. The Bruins, who had made the playoffs 29 straight years, missed the postseason in 1997 and were bad enough to earn the No. 1 pick in that June's draft. Mediocrity became a constant even after the Bruins got back in the playoffs in '98 and '99. And fans' distrust and disgust with Jacobs continued to climb. In 2000 he

Basketball's Brown Made a Hockey Impact

Financial troubles could've run the Bruins into the ground as the 1950s opened. But after the Boston Garden Arena Corporation purchased a 60 percent stake in the team and Weston Adams Sr. left to work as a stockbroker, Walter Brown was installed as team president. Brown, most famous for his role in the storied history of the NBA's Boston Celtics, had a love of hockey from his days as a coach and manager of the 1932 Olympic team. Under Brown, the Bruins missed the playoffs just once from 1952 to 1959 and were only denied more glory by powerhouses in Montreal and Detroit.

Brown is the only man in both the Hockey Hall of Fame and the Naismith Memorial Basketball Hall of Fame.

"His heart was into hockey long before basketball. Basketball was a way to fill dates at the Garden.... Walter Brown is the most overlooked figure in Boston Bruins history, and it's important to give him credit," said New England Sports Museum curator Richard Johnson.

answered for the Bruins' decision to not spend money the way the New York Rangers, Detroit Red Wings, and Colorado Avalanche were (to different levels of success).

"Harry Sinden can spend whatever it takes to put that team out there," Jacobs said. "But it's been proven in hockey that you can't buy a team. Well, you can buy a team, but you can't buy a winner. I mean, look at Edmonton and Buffalo this year. They've beaten the shit out of us this year, they've kicked our ass, and look how cheap their payrolls are—all lower. The same with Florida.

"On the same hand, look at St. Louis with a $30 million payroll, and they're terrible; Pittsburgh at $35 million, and they're terrible. Even the Rangers, the epitome of someone buying a team, and they've got nothing to show for it."

So while the blame was often thrown at Sinden's feet, Jacobs wasn't exactly clamoring for Sinden to change course in pursuit of the Cup. Many longtime fans actually were pushed to the brink by Jacobs' running of the club.

"A lot of the decisions were made for money, and it started to become so transparent," said one longtime fan who relinquished his season tickets in the '90s. "If they don't care about winning, why should I care about going?"

Contract holdouts and trades made to rid the team of players making more money than the Bruins were willing to pay ruled the days of the '90s. Getting anyone to criticize Jacobs, who in addition to owning the Bruins is now the executive director of the NHL board of governors, is virtually impossible these days. The salary cap has made it difficult to call him cheap, and most players and management types would rather not risk facing the wrath. But back in that streak-ending season of 1997, star center Adam Oates had had enough.

"I don't know if the owner is telling Harry he can't spend the money, or if it is Harry's own decision. All I know is we've gotten worse every year since I've been here. You can't blame anybody except them," said Oates after a difficult loss at Colorado.

Of course, there were times Jacobs appeared at the Garden and even addressed the media. Those times, often, were much to his detriment. He definitely didn't win any fans or make Boston any more appealing to star players when he took veiled shots at star center Joe Thornton in December 2004.

"There's a whole body of thinking by a lot of people within the sport who feel the high-priced players don't necessarily play every day," Jacobs said. "They play intermittently, and that has added to some of the dullness. When you pay a lot for a player, you expect him to play a lot, so we're playing a lot of guys who maybe we shouldn't be playing, who aren't really giving it the kind of interest that needs to be shown in this game."

At the turn of the century, Jacobs brought in his son, Charlie, to help run the show—first as executive vice president and then as principal. In Los Angeles Charlie Jacobs had worked for Bruce McNab with the Kings and also been around Lakers owner Jerry Buss. Neither was known for being shy around the public or the media. Little by little, Charlie tried to get his father into a positive light, where he could show that he truly did care about winning without publicly tearing his employees—players and coaches, mostly—down.

"Having heard some of the former Bruins say now, 'Gee, if I had only known how much your dad and you are so into this game at the time, I would've felt differently,'" Charlie Jacobs says now about his interaction with players who obviously had long-held negative thoughts about the elder Jacobs.

Changing 25 years of opinion, however, takes more than just a few public appearances. The Jacobs' efforts to reverse public attitudes were dealt a blow leading up to and after the lockout that 2004–2005 season. Despite the elder Jacobs' close relationship with commissioner Gary Bettman and the board of governors, the Bruins badly misread what the post-work-stoppage league landscape would look like. Instead of re-signing key players or important talent from other teams before the lockout, the Bruins banked on a glut of players hitting the market after the establishment of a salary cap. Instead, a 24 percent rollback on salaries allowed teams to retain their players, and the Bruins were left to re-sign a few of their own guys and add just B-list free agents as a supporting cast.

Boston missed the playoffs each of the first two years after the lockout. With their franchise a disaster, and the Red Sox and Patriots building championship clubs that took over the town's interest, the Jacobs family found out what life at the bottom of the Boston sports pecking order felt like. Finally, it was time for a change. In replacing fired general manager Mike O'Connell, the Bruins went outside the organization for the first time in more than 30 years to hire Peter Chiarelli away from Ottawa. Then Boston spent an unheard of sum of money—some $58 million—to sign the top two free agents available, Zdeno Chara and Marc Savard.

"It is something new to me and new to others. We probably sat back too long. I'm looking for them to do well," said Jacobs at training camp in 2006.

While that first season under Chiarelli was nothing short of a disaster, the Jacobs men stuck with their new GM. They allowed him to make a coaching change and continue to spend to the salary-cap maximum. The Bruins got back in the playoffs in '08, won the regular-season Eastern Conference title in '09, and won the Stanley Cup championship in 2011.

Jacobs might never win back all the Bruins fans who were alienated over the years. But if only a percentage comes back, that's better than nothing. And free agents haven't avoided Boston the way they did in the 1990s, as evidenced by the re-signings of players like Savard, Tim Thomas, and Milan Lucic. Jacobs has shot down every rumor of a possible Bruins sale throughout his decades in command. When the Bruins finally won that '11 Cup, Jacobs celebrated on the ice in Vancouver with the team and finally got to break with his father's tradition and tell his players, "Good job."

37 The Turk

No matter how many times current Bruins players get noticed out on the town and make appearances in the *Boston Herald*'s "Inside Track," they won't be able to ever match the off-ice notoriety of Derek Sanderson, center for the "Big, Bad Bruins."

In fact, in today's hockey world—where players are all encouraged, and nearly forced, to be as vanilla as possible and do nothing to distract from the team—you'll never see anyone on any team match "the Turk."

As the great Will McDonough wrote in the *Boston Globe* in 1988, "If Sanderson went 55 mph on the ice, he doubled that when the game was over. His whole life was speed. He couldn't live it fast enough."

Off the ice, Sanderson lived the high life by driving a Rolls-Royce, dating actresses like Joey Heatherton, appearing in a Hollywood movie (his scene didn't make it in the U.S. version), and hosting his own interview show on Channel 38 (Linda Ronstadt was one of the bigger-name guests on *The Derek Sanderson Show*).

He ran night clubs like Bachelors III, frequented numerous other establishments, and palled around with fellow star playboy-athletes Joe Namath of the New York Jets and Ken Harrelson of the Boston Red Sox.

And then there was the mustache. It's believed he was the first player in the NHL in 30 years to play with facial hair on his upper lip.

"I grew a mustache because my dad had one. That was it," said Sanderson, denying the idea that he wore the mustache as some sort of rebellious symbol.

126

Sanderson's father, Harold, did more for the Calder Trophy recipient and two-time Stanley Cup winner than influence his choice of facial hair. Harold Sanderson was the one who put his son in skates and taught him lessons about toughness, aggression, and skill. The elder Sanderson made sure Derek was turning both ways on his skates by the time he was seven years old.

"My dad was everything to me," Sanderson explained one day while taking a break from his job with Howland Capital Management. "He was my go-to guy, he was my mentor. He was the reason I played hockey. He was there for me every second of every day. He never forced me to do anything. He never made me do anything."

Sanderson's upbringing paid off in 1967–1968, when he became established as an NHL player and won Rookie of the Year honors. He continued to mature into a perfect blend of skill—he was a tenacious penalty-killer (often paired with linemate Eddie Westfall) and possibly the best faceoff winner of his day—and grit. In his first training camp with the Bruins, Sanderson had stood up to resident Boston tough guy Ted Green. Their relationship grew from there, so that Green always had Sanderson's back, and vice versa. In fact, all the "Big, Bad Bruins" had each other's backs, so that allowed Sanderson to really get under opponents' skin.

Before the Cup semifinals in 1969, the *Toronto Daily Star* headline read "Habs Fear Sanderson More Than Espo." Needless to say it wasn't because the Canadiens were worried Sanderson would score more goals than superstar center Phil Esposito.

"Sure, I'm a dirty player. I like playing dirty," Sanderson once said. "Anyway, that's the way the game should be played. I like fighting. Maybe I'll get beat up a lot, but I'll get the guy eventually."

Sanderson's extracurricular activities on and off the ice shouldn't take away from his standing as a highly productive player. After all, he assisted on Bobby Orr's Cup-winning goal in Game 4 of the 1970 Finals. And in the '72 Finals he shadowed Rangers star Rod

"The Turk" Derek Sanderson and his famous 'stache glide up the ice in a game against the L.A. Kings at the Boston Garden in the 1970s. The Turk was a vital part of the Stanley Cup–winning "Big, Bad Bruins" of the late '60s/early '70s.

Gilbert, limiting him to four goals for the six-game series and no scores after Game 3.

Unfortunately for Sanderson, that '72 Finals was really his last glorious moment in the game. After the Bruins won the Cup, he was the first player to jump from the NHL to the new World Hockey Association. While sticking around to defend the title might have been appealing, no one—let alone the fast-living Sanderson—could have been expected to turn down a $2.6 million, 10-year deal. Sanderson had been close to Bruins owner Weston Adams Sr. and was ready to turn down the Philadelphia Blazers' offer to stay in Boston for a small raise. But against his wishes, Bruins team lawyer Charlie Mulcahy showed up at the signing. Sanderson says he threw the pen at Mulcahy and stormed out.

Injuries and the misery of playing in a start-up league combined to make Sanderson's life hell away from Boston. By the winter of '73, he was bought out of his deal with Philadelphia after playing just eight games. He returned to the Bruins, but a suspension for fighting with teammate Terry O'Reilly prevented Sanderson from playing in the '74 playoffs, which featured a run to the Cup Finals against Philadelphia. And in the summer of '74 he was dealt away to the archrival Rangers.

After the 1977–1978 season, Sanderson was out of hockey, but that wasn't the worst turn his career had taken. He was also broke; he had burned through a lot of his riches in an alcoholic haze and had been swindled into bad investments by so-called friends and advisors. Sanderson was determined to get sober and turn his life back around. It took 11 trips to drug and alcohol rehab before he finally kicked the habit. His last trip to rehab, in 1980 at the behest of Orr and a few other former teammates, helped set Sanderson on the straight and narrow.

"I learned a lot, I really did," responded Sanderson when asked if he would live the same way if he could go back and do it all over. "I wouldn't recommend anybody risk their life learning what I learned. A lot of good things came from it. A lot of solid friendships were made; a lot of good people were around. So there were some good times. Not all of it is good."

Obviously, Orr played a leading role in Sanderson's hockey and non-hockey life. Sanderson is hoping to get a movie made that prominently features that relationship. One day when they sit down to take in the flick of Sanderson's life, modern-day Bruins players will be able to imagine living life in the fast lane. No one, however, will be able to match Sanderson's story.

 **Hitch**

Since the dawn of hockey, defensemen have struggled to get respect every bit as much as the late, great comedian Rodney Dangerfield.

There's no award to honor backliners who thrive in their own end and shut down opposing snipers. And the Norris Trophy, which is voted based on the best defenseman in the NHL each season, typically goes to the blueliner with the best offensive credentials to go along with some modicum of solid defensive-zone play.

After he retired from the Bruins in February 1934, Lionel Hitchman had no such problem gaining the recognition he deserved (even if his humble nature wouldn't allow him to ask for it). The first captain in Bruins history and the defensive rock of the 1928–1929 Stanley Cup–winning team was honored with the retirement of his No. 3. It was only the second number in NHL history to be retired.

Hitchman never made an All-Star team. He never recorded more than 11 points in a season. And in that fateful Bruins Cup season, he tallied just one goal in the regular season and one assist in the postseason. Obviously, his value could not be quantified with statistics. With Hitchman combining with the legendary Eddie Shore on the Bruins' back end—sometimes for the game's full 60 minutes—opponents managed to score just 52 goals in 44 games against Boston during that Cup-winning season of '29. "Without Hitch it would've been a different story," Hall of Fame goaltender

Cecil "Tiny" Thompson was quoted as saying about that stifling defensive campaign.

Hitchman actually started his working life as a Royal Canadian Mountie. But it has been written that "braving the snow on horseback in the hinterlands of the frozen north, subsisting on a diet of popsicles and snowball sundaes wasn't for him."

While not the intimidator that Shore was, Hitchman still played with heart and a physical edge that he honed during his first couple seasons with the Ottawa Senators. One famous incident involved Montreal tough guy Sprague Cleghorn cross-checking Hitchman, still with Ottawa, in the face during a 1923 playoff game—a move so egregious Cleghorn not only received a match penalty but caused the Canadiens to actually suspend their own player for the final game of the series. Hitchman, however, didn't miss a beat. He skated through the rest of the game with plaster protecting his broken nose. Ottawa went on to win the Cup that season.

During the 1925–1926 season, Hitchman joined the Bruins. Later that season Cleghorn became his teammate via a separate trade. Hitchman wasted little time burying the hatchet after the two were reintroduced by Bruins manager Art Ross.

"If we can team up on defense with as much vigor and energy as we did against each other, we should keep the league away from our net," Hitchman diplomatically explained.

While rarely retaliating, Hitchman was often the victim of opponents' stick fouls. In one playoff game against the Montreal Maroons Hitchman has his jaw broken by Hooley Smith. He returned to the game with a jaw brace and a football helmet but still was clubbed by Nels Stewart. The resulting injury sent Hitchman to the hospital, where he reportedly said, "It was just an accident. I got my head in the road of Stewart's stick."

As one author at the website Hockey Notes commented: "With comments like these, one has to wonder if [Hitchman] was nice or mentally disadvantaged."

While you could question Hitchman's mental state, you couldn't question his determination in keeping opponents off the scoreboard. And with Shore revolutionizing the defense position by attacking as much as protecting, he needed Hitchman to keep other teams honest and complement him as the perfect stay-at-home partner.

In the 10 years that Hitchman was a key player in their defense corps, Boston finished in first place five times and advanced to the Cup Finals three times. When he retired in 1934 with 417 NHL games under his belt, in addition to his number retirement, Hitchman received a reported $500 from the fans, $500 from Bruins owner Charles Adams, and a silver chest from Ross.

While he never was elected into the Hockey Hall of Fame, Hitchman inspired admiring words from his peers. Hockey Hall of Fame inductee and one-time teammate Frank Fredrickson might've summed up best what Hitchman meant to the Bruins and how he differed from Shore.

"To me, Shore was a country boy who had made good," Fredrickson said. "He was a good skater and puck carrier but was not an exceptional defenseman like his teammate Lionel Hitchman, who was better because he could get them coming and going."

39 The Voice of the Bruins on TV

How does one forge a career that lasts 44 years with one team—enough to earn the right to call one's autobiography *Voice of the Bruins*?

Well, first you start by single-handedly convincing a station to televise the games in the first place. Fred Cusick had been doing the Bruins' radio broadcasts for a decade when in 1963 he noticed the Bruins' had scheduled three straight Saturday night road games against Toronto (twice) and Montreal. After he was turned down by all the Boston stations, WMUR-TV in Manchester, New Hampshire, agreed to let Cusick have an hour on Sunday morning to rebroadcast the game.

"I taped the games in the CBC studios," wrote Cusick in his book a few years before his 2009 death, "drove all night to Concord, slept for a few hours, then got to Manchester in time to broadcast each game by adding a voiceover to the edited tape."

Cusick didn't stop there. He made an offer to send a Bruins calendar to any listeners who requested one by mail. What he received were pleas from more than 2,500 fans to "get the games on television." He took the fan mail to Ingalls Advertising, which also handled advertising for Volkswagen, and they agreed to have Cusick film or tape the rest of that season's games. The Bruins were born as a television entity.

Other than a two-season stint on radio from 1969 to 1971, Cusick described all the Bruins' action on countless television sets throughout New England and beyond for four decades.

"As clearly as Bobby Orr was the heart and soul of the great Bruins teams of the 1960s and '70s on the ice," wrote Stephen Harris of the *Boston Herald* after the Hall of Fame broadcaster's death, "Fred Cusick was the voice that made hockey the most popular sport in Boston."

Dan Berkery was the assistant general manager and then GM at Channel 38 over an 18-year span and got to know Cusick well. Surprisingly, he said, Cusick was a little different on and off the air.

"If you were in a room with Fred away from the hockey rink, he was one of the quietest people you ever met in your entire life," recalled Berkery. "You'd sit down, and he'd say 10 words in three hours. But when he would go behind that mic, and they'd drop the puck, he'd absolutely light up."

The first American to win the Foster Hewitt Memorial Award and earn induction into the Hockey Hall of Fame, Cusick also won the Lester Patrick Award, which is presented for outstanding con-tributions to hockey in the U.S. How he thought he earned the honor, however, is a bit of an odd story.

"[Philadelphia goaltender Ron] Hextall loved to roam, secure the puck, and shoot it or pass it down the ice," Cusick wrote. "In the game the Bruins were trailing by a goal with two minutes left, and their goaltender was taken out. They stormed the Philadelphia end, and Hextall moved out of the net, trapped the puck, and shot it down the ice. As always, he did it with such firmness and cer-tainty…. On the air I said, 'Hextall fires the puck so hard he'll score a goal soon.'

"The next time the Bruins drilled it in, Hextall cradled the puck in his stick and lofted the puck down the ice into the empty net…. The clip made the rounds of TV stations around the country, and I was identified as the forecaster. I'm sure the instant fame was a factor in someone selecting me for the Patrick honor."

Among Cusick's numerous famous calls was his signature response to a goal, where he would either say, "Score," or, "He scores." He adapted it from the legendary Foster Hewitt, who used to just say, "He shoots, he scores." Of course, when Cusick got excited or there was a particularly thrilling play, the word would sound more like "Scoooore." Four or five seconds would usually be the max.

"That voice is unmistakable, full and husky, like a tenor saxo-phone," wrote Stu Hackel in 1994. "At some moments, it is smooth, and at others, when play nears the goal, for instance, it is gritty. Each word is distinct. Listeners hear the final 'k' in Kirk before the 'M' in Muller. When the action is rough, Cusick gives each word a special punch. In moments of excitement—'Saaave, Caaseeeey!'—he sustains the tension by elongating vowels."

Longtime *Boston Globe* columnist Bob Ryan dabbled in televi-sion for a while and described his new understanding of Cusick's appeal in a column in 1995.

"I became fascinated with the grace and rhythm of his language while describing the game he loves," Ryan wrote. "You could count on finding a half-dozen plays or sequences in which he would tell the story—never overstating any case—in a spirited, yet controlled, and completely literate manner."

One call Cusick cherished more than any of his others was his description of the game-winning goal in Game 4 of the Stanley Cup Finals against St. Louis in 1970. The goal is famous for the way Orr seemed to fly through the air after scoring. As Cusick wrote about WBZ radio on that day, "Its clear-channel signal was heard in 38 states, and you can be sure that from whatever area they were listening, most of the audience on that hot May day was rooting for Bobby and the Bruins."

If they were backing Boston, it probably had a lot to do with their ability to tune in Cusick—and Bob Wilson—from such long distances. If there were Bruins fans outside of the Bruins' natural territory, Cusick and Wilson probably had something to do with their decision to adopt the Black and Gold as their team.

As longtime former PR man and assistant to the owner Nate Greenberg said, "Fans identified the Bruins through their announcing teams."

The Voice of the Bruins on the Radio

When he landed his dream job as the radio voice for the Bruins in 2000, Dave Goucher suddenly found himself having a dream meeting with his lifelong idol at the team's training camp that fall.

"What's [my] style like? I said, 'Well, I think a lot of it is like your style,'" Goucher recalled of his chat with Hall of Fame radio voice Bob Wilson. "He said, 'I always try to give first and last names as much as possible, and I don't like nicknames. What do you think of nicknames?' I said, 'I don't like them either, Bob.'

"He goes, 'Good boy.' It was almost like a vote of approval."

A vote of approval from Bob Wilson would go a long way toward boosting any would-be radio broadcaster's confidence. For all but two seasons that WBZ radio used the legendary Fred Cusick as its play-by-play man instead of Wilson in the early '70s, Wilson was the Bruins' radio voice for nearly 30 years.

Whether you're listening to old tape of Wilson's calls or talking to him on the phone more than 15 years after his retirement, there's a distinct sound entering your ears.

"First of all, he was blessed with one of the great voices of all time. He had a deep voice," recalled former Bruins longtime PR man and assistant to the owner Nate Greenberg.

"That deep baritone, in-command voice that you could tell by the urgency in his voice what was going on in the game," Goucher remembered. "Always in control, but when the big moment came, he delivered it."

Most Made Most of Bruins Broadcast

For almost 40 years Johnny Most and his raspy voice were hallmarks of a Boston Celtics radio broadcast. But Most, a good friend to Bruins radio voice Bob Wilson, once made a pinch-hit appearance alongside Wilson in the '60s for a game in Toronto.

"I decided to use some of my basketball phrases to describe the play," Most recalled in his memoir. "For instance, I had Boston defenseman Gary Doak 'shooting from downtown.' I also mentioned to my audience that Johnny Bucyk was 'tricky dribbling' the puck in front of the goal."

Most recalls that Weston Adams Sr., the Bruins' president, wasn't pleased with the broadcast, and he didn't call another Bruins game in his career. But that didn't stop some controversy from emanating from that evening.

"Boston was on the power play, and one of the Bruins' defensemen took a shot from the point. As I recall the broadcast, I told my audience, 'He hit the far right post,'" Most wrote. "However, some insist my call was: 'He hit the fucking post.' Personally, I'm 99.9 percent sure I didn't use the four-letter word on the air."

Wilson said his famous voice came naturally and was inherited from his father. However, he didn't aspire to use his voice on the radio until he got to college. "I didn't give it much thought until I was in college at Boston University, and I had to write a term paper on a vocation," Wilson explained one day. "I was involved in a junior achievement broadcast group at Boston University, so I wrote on radio broadcasting. This was in 1949, television was in its infancy, and who knew what that would bring? But radio was still king when I started, and it all started with a term paper at Boston University."

After a brief career-starting stint out of town, Wilson returned home to join WHDH. Over the years he accumulated tons of advice that he tried to put to use. Weston Adams Sr., the one-time owner and president of the Bruins, once told Wilson, "I want to hear the same game you're watching."

Wilson also took to heart some words he heard fellow legend Red Barber utter. "'In television you're a slave to the picture, and in radio you paint the picture,'" Wilson remembered.

Millions of New Englanders grew up listening to Wilson put all the words of wisdom to work. He crossed paths often with Cusick, who worked the Bruins' games for more than 40 years and was the full-time television voice from 1971 until his retirement in 1997. Wilson even said that "unconsciously there was a lot of Fred in my broadcasts."

"I've only heard Bob a few times, when I've had to miss a game because I was sick, but he's always had a great voice, a good command of the game, and [he] was an excellent announcer," Cusick once said.

Of course, Wilson made some calls unique to his broadcasts. Hall of Fame writer Kevin Paul Dupont recalled upon the closing of the Montreal Forum a night he got to sit next to Wilson during a game. The Bruins were heavy underdogs against the Canadiens, and Wilson opened his coverage by saying: "And who do the Bruins counter with? None other than Lyndon Byers—who couldn't put the puck in the ocean if he was standing at the end of the dock."

"He popped out the words 'Byers,' 'ocean,' and, 'dock' as if they were the three slashes of the sword that made up Zorro's 'Z,'" wrote Dupont. "I typed away the rest of the night, listening to 'The Wils' boom out his trademark, 'Game-coming-to-you from the Montreal Forum...'"

Wilson called the games of the Cup-winning season of '70 and many more historic evenings. Without singling out any particular night or player, he listed off the names of Bobby Orr, Rick Middleton, and others who gave him such a thrill while working. But Goucher recalled the night of May 3, 1979, when center Jean Ratelle helped the Bruins slay Montreal in Game 4 of the Cup semifinals with a hat trick.

"'This building is moving,'" is how Goucher recalled Wilson's description of the reaction to the third of Ratelle's scores, which won the game in overtime.

Whether talking about Wilson or Cusick, Greenberg knew exactly what he admired about them and why they were so beloved by Bruins fans.

"The one thing that Bob and Fred had in common was their love of the game. Among the many things I admired about both of them is their love of the game," he said.

"There were no aspirations to go any higher. Fred did the Bruins until it was time to retire; Bob did the games until it was time to retire. They weren't looking to move to another city or do another sport. That was their ultimate desire in life, to be the Bruins' announcers on TV and radio. They came to work every night excited to be there."

Wilson echoed those sentiments. "I was enjoying myself. I said to myself, *As long as you're having fun doing this, why don't you keep doing it?*" he explained. "The club agreed with that, several radio stations agreed with that over the years."

Even in retirement, no one would disagree that Wilson and Cusick were legendary voices who helped make the Bruins into must-watch, must-hear action.

41 Grapes

He was once voted the seventh-greatest Canadian of all time, ahead of even Wayne Gretzky. And he's still the most watched television personality in all of the Great White North.

But how big would Don "Grapes" Cherry be in Boston had his Bruins teams managed to win even one Stanley Cup? Well, an unthinkable too-many-men-on-the-ice penalty and a long-simmering feud with general manager Harry Sinden, which Sinden won by firing Cherry after that disappointing defeat in '79, prevented us from knowing if Cherry would've had a holiday named in his honor or a statue placed in the middle of Boston Common after a Cup triumph. All we do know is that the lack of a championship has done little to diminish Cherry's popularity among the fans and his former players in the decades since his departure from the Boston bench.

Cherry's teams earned the nickname the "Lunch Pail A.C." from the *Boston Globe* because the players never stopped working. Leigh Montville once wrote of Cherry: "His strategy called for simple, workmanlike hockey: throw the puck into a corner, beat up anyone in your path, get the puck out of the corner, shoot the puck at the goalie as hard as you can. He had a team of big players who could do that."

Seemingly every individual benefitted from Cherry's mentoring. One in particular was Rick Middleton, who went from just a point-scorer upon his arrival in Boston to a two-way stalwart who

Blue Was Bruins' Mascot

You can't think about Don Cherry without thinking about the "Lunch Pail A.C.," his loud sports coats, and his dog Blue. No coach in Boston history, and maybe in the history of the NHL, had a more prominent mascot both during his coaching and his broadcasting career.

In his book *Open Net*, George Plimpton wrote of Cherry's pet white bull terrier: "Cherry had a near-symbiotic relationship with his dog. I never met Blue while I was with the Bruins, but the dog was an overriding presence in camp in Fitchburg, and especially in Boston. When they saw Cherry in the morning, players would ask after him, 'How's Blue, Grapes?'

"'Pissed off.'"

To be compared to Blue in a media report or pregame speech was the highest compliment coming from Cherry, who once explained that he loved his dog because dogs "don't care if you win or lose." Cherry won more than he lost, and Blue was the dog behind the man.

could be relied upon to kill penalties and be on the ice at the end of games.

"Don was an old-school guy. He had the ability—I don't know if it was a conscious ability—but he had the ability to relate to people on their own level," said Rick Middleton, who as a Bruins forward benefitted greatly from Cherry's demands that he become more than just a scorer. "And he had the ability to understand how to push each guy's buttons, I think. I know, just for myself, it came through the attrition of ice time. He wanted me to be hungry. He wanted me to prove that I could play the type of game that he wanted me to play and thought in order to be a better NHL player I needed to learn to be. He did that by limiting my ice time."

One particular incident defined the Middleton-Cherry relationship. "It was a two-on-one, and somehow I was the only guy back," explained Middleton. "It's kind of foggy after all these years, but I remember the two players were Danny Gare and Bill Hajt. And Bill Hajt scored, like, two goals a year, and Danny was a 50-goal scorer. So I had to make a decision. I could cover my point, which was supposedly my job as a winger under the 'Cherry rules,' or go to a 50-goal scorer who's getting into position to score. So I went to Danny, and of course he dropped it back to Bill Hajt, who took the shot; it might've bounced three times before it went in the net. I didn't even want to go to the bench because I knew I let my defenseman score. And I think he benched me after a few sharp words."

Cherry was able to push the right buttons with almost every player, and he got results. The Bruins went to the Cup Finals in '77 and '78. And then the '79 Cup semifinals series against Montreal, which ended in overtime after the most famous bench minor in Bruins history, ended Cherry's reign. Some call it the most heart-breaking loss in team lore because the Bruins would've easily handled the New York Rangers in the Finals and, of course, Boston's Cup drought has now exceeded 35 years.

Had the Bruins won that game and the Cup, no one's life would've been more different than Cherry's.

"We'd have won the Stanley Cup, and then Harry wouldn't have been able to fire me," Cherry said years later. "My life might have been a little different. They liked me in Boston. We were tough. We were a Boston team. I was like a Southie to them. I was heavier. I had a big face. I'd say things."

Cherry's motivational weapons often involved more than just benching. His press briefings were classics, and his tongue-lashings of players packed a wallop.

"It can't get worse than to hear, 'You're the worst player in the goddamn universe,'" said forward Peter McNab. "You know, it's a big universe, there's got to be one other person worse than me."

He once called Middleton, who had reported to training camp a bit overweight, Porky Pig. Upon landing in Colorado to face a terrible Rockies team one season, Cherry was asked how his team would handle the mismatch.

"[Cherry] says, 'Yeah, it's probably going to be easy, I think I'm just going to have my guys wear their left skates,'" remembered

Middleton. "And, of course, it goes up in the dressing room. He did it to fire up the opposition to make sure we had a good game for them. He did it on purpose."

Cherry endeared himself to his players with plenty of encouragement, as well. And in the off-season, parties at his home were commonplace. Maybe the only one who couldn't tolerate Cherry's act was Sinden. Whether Cherry's philosophy on the sport didn't jibe with Sinden's or Sinden was just a tad jealous of the attention that was directed at his coach, the relationship began to really deteriorate during that '79 season. Cherry was in the last year of his contract and didn't hesitate to get a dig in at Sinden and the Bruins. He criticized the Bruins' use of practice pucks in games (player milestones reached at home were marked by a logo-less puck), their road-heavy exhibition schedule, and, of course, his salary.

As hard as they might've tried to ignore the rift, Bruins players couldn't miss it.

"I remember talking to Harry during the Stanley Cup semifinals [in '79], and Grapes saw me talking to him," said defenseman Mike Milbury. "And he said, 'Why are you talking to that guy? You're either with me or against me.' We were just talking about the penalty killing."

Over the years, his relationship with Sinden has healed, and any time he's back on Causeway Street, he gets a rock star's reception. On his popular *Hockey Night in Canada* segment "Coach's Corner"—during which he critiques players as though they should all be striving to make his "Lunch Pail" teams—he still talks of the Bruins as his favorite team. He sometimes even wears a Bruins tie or Bruins-colored jacket. The Bruins were the team he played his only NHL game for and the organization with which he cut his coaching chops. He holds no grudge against the Bruins.

"Have you ever heard of a coach who never got fired?" he asked. "Nobody goes on forever."

But Boston's love for Cherry, even without a Cup win, is everlasting.

Two Cups in Three Years

The Bruins' third Stanley Cup–winning team, which finished on top of the NHL in 1941, might be known more for what didn't happen in the years after the triumph than for what the club actually accomplished that winter and spring.

By the winter of '42, the Kraut Line left for the Royal Canadian Air Force, and after the '43 season, goaltender Frank "Mr. Zero" Brimsek joined the Coast Guard. The Bruins were left wondering what type of dynasty they might have been. But in '41 all they could think about was bouncing back after being upset in the 1940 playoffs and winning a second Stanley Cup in three years.

For the third straight year, the Bruins finished in first place in '41. They rolled off a 23-game unbeaten streak, which ended on February 25, 1941, with their record for the season sitting at 21–8–11. And then they finished the regular season on a 6–0–2 run.

Bill Cowley led the league in scoring with 62 points and earned the Hart Trophy as MVP, while Brimsek shut down opponents to the tune of a 2.01 goals-against average. Behind Cowley, the Bruins' offense was balanced and potent led by the Krauts—Milt Schmidt, Bobby Bauer, and Woody Dumart—and Eddie Wiseman. In one game Boston even pummeled Chicago goaltender Sam LoPresti with 83 shots and won 3–2.

Coming off their Cup win in '39, however, the Bruins had fallen in six games to the New York Rangers in the first round of the postseason in 1940. So they knew that all their regular-season accolades would be little consolation were they to fail again in the playoffs. Their first-round opponent was the second-place Toronto Maple Leafs, who allowed just 99 goals during the regular season.

After a 3–0 win in Game 1, the Bruins might have thought they were going to cruise to the Finals. Boston, however, lost Cowley to a knee injury that sidelined him the rest of the playoffs in that first game. And Bauer missed the second game with a cut suffered in a collision with Schmidt in Game 2, which the Leafs won 5–3. A 7–2 Leafs victory proved Boston couldn't take Toronto lightly. The Bruins rallied to force a Game 7, and then Mel Hill—he of the "Sudden Death" moniker earned during the 1939 Cup run—proved he could take care of business in regulation by scoring the game-winner with 5:43 left in the third period of the deciding game.

The battle-tested Bruins hit their stride in the Finals, despite some major pushback by Detroit. Boston orchestrated the first four-game sweep in Finals history, although they won two one-goal games and two two-goal matches. Schmidt finished the postseason with 11 points in 11 games, and Wiseman (proving the Bruins were shrewd to acquire him for Eddie Shore the season before) chipped in with six playoff goals.

No one knew at that time what WWII would do to the Bruins team and the NHL in general. Nor did anyone know Boston would have to wait 29 years for the next Cup. Cowley, the Krauts, and Brimsek seemed like they could carry the Bruins to a bunch of titles, and that's all anyone cared about.

43 Dryden Did Them In in '71

Drafted by the Bruins in 1964, Ken Dryden delayed the start of his professional career with Montreal by playing three seasons at Cornell University and skating for the Canadian National Team.

Two years after making his NHL debut, he skipped an entire season in a contract dispute with the Canadiens.

Unfortunately for the '71 Bruins, Dryden found time among his studying for a law degree and other life pursuits to launch his Hall of Fame career by leading one of the greatest postseason upsets in league history.

The '71 Bruins, looking to defend their '70 Stanley Cup crown, were a powerhouse that set 37 individual and team NHL records while losing just 14 times in the 78-game regular season. Seven of the top 11 scorers in the league that winter wore black and gold. In finishing atop the Eastern Division, Boston scored 399 goals (108 more than the second-place team) and accumulated 24 more points than the Habs in the standings. Boston won a club-record 57 games—the first team in NHL history to surpass 50 victories for a season. And in March the Bruins produced a 13-game winning streak. Then, after losing three in a row, they won their last three games of the season—including 6–3 and 7–2 games over Montreal.

All the records aside, the Bruins of Bobby Orr and Phil Esposito held an intangible edge by virtue of possessing so many stars right in their primes. On the other side, Montreal featured a roster littered with some of the game's greats. But, as Dryden noted in his classic book *The Game*, only Yvon Cournoyer could be considered a player at his peak.

The 6'4", 210-pound Dryden had just six games of NHL experience as the quarterfinal playoff series opened with him getting outdueled by Bruins netminder Gerry Cheevers in a routine 3–1 Boston win at Boston Garden. With the score 5–1 in their favor about halfway through Game 2, the Bruins looked like sure bets to make prognostications of their easily advancing to the next round. Allegedly, at some point during that second game, the Bruins were spotted "chuckling away without a care" on the bench. If a late-second-period Montreal goal didn't change the Bruins' mood, there was more to come. Dryden recalls that Montreal coach Al MacNeil convinced the players during the intermission that "the Bruins were too loose, that our chances would come, that the game was still unwon."

Five third-period goals later, the series was even.

"We were playing so well. And I played in that one particular game, we were leading 5–1 and wound up getting beat 7–5. I think that probably changed that series," recalled Eddie Johnston, who relinquished Boston's goaltending duties to Cheevers for the rest of the series after Game 2. "We were coasting along, had a nice lead, and then all of a sudden they caught fire and ended up winning the game and the whole series."

The Dryden mystique really began to grow in Game 3 with a 37-save performance by the rookie in a 3–1 win. The Bruins, however, solved Dryden to the tune of 5–2 and 7–3 for a 3–2 series heading to The Forum for Game 6. With Henri Richard, who had

'71 Records Still Stand

The 1970–1971 Bruins set 37 individual and team NHL records, including Phil Esposito's record-shattering 76 goals. But you can argue that might not have been the greatest offensive record set by the club that went on to become more famous for falling in a seven-game first-round playoff series.

Maybe more astounding was that the Bruins of '71 became the first team to feature 10—that's right, 10—20-goal scorers. Other than Esposito, Johnny Bucyk (51), Ken Hodge (43), Bobby Orr (37), John McKenzie (31), Derek Sanderson (29), Ed Westfall (25), Fred Stanfield (24), Wayne Carleton (22), and Wayne Cashman (21) each surpassed 20 scores. Esposito (152), Orr (139), Bucyk (116), and Hodge (105) became the first four teammates to pass the century mark in points in the same season, and Esposito and Bucyk (51) became the first 50-goal-scoring teammates.

That club still holds the record for fastest three goals by one team, as Bucyk, Westfall, and Ted Green all lit the lamp in just 20 seconds in a win over Vancouver.

When you see the statistical proof of Boston's overwhelming firepower from '71, what Ken Dryden and the Canadiens accomplished in upsetting the Bruins becomes even more astounding.

done a yeoman's job slowing down Esposito for most of the series, shifted to the wing, the Canadiens used a shadow-by-committee approach to contain the Bruins' 76-goal-scoring center and rode two-goal performances by Richard and Peter Mahovlich to an 8–3 rout—the largest margin of defeat all year for the Bruins.

So it came down to a seventh game and a matchup of the Cup-winning veteran Cheevers and the book-smart first-year pro Dryden in net. It was the pony player against the penal code studier. Well, what it turned into was a coming-out party for a goaltender who would go on to win six Cups in his career.

Dryden stifled the Bruins every which way. Boston outshot Montreal 48–34 but came up short, 4–2, on the scoreboard. Esposito—with 3–7–10 totals in the series—failed to register a point, and Orr, probably more banged up than he would let on, suffered a second straight pointless game. He finished the series with 5–7–12 totals.

"He was like an octopus in the net, we just couldn't put the puck by him," recalled Bruins legend Johnny Bucyk. "When you've got a good goaltender who's playing great and who's lucky—and you've got to be lucky to be great—he was…he was unbelievable."

Over the years the Bruins have taken little criticism for their trade of Dryden on or around draft day in '64 because it was widely believed the college-bound netminder would never pursue an NHL career. Dryden admitted he didn't even know he was once a Boston draftee until some 10 years later. So instead, Dryden wrote his name onto the nightmare pages of Bruins history with a breakthrough performance that rendered one of the greatest regular seasons ever mostly meaningless.

"The '71 season is probably the biggest disappointment that I think we had collectively as a team and as a team effort," Bruins forward Ken Hodge once explained. "I still think back on the '71 season, where we set all those records production-wise. Four guys scoring over 100 points…. We just reflect back and we say, 'Hey, what could've been; what should've been.' Montreal, they had a pretty good team. Everybody says we were better. They had a pretty good team with Dryden, [Serge] Savard, [Guy] Lapointe. They had a pretty good team themselves. I just wished we accomplished what we set out to accomplish."

44 Cash Earned All He Got

If all the back operations, shoulder procedures, knee repair jobs, and stitches weren't enough to prove that Wayne Cashman would do anything for the Bruins, he clinched his place as *the* player who would go the greatest lengths to help the club on April 21, 1977.

And his victim wasn't anyone in a Los Angeles Kings uniform during Game 6 of a quarterfinal round playoff series. The victim was Frank Mahoney.

Who's Frank Mahoney? Well, as the story goes, the Kings were facing elimination and decided they were going to stage the "greatest pregame show in hockey history" in an effort to stave off elimination. Mahoney walked to center ice across a carpet to cap the festivities by belting out "God Bless America"—Kate Smith, Philadelphia-style (as the Bruins found out in the '74 Finals)—to bring the crowd into a frenzy. Instead, he opened his mouth, and nothing came out.

No, Mahoney didn't lose his voice. It seems that someone just cut the microphone cord. As it came to be learned later, that someone was Cashman (with some help from Bruins trainer Frosty Forristall). The Bruins scored three goals in the first eight minutes of the game and outshot LA 30–7 through the first two periods. Although the Kings rallied to tie the score, Cashman made sure that

Gregg Sheppard's power-play goal stood up as a game-winner by breaking up a two-on-one featuring Butch Goring and Marcel Dionne in the closing seconds of a 4–3 Boston win. The Bruins advanced all the way to the Stanley Cup Finals that spring, until they ran into the Montreal dynasty.

"Talent above the shoulders and below the belt is as important as individual scoring totals," wasn't just a quote Cashman once uttered but the philosophy he played his career by.

Remarkably, he combined his guts and brains to be a high-caliber left winger for most of his 17 years in the NHL, all spent with the Bruins. He lasted 1,027 regular-season games from 1964 to 1983 and retired as the last player remaining from the Original Six era. He buried 277 goals, including a career-high 30 in 1973–1974. The line of Cashman, Phil Esposito, and Ken Hodge was one of the most productive in the NHL in the early '70s.

"Wayne would say to me, 'Throw it in my corner and get the fuck in front of the net,'" Esposito, who did as he was told, once wrote.

Few have worked the corners of the NHL's rinks with the proficiency of Cashman. And his teammates appreciated every bump, bruise, and break he suffered, digging out the puck to make sure it got where the team needed it to be.

"He's definitely one of the two or three best left wingers I've ever seen," said Bruins goaltender Gerry Cheevers. "And he was undoubtedly the greatest corner man the game has ever seen."

Sometimes Cashman had the battle in the corner won before he even got to the puck. "You could see a guy go into a corner after the puck, and just before he got to it, he stopped and flinched a bit when he saw Cash. That's when you knew you got him on the ropes," teammate Derek Sanderson said.

Cashman's place in Bruins history on the ice often gets overshadowed by his zaniness off it. In addition to the Los Angeles

Forward Wayne Cashman spent his entire 17-year NHL career as a Boston Bruin, posting 277 goals and more than 1,000 regular-season games played, while earning two Stanley Cups.

incident, Cashman played a leading role in some other Boston tales. There's the time he broke his foot swinging from a chandelier. There was the legal tiff with a taunting fan in Buffalo. Esposito recalled one time when Cashman stuck teammate Mike Walton with a fork when Walton reached for something on Cashman's plate. And, of course, there was the time Cashman was picked up by the local police. He was given his one phone call. A little later, the Chinese food delivery man showed up at the station with Cashman's order.

By the late '70s, Cashman took on the role of Bruins captain. The guy who once, allegedly, threw a television out the hotel window in reaction to the news of Esposito's trade now had to mentor young players. Don Cherry, the Bruins' coach back then, remembered that one of Cashman's goals was to make sure no one damaged anything in the hotels because Cherry would get blamed.

Cheevers recalled that before wearing the "C," Cashman was quiet. As captain, he opened up, "sometimes cheerleading, sometimes being brutally blunt." Cashman's leadership skills came in handy after his playing days, as he served as an NHL assistant coach for numerous teams, including the Bruins.

That his No. 12 isn't hanging from the Garden rafters and his off-ice antics are sometimes easier recalled than his on-ice performances and importance as a leader is an injustice to Cashman's legacy. However, it's not likely that he cares much. As then–Bruins general manager Harry Sinden said upon Cashman reaching 1,000 career games: "Cash doesn't like ceremonies."

45 Everyone Loves Normand

Any talk about Normand Leveille's place in Bruins history always starts with a pause and a tip of one's head.

After all, the Bruins' 1981 first-round pick seemed certain to hold a place among the franchise's all-time greatest forwards when he began his second NHL season in 1982. Instead, his story became one of tragedy and promise lost.

The Bruins selected Leveille 14th overall, and he rewarded their confidence with 14 goals and 33 points in 66 games as a rookie. Eight games into his sophomore campaign, he was on a torrid pace with three goals and six assists.

"Norm Leveille was a star in the making," said longtime hockey broadcaster and writer Stan Fischler.

Harry Sinden had drafted the Montreal native as Bruins general manager.

"He was destined to be a really, really great player," he said. "It might be easy to say something like that now, but believe me, he was destined to be a great player."

Destiny dealt Leveille, just 19 at the time, a cruel fate on October 23, 1982. In the first period of a game at Vancouver, Leveille was checked hard into the boards by Marc Crawford. He got up, but in between periods he told close friend and mentor Jean Ratelle (Leveille was in the early stages of mastering English) that he felt dizzy. When team physical therapist Jimmy Kausek and Vancouver's Dr. Ross Davidson took a look at the teenager, it was obvious something serious was occurring.

Leveille was wheeled right into surgery. It was discovered that since birth he had suffered from an arteriovenous malformation, or a defective blood vessel. While the Crawford hit could've been what caused it to rupture, doctors said it could've been something even less hurtful than that, "like a sneeze." Leveille suffered a stroke. Although the surgery saved his life, he endured severe harm to his brain and motor functions. He was in a coma for three weeks.

Some 26 years later, his wife, Denise, relayed to the *Boston Globe* what Normand has told her he remembers of that night.

"He was on the bench, and he wanted aspirin," she said. "He remembers going to the bench…and when he was there, telling Jean Ratelle that he had a headache. But it was Jim Kausek who said to him, 'You don't need aspirin—you need to get to the hospital.'

He could see the side of Normand's face was paralyzed, yes? And he remembers going to the [locker] room...and falling down."

The Leveille tragedy resonated with Boston fans, the entire NHL, and his home province of Quebec. Many believe the Bruins' solid playoff run to the '83 Wales Conference Finals was inspired by Leveille. When he managed to take one last spin on the Boston Garden ice during the "Last Hurrah" closing ceremonies—with Ray Bourque, Terry O'Reilly, and others aiding his movements— Leveille was able to feel the same love Boston would've shown him had his career included game-winning goals and dramatic victories instead of a tragic ending.

Leveille's tale, however, is more than just one of a Bruins player cut down on the cusp of a productive career. It's also one of perseverance. Leveille has made the best of his situation by running a camp for handicapped kids and a charitable foundation, playing golf with one arm (due to his stroke), and making several trips each season to Boston to check in on his old team.

That cements Leveille's story as one of triumph as much as tragedy in Bruins lore.

46 Post-Orr, Park Won Them Over

When the world's best defenseman seems to be too injured to play the game at levels only he has reached, what's the best way to make sure you're covered if he's never the same?

Well, acquire the world's second-best defenseman, of course. Brad Park might've had some stiff competition for that runner-up status behind Bruins superstar Bobby Orr at the time of his trade to Boston, but he definitely had the pedigree worthy of that classification when the Bruins shipped Phil Esposito to the New York Rangers for Park in a November 1975 multiplayer trade.

"I had our chief scout [Bart Bradley] follow [Park], and he went to New York, and he went to Montreal, and he went to Vancouver," then–Bruins general manager Harry Sinden recalled. "And Brad was the No. 1 star in all three games. So he called me and said, 'The guy is fabulous.'"

Orr had suffered an injury in training camp that clued in everyone to his mortality. The hope was that he and Park might team up for years to come (they only played 10 games together), but if not, at least Park would allow the Bruins to claim that the league's best blueliner was still in their uniform. Of course, turning him from a hated Ranger into a beloved Bruin took some time.

Orr and Park Were a 10-Game Dream

The "hockey gods" played a cruel joke on the Bruins and their fans in 1975. After Boston acquired Brad Park from the New York Rangers, the hope was that the two best defensemen in the league—Bobby Orr and Park—would team up for years to come and add some more Stanley Cup titles to the Bruins' collection.

Unfortunately, Orr's knees didn't hold up long enough to play more than 10 games on the same side as Park. And the next season Orr left for Chicago as a free agent after a contract dispute.

The 10-game peek at what life might've been like with Orr and Park patrolling the blue line (although both were hobbled by lower-body ailments) is quite amazing. Former Bruins coach Don Cherry wrote that NHL goaltender Cesare Maniago thought of facing the Orr-Park combo on the power-play points as "sitting there with two cannons pointed at you. And you never knew which one was going to go off." That pretty much paints the picture.

With Orr and Park in the lineup together, Boston compiled a 6–1–3 record. Orr posted 5–13–18 totals, while Park scored at a 2–7–9 clip. Boston's man-advantage was a remarkable 13-for-41 (31.7 percent), with Orr scoring three and Park two of the power-play goals. Reading those numbers must make every Bruins fans' mouth water. Unfortunately, the thirst for a longtime partnership between Orr and Park was never quenched.

On the ice, Park was undoubtedly a gem of a player. He came to Boston with one 82-point season and five NHL All-Star first- or second-team selections already on his résumé. However, selling Park to the Bruins players remaining from the two-time Stanley Cup championship clubs of the early '70s and to the Boston Garden faithful would still be difficult.

There was more to the backlash to Park's arrival than just the fact that he was brought in in exchange for the popular Esposito. Around the time the Bruins and Rangers were preparing to meet in the '72 Cup Finals, Park's book *Play the Man* hit the shelves. In it, he called the "Big, Bad Bruins" animals and took personal shots at the likes of Phil Esposito, Ted Green, and John "Pie" McKenzie. Of the Boston fans he wrote: "To begin with, Boston Garden is a zoo. The fans are maniacal, and the rink is downright grubby. Without question, it is the worst rink in the NHL. It's old and shabby and always looks as though it could use another coat of paint and at least two more vacuum cleanings."

That shabby rink was now his home arena. Park had been traveling in and out of Boston with an FBI escort ever since the book's release. But he soon won over the Boston faithful with his stellar play at both ends of the rink. Park became a point-producer and suffocating defender for Don Cherry's "Lunch Pail A.C." teams that used unrelenting hard work to reach two Cup Finals and one Cup semifinals before the close of the decade.

Park was twice named to the NHL All-Star first-team in black and gold, and he added two more Norris Trophy runner-up finishes to bring his career total to six. He posted a Boston-career-high 79 points during the 1977–1978 season. And in 1983 he scored the Game 7 overtime game-winner that catapulted top-seeded Boston into the Wales Conference Finals, where they lost to the New York Islanders' latest dynasty installment. Park, who also helped tutor a young Ray Bourque, left Boston third in points and fourth in goals all-time by a Bruins defenseman (until Bourque knocked him down a notch on both lists).

"Brad was not as flashy as he had been when he came to Boston from the Rangers, but he became a better player," Cherry once said. "If you could forget about Orr for a moment, there was no defenseman I would rather have had than Brad Park."

Knee injuries and then a contract tiff cost Boston Orr's services. So the Bruins and their fans learned to love Park as an alternative.

Jinx? What Jinx?

The almost annual rite of spring—the Bruins losing in the postseason to Montreal—lasted 45 years and 18 series between 1943 and 1988. The pains of those defeats equally afflicted front-office types, coaches, players, and fans alike.

So when the 1988 Adams Division Finals finished with a 4–1 Boston win over the Canadiens in Game 5, legions of people bathed in the joy of the Bruins finally conquering their most-hated rivals to the north.

"I remember coming back to the airport after winning Game 5 in Montreal, and there were thousands of people at the airport waiting for us," Gord Kluzak, a mainstay on defense for that club, recalled. "And it had been a tremendous relief to finally beat the Canadiens. [Breaking] the jinx, as it used to be called at the Montreal Forum, it sort of meant a lot to long-term fans, meant a lot to us as players to get that sort of nemesis off our back. And it's certainly one of the more vivid memories for me."

Sure, the members of the '88 Bruins hadn't been affected by *all* the losses during the 45 years of ineptitude against Montreal. But the Bruins' defeats at the hands of the Habs from 1984 through

1987 were recent enough to have every player in a Bruins sweater wondering if "the jinx" actually existed.

The Habs finished nine points ahead of Boston for first place in the division and finished 4–3–1 against the Bruins in the '88 regular season. Whether he was just trying to convince himself and his teammates that '88 could be different than the previous few seasons, or he really believed the Bruins were a more formidable foe than in previous years, Canadiens star Bobby Smith gave Boston tons of credit before the series started.

"I really believe that [the Bruins] believe that this is their year," Smith said. "And it's certainly the best team I've seen them with in the years I've been here."

In Game 1 Bruins head coach Terry O'Reilly decided to start late-season acquisition Andy Moog in goal. And the result did little to convince anyone '88 was the Bruins' year to get over the hump, as Claude Lemieux scored twice in a 5–2 rout at The Forum. In one of the timeliest switches of goaltenders in Bruins history, O'Reilly turned to Reggie Lemelin for Game 2—a 4–3 Boston win, despite the 30–14 advantage Montreal had on the shots chart.

Lemelin didn't relinquish the starting goaltender job the rest of the series, as he dominated the Habs in 3–1 and 2–0 wins back in Boston. The Bruins had a stranglehold on the series heading up to Montreal with 45 years of baggage packed on their flight. Just 10:20 into the game, Steve Kasper scored on a two-on-one. From there, the Habs seemed somewhat demoralized after putting so much emphasis on getting ahead early.

"We were so ready to play that if they had scored first, we would have come back," Kasper said after that game. "We know we would have. We beat them four straight, two in the Forum—we proved we're the better team."

Kasper scored once more, and Cam Neely added two goals before the night was done. Montreal, practically gasping for air, actually squandered a power-play opportunity by wrongly challenging the length of Lemelin's stick in the first period. When the final horn sounded on the 4–1 win, jubilation reigned.

Some Bruins players basked in the victory a little more than others. Kluzak had grown up a Bruins fan in Saskatchewan and suffered through years of heartbreak against the Habs as a fan and then player. Kasper and Ray Bourque both now had bragging rights in their hometown. "Going back in 1988, I just remember not hearing a thing. So that was a fun summer for me," Bourque said.

"I was born and raised in Montreal, and at that time I was spending my summer in upstate New York, about 75 miles from Montreal," Kasper said. "And I had family there. Every time I'd go back, I'd run into people that'd be like, 'What happened? You lost again.' So to finally eliminate them in that fifth game—and fortunately for me I played a prominent role, I had a couple goals that night—it was a great thrill…. To finally get the monkey off the back, I think it set the tone for future series."

Actually, the jinx wasn't completely eliminated, as Boston lost to Montreal in the playoffs the next spring. However, Boston then downed the Canadiens in the next four head-to-head series before 2002. Boston's '88 series win over Montreal might not have been achieved as dramatically as the one from '43, which ended on an overtime goal by Ab DeMarco, but it obviously resonated as much, if not more, in Boston history.

48 Bruins Trust in the Bradley Boys

To this day, Scott Bradley boasts that his late father Bart is his hero.

In many ways, the late Bart Bradley is a hero of Bruins lore—both for his actions as a Boston scout and for bringing his son into the black-and-gold family. While a lot of haggling between members of an organization goes on before trades are made and draft picks are selected—and though the general manager ultimately has the last word—both Bradley men have left their fingerprints on some of the biggest acquisitions in Bruins history.

The trades for Cam Neely and Brad Park? Bart Bradley, a Bruins scout for three decades, was at GM Harry Sinden's ear to promote both. The drafting of Glen Murray and Hal Gill? Bart Bradley was a driving force. The drafting of Patrice Bergeron, Joe Thornton, and Milan Lucic? Scott Bradley, a mainstay of the Bruins organization since 1993, campaigned for all of them as the team's director of amateur scouting.

"He taught me everything I know," Scott said upon his father's death. "His three great loves in life were his family, the Bruins, and hockey."

Hockey was a bit cruel to Bart Bradley, who appeared in just one NHL game—for the Bruins in 1949–1950—during a 17-season professional playing career. However, Bradley didn't let that sour him on the game.

"He always said there were so many good players and only six teams. And you talk to people about my dad as a player…," explained Scott.

A few years after his father's death, Bradley got his hands on some video of his dad's playing and put his scout's eye to work.

"I thought he was a pretty slick centerman," he recalled, taking a break from scouting to stop off in Boston. "I had a cousin, Brian Bradley, who played in the league for 10 years, and he [Bart] kind of reminded me of Brian's skating. Back then, he played with Guy Fielder out west in Seattle. He centered him, and they led the league a couple years in a row. In today's game I think he probably would've been a regular."

When a Bradley man makes a statement about any player, you listen. Along with chief scout Gary Darling, Bart Bradley advised general manager Harry Sinden on some of the most important deals the club made, including the exporting of Phil Esposito to New York for Park and the lopsided acquisition of Neely. Bradley watched Neely closely, or as much as he could with the bulky forward getting little ice time as the third right winger on the Vancouver depth chart. In June 1986 Sinden was swinging a deal with the Canucks to send Barry Pederson west. As for a player to go along with the first-round pick Boston would get in return, Bradley had no doubt who Sinden should choose. "He's the guy," Sinden recalled Bradley telling him of Neely. "Nobody thinks that much of him right now, but he's going to be great."

Growing up around the Bruins guaranteed Scott would love the game. He used to get the day off from school to visit the dressing room when Boston was in Vancouver. And he still remembers when he was four years old and his dad returned from training camp with Bruins jackets for his sons. A goaltender during his playing days, Scott even got to fill in during a Bruins practice one year.

There was little doubt Scott was going to stay in the game after his playing days were up, but at first it wasn't certain he'd follow his father into scouting and working for the Bruins. After a brief coaching career, however, he started traveling with his father and began easing into the family business.

"I'd go to a Friday night game with him, and after the game he'd talk hockey with me—'What did you see there? What did you see here?'—I think it rubbed off on me a little bit," said Scott Bradley. "I think he always knew because I was so keen on staying in the game. And you never know where life is going to take you, but the Bruins have always been a part of my life."

Scott likes to call his dad, Sinden, Tom Johnson, and other members of the Bruins organization from when he was starting out, "the smartest guys in hockey." That knowledge helped mold Bradley into a veteran of the Bruins organization who has climbed the ranks for almost 20 years. You don't stick with an organization for so long, and through a major regime change in 2006, without a solid track record. He got off to a great start in his first season as director of amateur scouting after a number of years as a scout. The Bruins held the No. 1 pick in 1997, and the debate was between star centers Joe Thornton and Patrick Marleau.

"Marleau was close. We had debates. But he just wasn't up to Joe's size. It wasn't me making the call. They were out seeing him. You get that top pick, you've got everybody going out to see him," said Bradley about a draft that also netted Boston Sergei Samsonov and P.J. Axelsson.

No one in the scouting business is perfect. But whether you're talking about Lucic, Bergeron, or defenseman Kyle McLaren, you're talking about selections that helped keep the Bruins highly competitive for the '90s and 2000s. The Bradley scouting eye has obviously been passed down from father to son.

"I can go into a rink and…I'm not always right, but if you can hit .350, you're a pretty good scout," said the younger Bradley.

Scott Bradley also keeps his father's best advice in the front of his mind.

"Be honest and true to your word. If somebody asks you about something, be honest," he said.

49 Turnaround Begins July 1, 2006

Never one to let things rattle him, center Marc Savard wasn't curled up on his couch waiting for the phone to ring on July 1, 2006, when he became a coveted unrestricted free agent.

Fresh off a 97-point season, Savard was on the verge of getting very rich from a team almost of his choice. On that day, however, he was splitting his attention between the next step in his hockey career and his second love—golf.

"To honest, I was in my club championship, I was out on the golf course, and I got a call from my agent," remembered Savard, who noted that he was "putting out quick" so he could take calls but that he didn't even make the cut at his hometown course in Peterborough, Ontario.

Defenseman Zdeno Chara, a one-time Norris Trophy–finalist at the time, was at his Ottawa home that same day. Reportedly, upward of 20 teams were in pursuit of his services when the market opened at noon. A handful of clubs wanted Savard.

The Bruins, in desperate need of a franchise makeover, signed both.

"[Director of player development Don Sweeney] was in there with me to help me. Chara was our No. 1 focus, and we went after him first and obviously made him a huge offer that day. And we got the sense that we had the market for him," said former assistant general manager Jeff Gorton, who was still serving as interim GM at the time. "He wanted to go to a place where he could be captain. He didn't want a big city, but he wanted something like Boston. His agent lived in Boston. So there were so many things working for us, so it wasn't easy, but to be able to land him was great. And then that eventually led to Savard because he was pretty happy to see us land the big guy."

The way the Bruins performed in the 2005–2006 season, some wished they had stayed locked out.

The first season after the work stoppage that canceled the 2004–2005 campaign was a downright disaster, starting with the assemblage of the team by signing mostly B-list free agents to complement the core of Joe Thornton, Glen Murray, Andrew Raycroft, and Patrice Bergeron. And then when that plan seemed destined for failure in late November, Bruins GM Mike O'Connell traded away Thornton—robbing the team of not only one of the best point-producers alive, but also a marquee name to associate with the franchise. The thought was that with Thornton gone, the Bruins could use his salary-cap space to ink a replacement. It was a risk O'Connell decided he had to take, and one that ultimately cost him his job—even though the Bruins were able to enact his plan after all.

After the Bruins missed the playoffs in the spring of '06, Peter Chiarelli was hired as the new GM, and he replaced coach Mike Sullivan with Dave Lewis. Chiarelli, however, wasn't able to officially take his position with Boston until mid-July because of a compensation dispute with his old club, Ottawa. So it was up to Gorton and his staff to make its mark July 1.

When the dust settled, Chara had agreed to a five-year, $37.5 million deal, and Savard a $20 million deal for four years. Gorton had to get the ultimate approval from executive vice president Charlie Jacobs, son of owner Jeremy Jacobs.

"And so it was, for all intents and purposes, $58 million. It was just a large investment and a lot of faith that things were going to work," said Jacobs. "But you know what? We had to jump in with both feet and make sure it would work."

"I think it was a little bit mixed emotions. It really was," he continued when pushed about how he was feeling about the two giant moves. "I didn't have buyer's remorse; I just wanted to make sure that they played well."

Chiarelli's obligation to Ottawa prevented him from getting directly involved in the negotiations. But his imminent arrival influenced both players: Chara had played in Ottawa for a number of years, and Savard's agent was once Chiarelli's boss in the GM's pre-hockey operations life.

After the deals were made official, Chiarelli was able to comment on them. "Let's just say what I set forth was very specific," he told the *Globe* about his limited discussions with Gorton. "I was surprised [at the Chara signing] and excited. I think it's a tremendous acquisition. Zdeno is a tremendous player, a large shutdown type of player. He's very competitive. He takes up that quarter of the ice in your defensive zone. It was interesting to say the least. [Ottawa] had reached a point where they were resigned that they couldn't sign Zdeno. As far as I know, in my discussions with [Ottawa] GM John Muckler, there were no ill feelings."

All that was left was for both players to live up to their salaries. But the 2006–2007 season was every bit as disastrous as the previous campaign. Chara only produced 43 points and was a ghastly minus-21 while dealing with the pressure of being the captain and skating 30 minutes a night. Savard tallied 96 points but looked disinterested in doing anything other than scoring.

Ownership granted Chiarelli a mulligan and allowed him to switch coaches to Claude Julien. A specific philosophy was established, and players who wouldn't buy into the coach's system would be jettisoned. Chara and Savard responded the way the team's top-earning players should. In 2007–2008 the duo led Boston to its first playoff berth in four years. And then the next season Chara won the Norris Trophy as the league's best defenseman, and Savard combined an 88-point season with a plus-25 rating to emerge as a solid two-way threat. Boston eventually won the 2011 Stanley Cup, the organization's first since 1972.

There were obviously other trades, signings, and drafting that contributed to the Bruins' turnaround. Without the actions of July 1, 2006, however, the Bruins might've been a laughingstock for years to come.

50 You Can't Sour the Kraut Line Legacy

All you need to know about the Kraut Line is that more than 50 years after Bruins stars Woody Dumart, Bobby Bauer, and Milt Schmidt played their last game together, *Sports Illustrated* Hall of Fame writer Michael Farber ranked the Krauts as the fifth-best line in NHL history.

The game has changed a lot over that half century since Bauer's one-game comeback from retirement in 1952, but the Krauts' mark on the game hasn't been altered, and their legacy continues today.

"They knew each other better than any other line in the history of the NHL in terms of idiosyncratic, off-the-ice personalities," longtime hockey writer and broadcaster Stan Fischler explained. "They were literally pals from childhood."

If the Dynamite Line was the Bruins' first trio with a catchy nickname, the Kraut Line was the first to sustain its success for a lengthy period of time and set the bar for every other line to come along.

Bauer was three years older than Schmidt, and Dumart was in between the two. Bauer's last season playing for the junior Kitchener Greenshirts was the first time he was on the same team as Schmidt and Dumart, who at that time was a defenseman. After Dumart and Bauer signed with the Bruins, they convinced manager Art Ross to sign a 17-year-old Schmidt, as well. The Kraut Line was on the road to formation.

When the trio eventually joined Boston's Providence Reds farm club, they formed a line, and head coach Albert "Battleship" Leduc gave them their name because of their German heritage. They became Bruins regulars in 1937–1938, and for the next eight seasons before they left for WWII—and for a couple after their return—no one could stop the Kraut Line. In 1940 Schmidt led the league in scoring with 52 points, and Dumart (43) and Bauer (43) finished second and third. That season the Bruins lost in the playoffs to the New York Rangers and failed to repeat as Stanley Cup champs. But the next season Boston plowed through the NHL and then registered the first-ever Cup Finals sweep against Detroit.

Bauer, a three-time winner of the Lady Byng Trophy, was known for his stick-handling on the line, while Dumart was the defensive stopper who was assigned to shut down some of the top opposing snipers in the six-team league. And then there was Schmidt, a two-way force who never backed down from a challenge.

"There wasn't a better defensive player in the world than [Dumart] was," Schmidt said. "[Bauer] was the brains of the line. We used to call him 'the Thinker.'… I said, well I had a strong back and a weak mind. So that's why we were successful."

If the chemistry the three players had built up since their junior hockey days wasn't enough to catapult them to the top of the

Krauts Get a Sensational Sendoff

No one could deny the "Kraut Line" of Milt Schmidt, Woody Dumart, and Bobby Bauer had a knack for drama. Playing their last game before joining the Canadian Royal Air Force on February 10, 1942, the Krauts torched the rival Montreal Canadiens for 11 points in an 8–1 Bruins win.

When the game ended, in front of a cheering Boston Garden crowd, the players were presented with their paychecks for the rest of the season, plus a bonus. Manager Art Ross made a speech praising his star pupils. Then players from both teams—that's right, even members of the hated Habs—carried the three Krauts off the ice.

"The attitude, feelings that the Montreal Canadiens had for the Krauts that night, they were fantastic," recalled Schmidt. "What more could you ask for? And that's one of those things that I can remember as clearly as it was yesterday."

charts, all three pushed each other every inch of the way on and off the ice.

"We would accept each other's criticism," said Schmidt about the trio who lived together in Brookline, Massachusetts, during the season. "That was one of the big reasons we got along so well. Bobby would criticize me for not doing something, or Woody would; we all did an equal amount, but we said it in real nice language."

There was more to just how close the Kraut Line was than their hometown ties and rooming situation. They even negotiated their contracts together.

"We felt if we went in together, asked for exactly the same salary for each, and took a stand in our dealings, we'd be better off," Schmidt once explained.

The only thing that prevented the Kraut Line from dominating the NHL for years to come after the '41 Cup win was the war raging in Europe. The trio decided to enlist in the Royal Canadian Air Force and was called up in 1942. But that didn't stop them from having on-ice success. They joined the Ottawa Commandos while stationed in Canada's capital city and went on to lead that team to an Allan Cup championship. The next year, while stationed in Halifax, Nova Scotia, the Krauts helped a team win the city championship.

During WWII, some tried to rename the Kraut Line the "Buddy Line" or the "Kitchener Kids," but those monikers never stuck. After their return from the service, the Kraut Line was back both in name and in action. In their second year back in 1946–1947 all the Krauts finished in the top 10 in scoring. The Bruins lost in the Cup Finals and then the semifinals in the two seasons after the Kraut Line returned, respectively.

Bauer pulled the plug on his playing career in '47, only to return for that one game in '52 as part of a tribute evening. The Kraut Line stayed close, however, as Dumart worked for Bauer's family hockey equipment company after his retirement, and Dumart and Schmidt were neighbors in Needham, Massachusetts, for years before Dumart's death in 2001.

The Kraut Line might have been the best line of its time, and it's definitely one of the best in Bruins and NHL history.

The Uke Line

Boston had always had its share of immigrant communities, but in the late 1950s and early '60s one trio of Ukrainian-Canadians were a little more important on the city's sports scene than any others.

The Uke Line of Johnny Bucyk, Bronco Horvath, and Vic Stasiuk, who had been linemates earlier in their careers with the Edmonton Flyers of the Western Hockey League, were a potent trio that kept Boston competitive and carried on a tradition of powerful triumvirates in Bruins uniforms established decades earlier by the Dynamite Line and the Kraut Line.

"The three of us worked well together," Bucyk, the left winger on the line, once explained. "Each of us knew where the other two fellows would be. Bronco and Vic turned out to be the big scorers, whereas my job was to get the puck out of the corners."

"I'd tell Vic and Bucyk, 'Get the puck and look in front for my socks.' That's how it worked," said Horvath. "But I wouldn't stay in there too long, because if you did, someone like Doug Harvey would cross-check you in the head or try to punch your lights out."

Technically, Horvath, the center, was Hungarian. But his family immigrated to Canada from Carpathia when the territory was ceded to Ukraine at the end of WWI. Horvath never tried to deny his place on the Uke Line—and who could blame him? The trio was together for four full seasons, including a run to the Stanley Cup Finals in 1958 and a playoff berth the season after. In that '58 season Horvath led the team with 30 goals and 66 points. Stasiuk and Bucyk both scored 21 goals, making the Uke Line the first to feature three 20-plus-goal scorers.

"As well-known offensive trios go, the Uke Line was different in that it lacked a true superstar," longtime hockey writer and broadcaster Stan Fischler wrote. "Stasiuk was a lumbering skater whose tenacity outdid his skills. Remarkably slow for a big-leaguer, Horvath nevertheless was a creative playmaker armed with an accurate wrist shot."

The Uke Line chemistry was forged on the ice, but it was nurtured away from the rink. All three men lived together in a place rented from former Bruins defenseman Pat Egan in Arlington, Massachusetts.

"We ate together and drove to the rink together, and that gave us the opportunity to discuss our play together," Bucyk said.

In 1960–1961 the Uke Line had its last hurrah. While Bucyk stayed in Boston all the way until his 23-season NHL career ended in 1978, Horvath and Stasiuk were both dealt away. Bucyk eventually was elected to the Hockey Hall of Fame, but for four years he couldn't have made as much history as he did without his Uke Line mates.

52 If You Hate Anyone, Hate the Habs

A great commercial promoting the Bruins' website during the spring of 2009 hilariously depicted a bear swatting down the popcorn bucket of a Bruins fan caught hanging out at the TD Garden with his Montreal-sweater-wearing girlfriend.

The tag line: "Don't date within the division."

The point: if you're a Bruins fan, you don't tolerate the existence of fans of the Habs, Toronto Maple Leafs, Buffalo Sabres, or Ottawa Senators. But the underlying point was that everything to do with the storied Montreal Canadiens is evil. Any Bruins fan, from any generation, knows that Montreal players, coaches, front-office personnel, fans, and anything or anyone associated with the Habs is to be hated.

"Hate's a powerful word, but we certainly strongly disliked them," explained Gord Kluzak, a Bruins' defenseman in the '80s. "Even in '86, when they beat us, they went on to win the Cup. We felt that we had a better team than them, and here they are carrying the Cup around again. And so, I think of Guy Carbonneau, Chris Chelios, Patrick Roy—they were extremely competitive, talented guys. Claude Lemieux—maybe I hated Claude Lemieux—but they were talented guys, a tough group to play against, and I don't think we had anywhere near a rivalry with any other team compared to the Canadiens."

No one should hate indiscriminately. So you have to learn why the Bruins-Canadiens rivalry has been aflame for more than 80 years.

As difficult as it is to give credit to the Canadiens, it was their powerful teams of the early 1920s, led by Howie Morenz, that helped boost hockey's popularity in the U.S. and first put the idea in the head of Charles Adams to bring an NHL team to Boston. Of course, that's the last time Boston should give props to Montreal.

Once Eddie Shore, Dit Clapper, and Boston's who's who list of future Hall of Famers rounded into a powerhouse club, the Boston-Montreal rivalry was on. Year in and year out, through the late '30s, the Bruins and Canadiens were among the best teams on the ever-changing NHL landscape. The Bruins downed the Canadiens in the semifinals on their way to their first Cup in 1929. But the next season the record-breaking 38–5–1 Bruins were limited to just three goals in the two-game Cup Finals. The Habs had won their second of their record 24 Cups, and as the decades rolled along, many of Montreal's triumphs would come at the Bruins' expense or at least feature the Canadiens going through Boston on their way to the ultimate victory.

Montreal repeated as Cup champs in '31 (beating the Bruins in the semifinals), but the Great Depression began to take its toll. The Canadiens were near extinction when their city-sharing partner Montreal Maroons were folded, which contributed to the saving of the Canadiens franchise. Before long, the Canadiens were icing teams with Maurice "Rocket" Richard, Elmer Lach, and Toe Blake leading the way, and the rivalry was renewed.

Bruins Cost Richard Lone Shot at Scoring Title

The Bruins weren't able to solve the hated Montreal Canadiens in any postseason series in the '50s, but one season they had an indirect hand in denying the Canadiens the Stanley Cup—and keeping one of the Montreal franchise's most iconic players from reaching a career-long goal.

On March 13, 1955, Maurice "Rocket" Richard attacked Bruins player Hal Laycoe with his stick, and other sticks, after Laycoe responded to a slash with a head blow that drew blood. Linesman Cliff Thompson tried to intervene, and the "Rocket" promptly punched the official twice. NHL president Clarence Campbell handed down a suspension for the rest of the season (three games) and the playoffs, an act that famously prompted the "Richard riots" during and after the Canadiens' next home game.

Richard's absence didn't stop the Canadiens from beating the Bruins in the opening round of the playoffs. But Montreal didn't have enough firepower to take down Detroit in the Cup Finals. Richard's chance to win his only NHL scoring title also went out the window, as teammate "Boom Boom" Geoffrion passed Richard in those last three games and won the title by one point.

Even if it wasn't much consolation for how much Montreal dominated Boston in that decade and for the better part of 60-odd years, the Bruins at least pushed Richard to the brink and cost the Habs a chance to add to their storied string of successes.

When the Bruins defeated Montreal in the Cup semifinals in 1943, Boston couldn't have imagined how long it would be until the next playoff-series victory over the Canadiens. However, they got an idea in the '50s, as six times Boston's season came to an end at the hands of their archrivals during that decade. Particularly painful were a seven-game loss in '52—a series the Bruins led, three games to two—and a Finals loss in '53 after Boston pulled an historic upset of first-place Detroit in the semifinals. The Boston-Montreal rivalry was now on the fast track to Hate-ville.

"There wasn't any friendship between them," said Eddie Sandford, a top forward on those 1950s teams. "You played 14 times a year, seven there and seven at home, so you knew that whatever your problem was one game, you were going to go up to Montreal and see the same guy again. It was very competitive. We didn't fraternize with them, and they didn't fraternize with us."

Even once Bobby Orr arrived on Causeway Street and the Bruins emerged from their franchise doldrums in the late 1960s, the Canadiens stood in the way. Jean Beliveau's overtime goal in Game 7 of the Cup semifinal series in '69 sent many a Hub child to bed crying because Orr and his "Big, Bad Bruins" would have to wait one more year to end the franchise's Cup drought. Boston won two Cup titles in the early 1970s, but neither run included a series with Montreal. And when the "Big, Bad Bruins" did face the Habs—in 1971—Ken Dryden stood on his head, and the Habs staged one of the great upsets in NHL history.

Don Cherry's "Lunch Pail A.C." teams of the late '70s didn't fare much better against Montreal—losing two Cup Finals series and a semifinal in '79. That '79 loss, of course, has gone down in infamy for the too-many-men-on-the-ice penalty toward the end of Game 7. Montreal tied the game during the ensuing power play and won the series in overtime. That loss was felt by Bruins backers across the continent, including Saskatchewan, where a young Gord

Kluzak—years before he would become Bruins property—was glued to his television.

"I remember being in tears as a 13- or 14-year-old watching that series," remembered Kluzak.

The Boston-Montreal rivalry had, and still has, the power to turn players into haters of their hometown team. Steve Kasper, a Montreal native, says he pulled on the Boston sweater and "it didn't take long to put [the Canadiens] in the rearview mirror." He remembered the third game of his rookie year, when the Bruins pulled out a thrilling 3–2 win over the Habs.

"All I can tell you is I was thrilled to beat the Montreal Canadiens," he said.

By the time the Bruins met the Canadiens in the 1988 Adams Division Finals, Montreal had won the last 18 series between the two franchises. Led by Cam Neely, Ray Bourque, Kasper, and goaltender Reggie Lemelin, the Bruins finally got the monkey off their collective back.

The Bruins and Canadiens met in the playoffs six straight years, from 1987 to 1992, with the Bruins actually winning four times. Montreal took three straight series from Boston to start the next century, but the Bruins closed out the decade with a four-game sweep in 2009.

"I think the rivalry's pretty healthy; I think it's pretty resilient in its own way…especially in Boston, there's a lot of hatred toward each team, and that's fun," said center Bryan Smolinksi, who played for the Bruins in the '90s and the Canadiens in the next decade.

The Montreal-Boston rivalry will never die. And from the days of Richard and Leo Labine colliding, to the days of Kyle McLaren knocking out Richard Zednik, through the physical battles between Milan Lucic and Mike Komisarek, Bruins-Canadiens games are always a grudge match with more on the line than just two points.

It might not be healthy to hate, but that's a chance Bruins fans are willing to take when it comes to the Montreal Canadiens.

Nifty Was Truly Magic

While watching Rick Middleton stick-handling, spinning, and weaving his way to his 448 career NHL goals—including 402 scored in a Bruins sweater—it was hard to say anything because his mastery with the puck would take your breath away.

Once you were able to speak, there were a multitude of adjectives you could use to describe Middleton's abilities. Most just called him "Nifty."

"I had a few different nicknames in New York, which I'm not going to divulge," Middleton explained. "But when I got to Boston, I had a couple. 'Magic' was another one. It always seemed that it depended on the players on the team—different guys seemed to have different nicknames for me. And 'Nifty' was the one that kind of stuck in the press, so it kind of was the one that lasted. But not all the guys called me 'Nifty,' but some do.

"What I thought was nice was that it did last all this time, and by the time I got on [television with] NESN, kids who weren't even born when I was playing would come up to me and say, 'Hey, Nifty, can I have an autograph?' So that name kind of lives on through a couple generations, and it was nice that it did. I kind of like it now."

Having witnessed what Middleton accomplished with a spoked "B" on his sweater, it's hard to imagine that when New York Rangers general manager John Ferguson decided he wanted to acquire Ken Hodge from Boston to reunite with Phil Esposito in 1976, Bruins GM Harry Sinden originally asked for left winger

Steve Vickers in return. When the deal was completed, it was Hodge for Middleton—straight up. Hodge barely made it through another season as a productive player, while Middleton went on to have a career that makes you wonder why YouTube wasn't invented decades earlier in order to display the spectacular highlights Middleton produced almost every night. *Sports Illustrated* in 2000 ranked Middleton among the top 10 break-away artists in the NHL since the 1967–1968 expansion. And he made his presence felt in Boston right away with a hat trick in his Bruins debut.

"Game after game he demonstrated stick-handling and skating talent that brought fans out of their seats," wrote late legendary Bruins play-by-play man Fred Cusick in his autobiography. "He often climaxed his maneuvers with a head-to-head meeting with the rival goaltender. Many times, Middleton would win the matchup by either drawing the goaltender out of position or, if he held the fort, picking a spot and firing it into the net."

Some argue now that Middleton, who claims to have learned all his "nifty" moves while playing street hockey as a kid, was the best steal Sinden ever made in a trade. Ferguson, who also said he made the trade because Middleton was taking "too big a bite of the Big Apple," called it his worst deal ever. One thing's for sure, Sinden still dotes a bit on the player who he brought to Boston in one of the league's all-time larcenies.

"He never played a bad game, ever, in his whole career," Sinden says now. "He was just one of those players who every night you knew exactly what you were going to get.... It's rare from a star player because they have their tough times."

Even when told about Sinden's glowing words, Middleton doesn't try to claim an error-free career as fact. He remembers one night in Chicago that earned him the ire of head coach Don Cherry.

"I don't know why, but I took the faceoff in our own end to the right of Gerry Cheevers. And I lost the faceoff so fast, the puck went back and was in the net before I took my stick off the ice," Middleton recalled. "I skated over to the bench, and Cherry looked at me and said, 'That's the last fucking time you're taking a faceoff.' I never took another faceoff."

The Middleton-Cherry relationship was that contentious throughout, but beneficial to both. With Cherry's constant barking at his ear, Middleton emerged as a two-way force without any drop-off in his offensive production and earned time on both special teams.

"It came step by step," Middleton once said. "Late in games I suddenly found that I was still on the ice. I got a whiff of confidence. I started to see how playing defense led into playing offense."

The Bruins with Middleton as one of their top producers and Cherry as coach reached two Cup Finals and a Cup semifinal (which ended in the infamous too-many-men game).

"He turned out to be something," Cherry once recalled. "Ricky turned out to be one of the best players in the NHL. Maybe I didn't get the champagne [for winning a Cup], but after I left the Bruins, I did receive a thank-you note from Middleton's parents. That was just as good."

54 Bourque Was the Star of Stars

The Bruins' inaugural season at TD Garden, then known as the FleetCenter, didn't do much to make people stop yearning for the old Boston Garden.

Although the Bruins advanced to the Stanley Cup playoffs for a 29th straight year, they finished second in the Northeast Division and bowed out in the first round of the postseason in just five games against Florida.

Sure, Cam Neely opened the place with a hat trick in a victory. And in December Adam Oates tied a team record with four goals in another win. But the highlights were few and far between.

Luckily, the NHL granted the Bruins and their new home the 1996 NHL All-Star Game—and in storybook fashion, future Hall of Famer Ray Bourque closed the festivities with a goal that to this day might be the most dramatic Bruins score in their most recent home.

Bourque's backhand shot from the inside edge of the right circle beat Toronto goaltender Felix Potvin high with 37.3 seconds left on the clock to clinch a 5–4 win for the Eastern Conference over the Western Conference. Although the vote had already been counted with him not winning, Bourque was still presented with game MVP honors.

"This will be the one, I'm sure, that I'll remember forever," said Bourque, who was in the midst of his 17th season with the Bruins. "Winning at the end like that, scoring the goal and just having the crowd go crazy, it's been a great relationship for 17 years. To have it happen here and in my building is extra special, I've got to say. I haven't been this nervous for a game in a long time. I don't get that way too often. I just wanted to go out and play well. I just didn't want to get embarrassed out there. In these games, sometimes, that certainly happens."

Bourque's pride might've been dashed a little the night before. At the league's annual skills competition he was dethroned as the shooting accuracy champion—he had won the previous three contests—by New York Rangers star Mark Messier. Bourque was also stopped on a breakaway attempt by Chicago's Ed Belfour that prevented the East from winning the team points race.

Bruins All-Star defenseman Ray Bourque reacts after tying for first place in the accuracy shooting competition during the skills competition at the 2000 NHL All-Star weekend in Toronto. Photo courtesy of AP Images

But Bourque more than made up for it the next night, when all the league's biggest superstars reported to Causeway Street for the midseason spectacle. In a rare defensive struggle for an All-Star Game, Bourque did something rare just before he scored the game-winner—he threw a hit.

As the *Boston Globe* described: "Just before connecting for the winner, Bourque threw one of the game's few checks—perhaps the only check—when he rubbed out [Paul] Kariya. The Bruins captain didn't want to see his name on the score sheet as a minus if Kariya had dashed up ice to score the winner. Bourque applied the body one moment, scored the next, and perhaps snatched the [MVP] trophy away from Kariya in the process."

The FleetCenter fans had been showering Bourque with adulation all weekend, to the point where he spent a great deal of his time misty-eyed. His heroics then really brought the house down in the first sign that maybe some of the old Garden electricity could carry over to the new arena.

One thing that definitely hadn't changed with the Bruins' move to a new venue was Bourque's greatness.

"I was hoping I'd get an opportunity to [score the winner], but if it wasn't me, I'm glad it's Ray," said Bruins and Eastern All-Stars teammate Cam Neely after the game. "It's great for Ray, believe me. I know how much this meant to him. I'm so excited for him. I knew it was something special for him. For the game to end the way it did makes it really, really special. Ray's been a great friend of mine for 10 years since I've been here. To see him get that goal and how the crowd reacted—it was great for Ray and for everyone involved with the team and the city."

It will always be the first truly great moment in the new Garden's history, and it was appropriate it was authored by the greatest player to wear a spoked "B" in that building.

55 Even Injury Couldn't Bring Bergeron Down

When Patrice Bergeron reported to Bruins training camp at the start of the 2008–2009 season, his career could have gone one of two ways.

Little did he know that in two years' time he would be an Olympic gold medal winner, and then one year later a Stanley Cup champion.

"[I feel] very lucky," said Bergeron days after his two-goal performance in Game 7 of the 2011 Stanley Cup Finals in Vancouver helped the Bruins end a 39-year title drought. "I feel blessed and, you know, that's what you fight for your whole career, and being able to do it so early, it's special. But that being said, once you taste it you want more. I'll enjoy this one right now but this summer I have to regroup and get back and get ready for next season."

Luck, however, had nothing to do with Bergeron's resurgence. It was all about hard work.

In the fall of 2007, Bergeron's third NHL season had been cut short by a Grade 3 concussion suffered after a hit from behind by Philadelphia's Randy Jones. There were fears that he could become yet another tale of Bruins misfortune, joining the likes of Gord Kluzak and Normand Leveille, promising young future stars whose careers were abbreviated by injury or illness.

However, Bergeron's nature didn't allow him to give up on his career. He used the same work ethic that earned him a spot on an NHL roster at 18 in 2003–04 to return to full strength as the team's best two-way center and alternate captain. By his second full season back from the injury, he had again emerged as one of the league's best young stars and earned a spot on the Canadian Olympic team for the 2010 Winter Games in Vancouver.

"I didn't get selected for summer [orientation] camp, but at the same time I was worrying about the Bruins and playing my game and making sure I was giving the Bruins a chance to win every game," said Bergeron about his dark-horse candidacy for the squad. "And that's what it's all about for me, it's about the team. And after that, well, I guess they liked what they've seen. And they said it, too, after the summer camp, that it didn't mean that if you weren't on that roster that you weren't going to get the call."

It shouldn't have been a surprise to anyone that Bergeron was able to turn nonexistent expectations into a spot on that team. He had done the same back in 2003, when he made the big club after he had been a second-round draft pick just a few months earlier. Bergeron wowed the Bruins' front office with his camp performances against players of his own experience level, and then impressed the established NHL guys by dominating them in drills and scrimmages.

Guidolin Set the Youth Standard

A bunch of the Bruins' brightest stars—from Bobby Orr to Joe Thornton, Patrice Bergeron, and Milan Lucic—got their starts in the NHL as teenagers. But in 1942 the Bruins were short players because of WWII, and the team made history by promoting 16-year-old Bep Guidolin to the big club. The late Guidolin remains the youngest player to ever skate in an NHL game.

"I hate to say this about myself, but what the heck, I could skate—I mean, I could really go, eh?" Guidolin told the *Boston Globe* about the night in November 1942 when he joined the Bruins against the Toronto Maple Leafs at Maple Leaf Gardens. "I got out there, and boy, I thought I was still in junior hockey, I was just flying. But Bingo Kampman caught up to me—not a fast guy, either, Bingo—and, boy, did he lay me out. Welcome to the NHL."

Rules that prohibit a player even being drafted before his 18th birthday pretty much guarantee that Guidolin's place in history will last forever.

"The first three or four practices I saw him play, I said, 'This kid knows how to play already,'" recalled former Bruins president Harry Sinden. "His junior coach didn't teach him, and neither did anybody else, and neither has anybody else since. But instinctively, he knew how to play. And you can see what he does."

Bergeron admits he might've even surprised himself that fall.

"I was just trying to come here and learn as much as I could, get the experience, and see what happens," he said. "But, I mean, with a couple exhibition games under my belt, I felt that I could stay. So I sort of told myself, *If I give a little more, I might have that chance.* Especially at that time, they had some space in the middle here at center, so I was just trying to go out there and play and see what happens, and it was sort of up in the air at that point."

As an NHL rookie, Bergeron put up 16 goals and 39 assists in 71 games and even netted an overtime goal in the 2004 playoffs during a series the Bruins eventually lost in seven games to Montreal.

After the lockout, the Bruins struggled, but Bergeron's dedication to a taxing workout regimen and stringent diet put him at the brink of stardom. His rise was sidetracked a bit after the Jones hit and then a second, but unrelated, concussion suffered in 2008. He finished the 2008–09 season healthy and helped the Bruins finish atop the Eastern Conference in the regular season and win a round of the playoffs for the first time in 10 years. In 2009–10, he missed just nine regular-season games and recorded 52 points—his most since 2007. But he also was on two different ends of some historic team experiences.

In February he won the gold medal at the Winter Olympic Games in Vancouver when Team Canada defeated Team USA in overtime.

"It was a great experience. It was a lot of fun, and obviously winning that gold medal means even more and it was really a special moment," he said upon returning from the Games.

After suffering a career-threatening concussion in 2007, Bruins center Patrice Bergeron returned to the form he showed in his first three seasons, putting up 19 goals and 52 points during the 2009–2010 campaign.

In the spring of 2010, the Bruins upset Buffalo in the first round of the playoffs and led the Philadelphia Flyers three games to none in the second round. After a confluence of occurrences, the Bruins became the third team in NHL history to squander such a commanding lead.

Bergeron returned for the 2010–11 season as a member of an almost identical Bruins core from the one that went down in flames the previous spring. Combining with Mark Recchi and Brad Marchand to give the Bruins a solid second line and flaunting polished defensive skills that had him in the Selke Trophy race all season long, Bergeron helped the Bruins win the Northeast Division.

The Bruins got by Montreal in the first round and then faced those Flyers again in the second. This time, the Bruins finished things off in four straight, but in the clinching game Bergeron suffered yet a third concussion.

This head injury wasn't as serious as the prior two, and he missed just two games of the Eastern Conference Finals against Tampa Bay. He returned to play a starring role in a seven-game win, and the Bruins were back in the Stanley Cup Finals for the first time since 1990. Bergeron helped his team overcome a 2–0 series deficit against Vancouver, and then he buried two goals in the deciding Game 7.

The doubts about Bergeron's ability to reach his career potential were completely eviscerated in just four years.

56 Sudden Death

A lot of things rhyme with Mel, and a lot of things rhyme will Hill, both complimentary and derogatory.

However, when it came time to find a nickname for Bruins forward Mel Hill, there was only one term that could fit—once the Stanley Cup run of 1939 was over, that is. After that spring, he was "Sudden Death" and there hasn't been another "Sudden Death" since.

"It wasn't an easy tag to carry the rest of my career. It seemed like I was expected to be the hero in every playoff game from that moment on," Hill once explained. "The name 'Sudden Death' was easier to live with after I retired."

Hill's heroics in '39 weren't just dramatic because they propelled the Bruins to their first Cup title in 10 years. His three overtime goals against the New York Rangers made sure Boston avoided the utter embarrassment that would have arrived had the Bruins failed to close out the series after jumping out to a 3–0 lead in that series.

It all started March 21 with the Bruins, who finished atop the one-division, seven-team NHL, hosting the Rangers in Game 1 of the Cup semifinals. The 25-year-old Hill was in just his first NHL season and making his first foray into postseason hockey at the sport's highest level. No doubt, Hill wanted to impress during the series because a few years earlier the Rangers had deemed Hill too light and lacking of the talent necessary to play in the NHL after a tryout with the club.

After regulation and two overtimes in Game 1, the score was tied at 1–1. It was around the time of the third overtime's start that coach Art Ross mentioned to Bruins star center Bill Cowley that with New York focused so much on winger Roy Conacher, the third member of the line—Hill—might be available for a scoring chance.

Late in the session, that advice paid off. Cowley stick-handled into the New York zone, drifted to the corner, and then found an unguarded Hill in front of the Rangers' crease for a shot that beat goaltender Davey Kerr high for a Bruins series lead.

Had Hill's heroics ended there, his revenge on the Rangers and his place in the Bruins' history would have already been secured. But before the series was done, he tripled his pleasure. He ended Game 2 early in the first overtime with a 40-foot shot off a drop pass by Cowley. Boston handedly won Game 3 4–1 and seemed poised to capture the Cup without any more dramatics. But the Rangers wouldn't go away. The Rangers won consecutive 2–1 decisions and then took Game 6 3–1 to force a do-or-die Game 7.

Another tight affair didn't produce a winner after five periods, until Cowley and Hill worked their magic again. Cowley tracked a rebound to the corner and then, from behind the net, he fed the puck in front for Hill to beat Bert Gardiner for the series-clinching goal.

"I held the puck for a second, then flipped it up into the net on the short side. The fans went wild, and it was a tremendous thrill to win a series for my team," Hill recalled.

Although he had a nondescript career after '39, Hill carried his outstanding play from the semifinals into the Cup Finals with a couple assists in a 2–0 Game 4 win and the game-winner in the clinching Game 5 against Toronto. In '41 Hill didn't produce any overtime fireworks during the Bruins' second Cup run in three years. But he did clinch the semifinal series against the Maple Leafs with a clutch goal.

After '41 Hill was sold to Brooklyn and never played for the Bruins again. Mel's play was swell, and Hill's goals gave them a thrill, but there was, and will always be, just one nickname for the heroic Mel Hill: "Sudden Death."

57 Gallery Gods Had the Bruins' Backs

Boston Garden always provided the Bruins with an overwhelming home-ice advantage. But that "seventh player" effect wasn't just caused by the proximity of the fans to the ice surface and the ability of the Bruins backers to make noise as loud as a jet engine.

Sometimes, there were pithy comments that emanated from the second balcony. And the voice behind those insults and put-downs usually belonged to one of the Gallery Gods, who legendary Bruins play-by-play voice Fred Cusick described in his autobiography as a "collection of die-hard and voluble fans."

Nowadays the Gallery Gods number in the hundreds and sit mostly in section 325 of TD Garden. In the heyday of Boston Garden they sat in the first two rows of the second balcony on either side of the rink—until the early '80s, when luxury boxes were installed and forced the Gods higher into the "heavens"—and numbered in the thousands.

The Gallery Gods came to prominence in the 1930s, but there is evidence of their emergence from the time Boston Garden opened. Roger Naples, a Revere resident, first interacted with them as a teenager in 1938, and he has now served as president of the Gods for more than 45 years. His role with the oldest fan club in all of hockey has led him to forge friendships with some of the greats of the game, including Bobby Orr and Milt Schmidt, who Naples calls his role models. A picture of the Kraut Line of Schmidt, Woody Dumart, and Bobby Bauer still decorates the front of Naples' refrigerator. "The Gallery Gods are special people and have always been special people," Naples, now pushing 90 years old, said. "Everybody has been beautiful throughout all the years."

If you're a Bruin, the Gods love you. Otherwise, they despise you. Among those in black and gold, some have been more beloved than others. "I was never booed there ever," recalled Bronco Horvath, a star Bruins forward in the late '50s and early '60s. "I had a guy about 6'8" walking around. He said, 'You boo Bronco, you're going for a flip.'"

Longtime Bruins season-ticket holder and author Kevin Vautour remembered hearing the Gallery Gods give forward Eddie Shack the business more than 40 years ago.

"The one that I've never forgotten is, they were playing the Toronto Maple Leafs one night, and Eddie Shack, who later played with the Bruins, was with the Leafs at this time. And Shack had this huge, bulbous nose on him.... And there was a play Toronto was blown for an offside. And a fan up there yelled out, 'Eddie, you weren't offside, your nose was.' And the place just broke out laughing. It seemed like the energy in the building came from the second balcony."

Bruins players were as apt as opponents to hear a comment or two directed their way. When left winger Orland Kurtenbach mentioned to the media one autumn that he had problems finding his legs before Christmas, the Gallery Gods sang him a rendition of "Jingle Bells." When the Bruins were having a particularly rough game in 1966, a God famously yelled at head coach Harry Sinden, "There's a bus leaving for Oklahoma in the morning. Be there—under it."

There's more to the Gods than just their Don Rickles-like sense of humor. They donate their dues to charity and help out at events like the Bruins Wives' Charity Carnival. Over generations, season tickets and memberships get passed on within a family to make sure their ranks are replenished as best as possible. And if you don't believe the Gods are a family, listen to this tale from Naples.

Years ago he saw some ticket scalpers trying to hassle a couple teenagers for an extra buck or two on tickets. Naples tried to get them to sell the kids the tickets for face value because they were just kids. When the scalpers refused, Naples reported the incident to Bruins owner Weston Adams Sr., who had the Garden crack down on anyone trying to bilk kids out of anything more than face value. But that's not the end of the story.

One of those kids was Bill Stillwell, who Naples befriended and sat with at a number of games in the years after. Stillwell is now Naples' nephew by marriage after marrying Naples' niece.

The Gallery Gods might not have the same effect on a Bruins game they had years ago, but they're still as tight-knit a bunch as ever.

58 Flaman Made You Keep Your Head Up

The "Big, Bad Bruins" were still a few years ahead on the horizon by the time Ferny Flaman was done punishing players with body checks for the Bruins.

There's no doubt had he been a generation younger, he would've fit in well on the two Stanley Cup–winning clubs with his ability to inflict pain and do it cleanly.

"He was one of the purest—alongside Johnny Mariucci, 'Black Jack' Stewart, and Bill Barilko—the purest defenseman in history," said longtime hockey writer and broadcaster Stan Fischler. "He was a phenomenal fighter. And when I say pure, he was not dirty. He played tough, but as clean tough as you can play. He would fight anybody. And he was what I would call—and I'm talking about pre-rushing defensemen—he was a defenseman's defenseman. He played defense the way a defenseman would like to see anybody else play defense. A coach's dream and a pure competitor."

He was a fan's dream, as well.

"His lusty body checks and potent fists endeared him to the Boston Garden faithful," Fischler once wrote.

And the Hub spectators lavished their love upon Flaman. Even though his two stints in Boston were separated by a three-plus-season stay with rival Toronto (including a Cup-winning year in '51, the same year he was traded), Flaman was honored by the Boston fans in 1959 with "Ferny Flaman Night" even though he was still playing. The biggest part of the festivities came when he was presented with a car. "They drove the car on the ice with my mother in it. She had flown in from Canada, from Saskatchewan,"

Flaman recalled. "It was a big surprise, and there were a lot of tears in the eyes of a lot of people."

Flaman was rushed to the NHL as a teenager because of WWII and, after playing 25 games over his first three seasons, he established himself as a regular on the back end in 1947–1948. Unfortunately for him, Flaman replaced one of his childhood heroes upon promotion to the NHL. Flaman wore a Babe Pratt No. 4 sweater as a kid playing pond hockey, but Pratt was demoted to the minors to make room for Flaman in the 1946–1947 season.

Any defense pair featuring Flaman would be the most feared on the ice, but when Flaman teamed with fellow body-cruncher Leo Boivin in the late '50s, everybody kept their heads up at all costs. Flaman said in retrospect that he played like "every shift was a playoff shift." But maybe games with hated Montreal were when he was at his absolute best. His battles with Henri "Pocket Rocket" Richard and Jean Beliveau were legendary.

"That Flaman," Richard once said, "he bothers me more than anybody else in our league. I can't think of anyone else who gives me such a bad time. He's always got his stick between my legs or hooks my stick or something."

"Any other player I do not worry about," Beliveau once told writer Jim Proudfoot. "But when I go near that fellow, believe me I look over my shoulder."

Mr. Hockey, Gordie Howe, had similar praise for Flaman in the aftermath of their longstanding rivalry. Although his penalty-minute totals often surpassed 100, Flaman never lost the respect of his opponents. He never went looking for a fight and did his best to stay within the rules. "I gained a lot of respect for that. I was more or less a policeman of the team. We didn't have much trouble at all," he said.

It'd be difficult to find a comparable player in Bruins history, but one modern-day NHL star is often referenced to describe Flaman's play. It's kind of ironic that as a longtime scout for the New Jersey Devils, Flaman got to know and respect this player—

fellow Hall of Famer Scott Stevens. "If I would be compared to him," Flaman said, "it would be an honor, really."

Flaman is retired almost 50 years, and the honors just keep coming his way.

59 Milbury Made It the Hard Way

Everyone knows about Mike Milbury's role with Don Cherry's "Lunch Pail A.C." teams of the late '70s as a hard-nosed, stay-at-home defenseman who played every shift as though it were his last.

But what about Milbury's off-ice role with those clubs? Well, Milbury just happened to live in the same area as Cherry, so the two would ride to the Boston Garden together on game day.

"Grapes used to make me come to the rink with him and practice his pregame speech," recalled Milbury, noting that as a second-year pro all he could do was sit and listen. "Which was a little uncomfortable because I'd get in the room, and there were certainly no surprises when I got in there.

"It was a little uncomfortable showing up at the rink with the coach driving me in."

It's a tribute to Milbury's work ethic and rugged play that he was able to earn enough respect among his teammates to counteract the impression that he was a "coach's pet."

"You respected Mike because you knew his path to the NHL wasn't an easy one," explained former teammate Peter McNab, who remembers Milbury warning him when a speech would be particularly scathing. "He worked and worked and worked. You'd think because he was one of Don Cherry's favorites, there would be guys talking behind his back. That wasn't it at all. Can you imagine driving in with the coach?... Wouldn't you expect to just get your ass kicked? Absolutely not.

"He worked so hard and just fought for everything he got out of his career. He turned into a really good defensive defenseman with some really good offensive skill. And you look at his numbers. Anytime there was anything needed on the ice, he did it. He worked his tail off to get to be that."

Those speeches helped Cherry coax a number of Bruins teams that were maybe at a disadvantage talentwise against some teams to two Stanley Cup Finals appearances and one semifinals berth during his tenure. And Milbury was a main cog on those clubs.

The Walpole, Massachusetts, native, somewhat remarkably, established himself as an NHL regular for 12 seasons after not getting drafted. The '70s were a difficult time to break in as an American-born player, let alone one who played at Colgate. A little bit of luck was involved in Milbury getting his initial opportunity to make the Bruins. After a five-game tryout with the Boston Braves of the American Hockey League didn't go so well, it didn't figure Milbury would be back in the organization. But when Cherry was putting together his training-camp roster in 1974, he remembered someone his friend John Hoff had seen playing at Colgate. Milbury was added as the 61st guy on the 60-man roster.

At his first training camp, he impressed with his guts and brains. He spent that season and most of the next with the Rochester farm club before a spot opened up with the Bruins in the spring of 1976. Milbury never left after that. Lambasted by Cherry for playing soft in his first game of his first NHL stint, Milbury responded to his coach's taunts in his second game.

"Sure enough, we're playing in Toronto," Cherry recalled, "he starts the game, and the first guy who comes down, I think it was Pat Boutette, and Milbury does a number on him. And his career took off from there."

The philosophy under Cherry was for every defenseman, except for Brad Park, to move the puck up the wall to the wingers. Milbury did as he was told, and did pretty much anything else the Bruins asked of him.

"He was a good teammate, he was very analytical. He would do what needed to be done," said Bruins legend Terry O'Reilly. "For example, if we were losing, and he thought we needed a spark, he would do something to create a spark, even at the risk of getting beat up. He was very analytical that way.

"He was a guy who didn't like to fight, but he would fight in defense of himself or a teammate or to motivate his team. So he was smart and loyal in that aspect."

For 754 regular-season games and 86 postseason contests, Milbury wore that loyalty on his sleeve. Even late in his career when the hometown fans turned on him, Milbury exerted 100 percent of his energy.

His numbers weren't impressive—which probably led to *Boston Magazine* naming him as the city's worst pro athlete one year—but his effort and intangibles were second to none.

"But when you think about it," Milbury once said, "assuming that what [the magazine] said was true, it certainly must be to my credit—my ability to adapt—that I was able to survive in the NHL for 12 years."

When Milbury retired from playing, he stayed in the Bruins organization, first as coach of the Maine farm club for two seasons and then as O'Reilly's replacement as the bench boss in Boston. In his rookie season the Bruins advanced to the Cup Finals. Most impressive, the Bruins—while playing for a guy who once accumulated 222 penalty minutes in a season—finished second to Buffalo in fewest PIM. Milbury applied the same wiliness that allowed him to survive as a player to his coaching. He urged his players to "turn the other cheek" and implemented a few other innovations—days off during the week, momentum-stopping timeouts—to maximize his players' potential for success.

"I think Mike was a really good coach. I think he had a pulse of his team and he brought the emotional side of getting a team ready but also the Xs and Os to break a team down and to make changes," said former Bruins defenseman Don Sweeney. "I think he had a good feel for the intangible guys but also knew how to kind of let the horses out of the gate with the upper-echelon players, as well."

After two seasons, Milbury moved into the front office for a few seasons before he got the itch to coach again and wound up spending a number of years with the New York Islanders. When he left Long Island, he returned to the Bay State, which has served his home base in between television gigs.

Working for no fewer than three networks at a time, Milbury has brought the same work ethic and competitive nature that he used to carve out his career as a player, coach, and front-office guru to his second career.

60 "Terrible Ted" Made Terrible Years Tolerable

During arguably the lowest point in Bruins history, "Terrible" Ted Green made it worth it to go to Boston Garden and stand up and cheer.

He was as mean and physical as his nickname indicated—longtime hockey writer Stan Fischler called him "pound for pound the toughest post-WWII Bruins player"—but over the years developed enough skill to become one of Bobby Orr's defense partners during the '72 Stanley Cup–winning season.

"There was no question he was underrated," said Eddie Johnston, a Bruins goaltender during the lean '60s and celebrated '70s. "When I was playing, when Orr came along, he took over. But there's no question in my mind that when Teddy was there, he was the closest thing to Orr. He had tremendous talent, Teddy."

Green was known as one of the toughest junior players in all of Manitoba when the Montreal Canadiens let him go to Boston in the interleague draft in 1960. While it took time to bring the other aspects of his game up to NHL caliber, Green was the embodiment of Eddie Shore's win-at-all-cost spirit from three decades earlier and the all-for-one attitude of the "Big, Bad Bruins" from the second half of his career.

Green Survived Maki's Stick Swing

When Ted Green was able to step out to the bench area and celebrate the 1970 Stanley Cup win with his Bruins teammates, it was nothing short of a miracle.

"I did all I could do not to cry because of the happiness, but to see Greenie. I couldn't believe it," said Bruins star center Phil Esposito.

With Green in their lineup, the Bruins might've had an even greater season in 1969–1970. But a stick-swinging incident with St. Louis's Wayne Maki in the exhibition season ended Green's season…and nearly his life. The Green-Maki exchange is still the ugliest bit of violence against a Bruins player ever.

On September 21, 1969, in Ottawa, after an exchange of punches and slashes, Green turned to go to the penalty box. Maki then hit Green over the head. Players remember Green's face being horrifyingly distorted from the blow. He was unconscious and taken off on a stretcher. Emergency surgery had to be done to move bone fragments away from his brain. It wasn't known whether he would walk or talk again, but after a total of three surgeries and a lot of determined work, he was able to return to pro hockey for another decade.

Amazingly, the NHL suspended both players for the incident. Maki for 30 days and Green for 13 games "if and when he returns" to hockey. They were also fined $300 apiece.

Green's post-playing days featured a host of success as an assistant coach, most famously with Edmonton in the '80s. Maki's playing career ended in 1972, when he was diagnosed with brain cancer. He passed away in 1974.

Despite starting his career with Boston teams that finished last five times and missed the playoffs eight straight years, Green would sacrifice life and limb and fight all comers.

"I had one philosophy," Green, who six times exceeded 100 penalty minutes in a season, once said, "and that was this—the corners were mine. Any man who tried to take a corner away from me was stealing from me. I get mad when a man tries to steal from me."

That usually meant a fisticuff. Green would stand toe to toe against the likes of Chicago's Reggie Fleming, Montreal's John

Bruins defenseman Ted Green battles the Rangers' Brad Park during a game at Madison Square Garden in the early 1970s.

Ferguson, and Dave Richardson of the New York Rangers, among others, without hesitation.

"He was a very, very good fighter," recalled Fischler. "At one time, he was, without question, the most feared fighter in the league. It wasn't until John Ferguson beat the shit out of him, deliberately, in the first period of [Ferguson's] rookie year, the first game that Fergie played, that took a little bit of Green's luster away."

Boston loved Green during a period when there was little to love about the Bruins. Longtime Bruins fan and historian Kevin Vautour remembers going to the Garden just to see Green and what he would do on a given night.

"He was rough when he first came up, but as he matured he became a very good power-play player, he'd be one of the point guys on their power play, which wasn't very good in those days," said Vautour. "If you tried to skate by him, he was going to hit you."

As much as Boston loved Green, other cities hated him—in particular New York. One incident involved Green spearing Rangers player Phil Goyette. Rangers president William Jennings went as far as to put a bounty on Green's head.

Green toned down his act a bit after the arrival of Orr and the ascension of the Bruins to the elite levels of the NHL. He took a mentoring role with the younger players like Orr and Derek Sanderson.

Maybe Green's greatest act of toughness came after a gruesome stick-swinging incident with St. Louis' Wayne Maki during a 1969 exhibition game that nearly ended Green's life and career. It took three surgeries to repair his facial fractures and keep him alive. At one point it looked like Green might never walk or speak again, but remarkably he was back in the NHL the next season. He obviously attacked his rehabilitation and recovery the way he went after opponents.

"There were games that the injury bothered me—mentally, not physically," said Green, who had to have a metal plate implanted in his head after the incident. "But I got over most of that."

In addition to aiding the Bruins' Cup cause in '72, Green went on to succeed for a number of years in the new World Hockey Association. Regardless of his team or league, Ted Green was always the "Terrible" type of player anyone would want on their team and fans would root for, no matter the struggles of that team.

61 Lockout Plan Set Franchise Back

On the day Mike O'Connell was fired as Bruins general manager in March 2006, team president Harry Sinden explained how his long-time protégé had been "dealt the nine of hearts" by Boston's failed business plan leading up to and after the lockout that wiped out the 2004–2005 NHL season.

Well, if that was the case, then the Bruins' decision to enter the lockout with a skeleton-thin roster and then try to buy up other teams' discards once the labor dispute ended was a crapshoot that bankrupted the entire organization and fan base.

"That was a philosophy that I don't think anyone saw coming. A [24] percent reduction in current contracts, a giveback basically. Had we known that, we would've signed a whole roster," said Bruins principle Charlie Jacobs, looking back at the lockout five seasons later. "But you didn't know. We were told that this stuff wasn't going to fly. Guys were going to have to be at a certain [salary cap] number; they'd be buying out players left and right."

The eventual reality was that with the rollback on salaries, teams were aided in their attempts to get below the cap ceiling. And those that were still over the limit were hardly penalized. The Bruins miscalculated. And what a team they would've had were it not for that misjudgment.

Remember, the Bruins finished the last regular season before the lockout as the top team in the Northeast Division and second-best team in the Eastern Conference. They had bolstered their roster around All-Star center Joe Thornton, high-scoring winger Glen Murray, two-way defenseman Nick Boynton, and eventual Calder Trophy–winning goaltender Andrew Raycroft, with the additions of defenseman Sergei Gonchar and center Michael Nylander at the trade deadline. Although the Bruins collapsed against Montreal in seven games in the first round of the playoffs, the future looked bright.

Patrice Bergeron had emerged as a budding star in just his first pro season out of junior hockey. Looking back at the Bruins' reserve roster of prospects, it reads like something of a who's who of future stars and solid NHL players. The June 2004 draft annexed David Krejci, Matt Hunwick, and Kris Versteeg for the Bruins. One year later Boston drafted Vladimir Sobotka. Mark Stuart, Byron Bitz, and Nate Thompson were all already property of Boston from the '03 draft.

With the exception of Versteeg and Thompson, the players acquired by O'Connell's staff—including assistant general manager Jeff Gorton, amateur scouting director Scott Bradley, and scouts Daniel Dore, Nick Bobrov, and Adam Creighton (among others)—all played prominent roles in the Bruins' resurgence under new general manager Peter Chiarelli in the latter part of the 21st century's first decade. Had you added them to the Bruins' powerful '04 squad, maybe there would've been more than two playoff-series victories in the decade.

Instead, the Bruins were outbid for Nylander and forwards Mike Knuble, Brian Rolston, and Ted Donato, and defenseman Sean O'Donnell were allowed to sign elsewhere that summer. After the lockout, Gonchar also departed. All but Donato became key contributors on winning teams.

Thornton and Murray were re-signed, but Boston was rebuffed by primetime free agents Mike Modano and Peter Forsberg and had to settle for B-list signees for a supporting cast. The talent projections for most of the Bruins' players were so far off that O'Connell decided he had no choice but to begin the franchise's biggest shake-up in years by dealing Thornton.

"I think with that group that we had there, we felt if we could've kept some of it together, it would've been really a group to move forward with. I know the lockout caused…people could debate if that was the right theory or not," said Knuble. "They let a lot of us go, which was the way it was at the time. To be honest, I was pretty disappointed at the time. I didn't want to go anywhere. I liked the group of guys."

In the aftermath of O'Connell's firing, a lot of "he said, he said" went on over who was to blame for the faulty plan. Only those privy to the conversations between ownership and management know for sure, and they disagree on the specifics. Obviously owner Jeremy Jacobs had ultimate say over whether the money should've been spent prior to the lockout. As the hockey guys, Sinden and O'Connell were just as culpable. When it came time to fill out the roster post-lockout, O'Connell made some mistakes, which ultimately combined with the Thornton trade to cost him his job. One would've hoped Jacobs had a better idea of where the collective bargaining talks were going, considering his closeness to the league's board of governors.

Regardless, the Bruins missed the playoffs for two years out of the lockout and didn't get back into Cup contention until their fourth post-lockout season. Anything could've happened, but the Bruins sure looked on the cusp of something huge had they dealt themselves a better hand.

62 Orr's Impact Sparked U.S. Hockey Growth

There's a chain reaction of fantastic hockey in the U.S. that carries all the way through today, and it traces straight back to none other than Bruins Hall of Famer and No. 4 Bobby Orr.

The modern-day star U.S.-born players, like Zach Parise, Ryan Miller, and Patrick Kane, had Jeremy Roenick, Tony Amonte, and Mike Richter to idolize as kids. Those stars of the '80s and '90s were inspired by the 1980 "Miracle on Ice" gold medal–winning team from the Lake Placid, New York, Olympic games. And where did those players who shocked the Russians and then topped the Finns to make everyone believe in miracles take their inspiration?

"I saw the same phenomenon in Chicago when Michael Jordan came to Chicago," said 1980 Olympic team star Jack O'Callahan when asked about Bobby Orr and the "Big, Bad Bruins." "And the town lit up like a lamp. But I think in Boston it was even more pronounced. When Bobby Orr came to Boston, and the Bruins were competing after having many down years, all of sudden they were competing for championships, they won a Stanley Cup [in 1970 and 1972]. Bobby Orr just lit it up around New England. So it was real easy to be a hockey player once Bobby Orr came to town. And you couldn't have a greater sort of person to look to than Bobby Orr. He just lit New England up and drove a lot of people into hockey. I think that really led to, when you look at 10 years later, we were all with that Olympic team…and I don't think Bobby Orr just drove New England guys…. That's what it was all about."

Everyone wanted to be Bobby Orr. His grace, his dignity, and his ability to do the remarkable with a puck on his stick captured everyone's imagination. The Bruins became must-see TV on Channel

38, and the Boston Garden was *the* place to be. If anyone was hedging their bets about joining the hockey craze, Orr's Stanley Cup–clinching goal in Game 4 of the 1970 Finals sealed everyone's fate.

"After the game was over, my friend, Billy Riley, and I were driving through Charlestown," said Boston University coach Jack Parker, who attended that historic game as a fan. "And there were kids out on the streets of Charlestown all playing street hockey right after the game. Five minutes after the game, we were out of there so fast, it's unbelievable what happened. That's why we got all these great NHLers, like [Tony] Amonte and [Bill] Guerin and [Shawn] McEachern and Scotty Young. Those were all guys who were infatuated with Bobby Orr and the Bruins. And I'd say more Bobby Orr."

Participation in hockey went through the roof. Record-keeping is shaky from that era, but approximately 16 Metropolitan District Commission rinks were standing in 1970, and six more went up in the next five years. Longtime Bruins fan and historian Kevin Vautour remembered how the existing rinks also felt the Orr impact.

"The rinks that were in effect back then, the old Metropolitan District Commission rinks, I would say that practically none of them—Arlington, Everett, Brighton, Allston—had roofs," said Vautour. "All of a sudden, the demand for ice time came that they needed to keep the places open 24 hours a day, seven days a week. That's the first thing that happened, that they all had to get roofs and dressing rooms and things like that."

If Orr's imminent arrival in the NHL didn't totally inspire the league's first expansion in 1967, it definitely set the next two expansions in motion. By the end of the decade, the likes of Mike Milbury and Bob Miller were making their names as Americans in black and gold. And then came the U.S. triumph.

"The Orr-Esposito era Bruins were sort of the godfather to the '80 Olympic guys," said New England Sports Museum curator Richard Johnson. "All of them, not just the Boston guys, but the Minnesota guys, too, because the Bruins were on national television, they were on Sunday afternoons. Kids were coming in with their sticks and probably with their skates on, and were watching the game. And those teams with Bobby Orr and Esposito got those kids to work a little harder, to play a little better, to want it a little more because an American team had now supplanted Montreal and Toronto as the top team in the league. That was huge."

It was huge, and it kept growing. The increase in U.S. stars, and players in general, opened the door for more hockey expansion into Sun Belt cities in the '90s and 2000s. Now players come from Arizona, California, and Texas in numbers that challenge some of America's more hockey-centric areas.

Orr's appearance on the Boston scene created a ripple that's still felt in hockey today and should continue for generations to come.

Vote for the Seventh Player

If you're a true Bruins fan, you must exercise your democratic right to vote—and not every two or four years in some election involving politicians.

The annual selection of the Seventh Player Award started in the 1968–1969 season and is voted by the fans to the "player who performed beyond expectations as voted by the fans."

Every season fans flock to a local car dealership to make their picks. And that's just how Channel 38, the television home of the Bruins from the late '60s through the early 21st century, expected the award to go over. It started as just a promotional tool and morphed into something so much bigger.

"Lo and behold, we put it on the air, and then people would write in and everything like that. And, my god, we knew we had lightning in a bottle right away because the people would just flock," recalled longtime Channel 38 general manager Dan Berkery. "The postcards that came in were absolutely unbelievable. And it turned into a very positive thing with the Bruins themselves, the players. They liked it, seeing who should be recognized."

Versatile forward Ed Westfall was the first winner. Over the years the award has gone to popular players like Terry O'Reilly, Derek Sanderson, John "Pie" McKenzie, Mike Knuble, and Milan Lucic. Hall of Famer Cam Neely won the award twice—after his first season in Boston and his comeback year of 1993–1994.

While Bruins fans are some of the most knowledgeable in the NHL, they can sometimes neglect the spirit of the awards' description. How else can you explain high-scoring winger Bill Guerin and star goaltender Tim Thomas not only winning the award twice but winning it in consecutive years? Thomas explained. "I guess their expectations of me weren't very high," he said of both times he won. However, there's probably a better reason for the repeat victories.

"The issue would always be, 'Was it the most popular player?' It was supposed to be the player who went above and beyond the call. Certainly it was a popularity contest," said former Bruins public relations guru and senior assistant to the president Nate Greenberg. "Some years it was right on; some years it was a little off. It was a terrific selling tool."

As a native of Wilbraham, Massachusetts, Guerin was particularly appreciative that the fans picked him once, let alone twice.

"I knew a lot about it, and I knew it was a big deal and how important it was to the guys," he said. "And just to Bruins fans, it's pretty important. I was really happy because I remember watching on TV, seeing the guys get it and win it. My dream was to play for the Bruins, never mind win the Seventh Player Award."

Mike O'Connell went on to serve as coach, assistant general manager, and GM of the Bruins in the days after his playing career. He won the Seventh Player Award in 1983–1984 and obviously knew its meaning because he grew up as a Bruins season-ticket holder in Cohasset, Massachusetts. But he also remembers not being able to relish the award after the presentation.

"It was terrific. But you know when you're playing and you win it, you're toward the end of the season and you really don't get a chance to enjoy it. It's a team game, and you've got the Stanley Cup playoffs coming up, and that's really your focus," he said. "So you look back at it and it was nice, but at the time it was more like, 'What's next?'"

Once the season is over, however, the player has a constant reminder of winning the vote. The winner of the award, which is now presented by the team's television home, NESN, comes with a free car from the sponsoring dealership. As of the 2009–2010 season, Knuble still owned his car. David Krejci, who won in 2008–2009, traded his pickup for a Dodge Charger. Barry Pederson remembers driving his Toyota hatchback around for years. After all, up until a certain point in history, players weren't making astronomical salaries, and a free car could come in handy. Rookie goaltender Tuukka Rask won the award in 2009–2010.

So as winter starts to turn to spring this season and every season after, make sure you get out to vote for the Seventh Player Award. You'll make some player very happy and one vehicle richer.

64 Pie

It takes courage to ride in the rodeo.

Luckily for the Bruins, John "Pie" McKenzie played with that same bravura from the second he joined the club in a trade on January 10, 1966, until he left for the WHA after the 1972 Stanley Cup–winning season.

John "Pie" McKenzie (left) loiters around the net with teammate Bobby Orr before a game at Boston Garden in January 1970. Though only 5'9",
McKenzie was an integral part of the "Big, Bad Bruins" Cup-winning teams.

"My custom at the start of games was to take a run at somebody on my first shift. I just wanted to stir things up and plant the idea that if a squirt like me can go after them—particularly if my target is a big star—then why not everybody?" the diminutive McKenzie—at 5'9", 165 pounds—once explained. "I tried to act the same when we were sagging in a tight game."

McKenzie was known for riding broncos and roping calves in the rodeo during his off-seasons. In season he played with a physical style that somehow didn't earn him a regular spot with

Chicago, Detroit, or the New York Rangers. In fact, the only positive thing to come out of McKenzie's first few years in the NHL was his nickname.

Early in McKenzie's career, teammate Gerry Melnyk noticed a resemblance between the forward and a logo for a Canadian chocolate bar. The character, with a small body and big head, was called "Pie Face." Melnyk started calling McKenzie "Pie Face," and later it was shortened to just "Pie."

Boston proved to be the perfect place for Pie to play. The small Boston Garden ice surface and the style coach Harry Sinden wanted to play when he took over the next season suited McKenzie well. After Bobby Orr's arrival and then the trade for Phil Esposito, Ken Hodge, and Fred Stanfield was completed, the "Big, Bad Bruins" were born—even if one of their toughest customers wasn't all that big.

McKenzie battled his way through opponents and into the hearts of the Garden faithful. Banners at Bruins home games sang his praises and a famous bumper sticker read: "No matter how you slice it, Pie is the greatest."

"It was their belief that Pie McKenzie reflected them. In other words, nobody you knew could play the game like Orr. Nobody. But you'd go out in the street, and there'd be 10, 15 guys who think they can play like McKenzie," said longtime Bruins fan and historian Kevin Vautour. "Not the most talented guy in the world, but the guy who was willing to go in and sacrifice himself for his teammates. He was kind of sneaky on occasion, you'd see him start a little brouhaha, and all of a sudden one of the bigger guys like Don Awrey or Ted Green would have to come in after the trouble he started. But McKenzie could pretty much take care of himself."

While his physicality never waned, McKenzie added an offensive element to the Bruins that he hadn't shown at his other stops. He became a fixture on the wing of a line centered by Fred Stanfield and completed with Johnny Bucyk before and during the '70 and '72 Cup-winning seasons. He produced 70-, 77-, and 69-point seasons from 1970 to 1972. Previously, general manager Milt Schmidt had asked McKenzie to give up the rodeo—and he obliged with little fight.

"I considered it a compliment," he said. "Let's face it, they had to be interested in me to show that kind of concern. It was nice to feel wanted."

McKenzie's style of play came at a price. Early in his career he had to have his spleen removed, and he played much of the '71 season with a fractured skull. Other injuries occurred, as well. However, he fought through them and left everything he had on the ice.

After the Bruins won the '72 Cup, McKenzie was offended that the team didn't protect him in the expansion draft. Although he wasn't selected, he joined a number of his teammates in jumping to the WHA. The era of Pie ended in Boston, although he returned to the region with the New England Whalers years later and became a fixture at alumni games and events.

"His round face and innocent blue eyes and apple cheeks mask a tiger, I'll tell you," goaltender Gerry Cheevers once wrote.

Boston loves anyone who plays like a tiger, and its fans were always in love with Pie.

65 Remembering Ace

A role player who found his niche by playing the body in a way befitting of the "Big, Bad Bruins," and an affable sort away from the rink, Garnet "Ace" Bailey was one of the Bruins of the early '70s who the Boston faithful really embraced.

"On so loveable a gang of players, loveable personalities as a team at the time, Ace fit in," said longtime *New Bedford Standard-Times* Bruins writer Mick Colageo.

After his four-plus seasons (including two Stanley Cup–winning seasons) with the Bruins, through the rest of his 10-season playing career and then his years as a scout and then director of pro scouting for the Los Angeles Kings, Bailey endeared himself to legions of people in and out of hockey. Tragically, Bailey and his Kings scouting colleague Mark Bavis were passengers on United Airlines Flight 175 when it struck the South Tower of the World Trade Center on September 11, 2001.

"That was probably the hardest day of my career in the NHL," recalled Dave Taylor, who was then the general manager of the Kings.

Bailey had become a fixture on the ninth floor of TD Garden, where he scouted the Bruins and their opponents, just as he had been a mainstay with the two Cup-winning teams. He potted 11 goals in 58 games before a broken ankle ended his season in 1969–1970. Even injured, he showed up for practices, games, and road trips with the team.

"Ace was a joy to have on the team," explained former Bruins coach/GM/president Harry Sinden. "He was one of those second-tier players who every team needs. On the days he didn't play much, his attitude didn't change."

Established as a full-time NHL player by the Bruins' next Cup-winning season, Bailey skated in 73 regular-season games in 1971–1972 and posted 9–13–22 totals. He saved his most dramatic moment as a Bruin, however, for the largest stage. After the Bruins squandered a 5–1 lead in Game 1 of the Cup Finals at Boston Garden, Bailey scored the game-winning goal with just 2:16 left in regulation.

"I remember that goal like it was yesterday," remembered Bruins teammate Phil Esposito. "I can still see it, see Ace going around Brad Park. That goal turned the series around, and I told him that."

The Bruins won that series in six games after getting a boost from Bailey's goal, which might have been a bit of an accident.

"I had told Ace specifically not to go on the ice because I didn't think he was checking that well," explained then–Bruins coach Tom Johnson. "Then somebody came off and nobody went on—there was a little miscommunication. So Ace jumps on, goes around Park, and scores the winning goal. I told him later, 'This is a secret between you and me.'"

To fans of the "Big, Bad Bruins" who won two Cups in three years, all the images of those glorious seasons are unforgettable. For Colageo's brother, Don, Bailey's goal inspired a painting. Years later, with Colageo working in the media often crossing paths with Bailey the scout, Colageo presented the former Bruins player with a print of his brother's painting. Of course, Bailey was thrilled with it. He was so thrilled he wanted his wife Kathy to make sure it would be hanging when he returned from training camp on the West Coast. Before he boarded that ill-fated flight on September 11, Bailey called home and "the last thing he said to her before getting on that plane," Colageo explained, "was, 'Got to get this framed.'"

Bailey's absence will always be felt by those who knew him.

"Ace is one of those guys, whenever I think of him I start to smile," said Taylor. "He had a talent to get everybody involved with the group, to make everybody feel they were part of the team. And he had a very, very competitive side to him. But on the other side, he also was soft and had a lot of time for kids and loved to really enjoy himself away from the ice."

The Kings honored Bailey by naming their Most Inspirational Player Award after him, as well as naming the lion mascot "Bailey." The Ace Bailey Children's Foundation was started in his memory after his death "to perpetuate his deep caring for the happiness of children." And a plaque marking the seat he usually scouted from at TD Garden now covers the tabletop in front of that chair. "Everybody remembers him, and it's nice to see his name up here," said Taylor.

66 Johnston Survived Last Full Season

Nowadays if a goaltender just plays in games on back-to-back nights, it's considered a remarkable feat, especially if the netminder in question performs at his best and earns a pair of wins.

If a goaltender's games-played column on the stat sheet starts to swell past 60 and head toward 70 in an 82-game regular season, talk radio voices and columnists often start to lament the wear and tear on that puck-stopper, who might not be able to be at his peak when his team needs him the most.

There was no such controversy around Eddie Johnston during the 1963–1964 season because the Bruins finished dead last in the six-team NHL, 23 points out of a playoff berth. After playing all 70 games and 4,200 minutes of the Bruins' season—the last goaltender in NHL history to do so—Johnston might not have had much left in the tank. Of course, with a better team in front of him, he might've been fresher at the conclusion of the season and received some support in trying to allow less than the 211 goals opponents beat him for that season.

As longtime hockey writer Stan Fischler once wrote, "It was difficult to determine just how good—or bad—Johnston's goaltending was because Boston's defense seemed to be competing with its offense for some sort of ineptitude award."

A barrage of pucks from opposing sticks against Boston's porous defense wasn't the only challenge Johnston had to meet in maintaining his status as the Bruins' only goaltender that year.

"In that particular year, I wound up breaking my nose three times," said Johnston, now retired after a five-decade NHL career as player, coach, and executive.

The treatments Johnston had to endure to keep playing aren't for the squeamish to experience or even read about, so feel free to skip down a couple paragraphs if you're of a weak stomach.

"I remember the one time I broke it on a Wednesday at home, and then I broke it again on a Saturday in New York. There was a doctor there, a Japanese doctor, and what they'd do is stick cod sticks up your nose," Johnston recalled. "You'd finish the game, and then they'd straighten you out after. I remember calling him quite a few names because he grabbed my nose and twisted it and put it back in place a little bit.

"When I broke it, then I came home, and both my eyes were shut, and they took me to Mass General. And he put leeches on my eyes, and they would suck the blood out. You would stay there for about an hour, and then they would throw the leeches back into the jar."

The '67 Draft Sidetracked Bruins Dynasty

President Weston Adams Sr.'s efforts to get his scouts to scour the land for talent and restock the farm clubs in the 1960s did more than just land Bobby Orr's services for the Bruins. As the Orr era started, the Bruins were overflowing with the type of talent that could have made them a dynasty in the early 1970s. Unfortunately, the 1967 expansion draft decimated the Bruins' stock of reinforcements, starting with future Hall of Fame goaltender Bernie Parent. A two-time Vezina Trophy winner, Parent led Philadelphia to two Stanley Cup titles, including the '74 win over the Bruins.

Although the Bruins won the Cup in '70 and '72 and probably would've captured the title in '71 were it not for one of the game's greatest upsets in the first round against Montreal, imagine what Boston would've looked like if Parent, defenseman Joe Watson, centers Ron Shock and Terry Crisp, right winger Gary Dornhoefer, and left winger J.P. Parise (among others in the 20 players lost) had been retained to contribute to the Bruins' cause or used as trade bait. Sure, the 1972 defection of four stars players to the WHA and the loss of Eddie Westfall to the New York Islanders in that year's expansion draft pulled the rug out from under Boston's hopes to repeat as Cup champ, but the '67 expansion draft was the first blow to the Bruins' hopes of dominating the upcoming decade.

It was a long, awful season for Johnston and the Bruins, who started off 1–7–1 in October and only won consecutive games three times all season (with one three-game winning streak all year). One stretch from late December into January saw the Bruins suffer with a 0–10–1 record.

When the curtain fell on the Bruins' season in March, they missed the playoffs for the fifth-straight season. The losing aside, Johnston wouldn't have approached that season any other way.

"Back then, if you got hurt, you didn't dare relinquish your job to anybody," he explained.

Johnston made just $8,500 that season but then asked for and received a $1,000 bonus.

"After the season I went to see the manager, Lynn Patrick, and told him I thought I had a thousand dollars coming to me because they would give me a bonus if I had an average of 3.00," Johnston once explained to Dick Irvin. "He said, 'Did you read the fine print? You had a 3.01.' But he gave it to me!"

There were more rewards in Johnston's future, as after two more lousy seasons, the Bruins would combine Bobby Orr with Phil Esposito and start on a remarkable run of team success, which included two Stanley Cup titles in 1970 and 1972. By then Johnston didn't have to do all the work himself with future Hall of Famer Gerry Cheevers around to share the load.

67 Flyers Became Bigger and Badder in '74

To call it a "passing of the torch" would be inaccurate because a passing implies an exchange that's way too neat and polite.

When the "Broad Street Bullies" defeated the "Big, Bad Bruins" in the 1974 Stanley Cup Finals, the sight was more like a battle royal to determine not only which team would be the champion of the NHL but also prove to be the toughest, meanest team in the league.

Ever since the arrival of Bobby Orr and the trade for Phil Esposito, Boston—even in the years the Bruins didn't win the Cup—was known as the most intimidating club to play against. That '74 series brought down the curtain on that era.

"It was a monumental event because [the Flyers] were the first expansion team [to win the Cup], they were huge underdogs, and to beat Orr and Esposito was a phenomenal accomplishment," said longtime NHL writer and broadcaster Stan Fischler. "And it was exactly a passing. The irony was that the Flyers stole the toughness image away from the Bruins. The Flyers were bigger and badder, in a sense, than the Bruins were."

The Flyers featured seven players who exceeded 100 penalty minutes that season. But as with the "Big, Bad" teams that brought the Cup home to Boston in 1970 and 1972, there was more than just toughness in the Flyers' favor. Future Hall of Fame center Bobby Clarke was in the midst of his prime at both ends of the rink, and goaltender Bernie Parent was at the end of the first of two Vezina Trophy–winning campaigns. Rubbing salt in the Bruins' wounds was that the netminder, who won the Conn Smythe Trophy that spring, was once their property. Parent was one of a bunch of talented players the Bruins lost in the '67 expansion draft. In fact, four expansion-draft losses—and seven players total who were once Boston property—chipped in for Philadelphia that championship season.

So it was no surprise that some of the Bruins' brutality had infiltrated the Flyers' philosophy. But that combination of skill and sandpaper had to be harnessed, and the man who did that was coach Fred Shero. In general, Shero liked tough teams. The Flyers' drafting of Dave "the Hammer" Schultz (348 PIM in '74) and trade for "Moose" Dupont (216 PIM) proved that. But then the bench boss came up with the best way to use that rugged play to slow down the game's best player—Orr.

Instead of avoiding Orr, Shero wanted his players to attack the star defenseman. He wanted to dump the puck into Orr's corner and take it to him. He wanted to forecheck with two, three forwards, and deny Orr his usual paths up the ice. He wanted to make Orr hurt.

With Clarke playing an instrumental role, the strategy worked to wear Orr down and, in turn, slow down an offense that led the league with 349 goals that season. Clarke also dominated Esposito in the faceoff circle and limited the Bruins' 68-goal sniper to just two scores in the Finals.

"They had Orr, and he can do an awful lot," Shero said in retrospect. "But we've got 17 good hockey players, and every one of them put out. It was 17 against one."

As a reminder, Flyers general manager Keith Allen taped a sign onto his own suitcase: "Orr's Not God. Hit Him!" And hit Orr they did, except they couldn't stop him in Game 1. Orr's goal with just 22 seconds left in regulation proved the game-winner. Game 2, however, turned the series from a cakewalk to a broo-ha-ha. Clarke's overtime goal capped a comeback from 2–0 down and ended the Flyers' 0–16–2 slump at Boston Garden (dating back to their first-ever game played there).

"That was a big win for them coming into Boston and beating us in Boston," said then–Bruins forward Ken Hodge. "That was a very big win. Everybody talks about home-ice advantage and whatever...it just reversed the tables a little bit. They took home-ice advantage away from us. We battled hard."

The Flyers pushed Boston to the brink by defending their home ice in Games 3 and 4. Back in Boston for Game 5, the Bruins sent a message that they wouldn't go down without a fight. In fact, it took just 24 seconds for Carol Vadnais to drop the gloves with Schultz. The game featured four fights and a single-game record, for a Cup Final game, 43 penalties combined by both teams. More importantly for Boston, the game featured vintage Orr—playing through the serious knee injury that would allow him to play just one more full season—with two goals and one assist in a season-saving 5–1 Bruins win. "You can have all the Bobby Clarkes in the world," general manager Harry Sinden famously said after that game. "I'll take one game like that from Orr. He made 30 moves no one has ever seen before."

With the Cup one win away, the Flyers pulled out all the stops. Instead of a recording of their good-luck charm Kate Smith belting out "God Bless America," the Flyers had her sing in person. Even a pregame handshake and presentation of a bouquet of flowers from Orr and Esposito didn't change Philadelphia's fortunes.

Rick MacLeish, another former Bruins farmhand, scored the game's lone goal at 14:48 of the first period, and Parent made 30 saves. When Orr was whistled for holding by Art Skov—Schultz still calls Skov his "favorite referee"—with 2:22 left on a Clarke breakaway, the Flyers knew they were on the cusp of history.

The Flyers' victory was a breakthrough for expansion teams, a tribute to how far a team could go with the right amount of talent added to an overall philosophy of physical punishment, and also drew up a blueprint for teams—no matter how healthy or hobbled he would be—to slow down Orr.

68 Offensive D-Men Owe It to Orr

Flip through current NHL media guides, where media relations staffs combine statistical information about their franchises with trivial material on their players that helps announcers add color to television and radio broadcasts.

Although most players were born a decade or more after Bobby Orr retired, you'll spot pages and pages of guys—both defensemen and not—that claim the famous No. 4 as their favorite player. They were but a proverbial glimmer in their mothers' eye when Orr was flying around the Boston Garden rink, changing the way the game is played for generations, but still through the power of DVD and folklore, players know that to be great is to be Bobby Orr.

New York Rangers blueliner Michael Del Zotto was a 19-year-old rookie in 2009–2010 when he skated around in uniform No. 4 in Orr's honor. He and many others in recent years know that without the career of Robert Gordon Orr, the exploits of defensemen in all three zones might not be possible. Without Orr, there might not have been Ray Bourque, Denis Potvin, Paul Coffey, Chris Chelios, Brian Leetch, or Al MacInnis. Orr's accomplishments were just that groundbreaking.

"I think defensemen in general tried to be more offensive [after Orr came along]," said Boston University coach Jack Parker. "He did to hockey, to the position of defense, what Bill Russell did to the position of center in basketball. Bill Russell made defense something cool in the NBA. And Bobby Orr made offensive defensemen something cool in the NHL. Nobody did it better than him, that's for sure."

A defenseman winning the Art Ross Trophy? Twice? And recording more than 100 points in a season *six* times?

"If anybody had told anybody, prior to Bobby, 'You know, within the next three years a defenseman is going to win the NHL scoring championship?' they would look at you like you were out of your mind," explained Wren Blair, the scout who lobbied Orr's family until the prodigy finally signed with the Bruins organization in the '60s.

There wasn't too much room to roam for defensemen before Orr came along. As Stan Fischler once wrote, "Defensemen were essentially dedicated to patrolling their blue line and keeping the enemy from threatening their goal. Rare was the backliner—that's precisely why they were named *back*-liners—who took off on an offensive foray." Eddie Shore had been as offensive as they come while leading the Bruins to two Cups. Red Kelly, Flash Hollett, and Doug Harvey all could put points on the board. Kelly once even posted a 70-point season. However, none was Orr.

"The closest player to come closest to what he did was Doug Harvey of the Canadiens," said New England Sports Museum curator Richard Johnson. "But Doug Harvey slowed the game down and had the game suit the Canadiens. Whereas Orr, he sped the game up. It went from 33 RPM to 78 when he was on the ice because his wheels, his skating ability, and his innate talent were just like he was playing a different game. It was like everybody else was playing the old game, and he was playing a different sport."

There was no way to pull back the reins on Orr's skating ability and his acceleration. And why would anyone want to? Well, there was *some* backlash to the way Orr played the game. None other than future Bruins coach Don Cherry, who was playing minor league hockey in Rochester when Orr came on the scene, wasn't too fond of Orr, his future pupil.

"At first, I couldn't stand Bobby Orr. He stood for everything I was against," explained Cherry. "I was a big defenseman, and I would see him on TV sometimes, and I would think that this guy isn't a defenseman, this guy is a rover. He's all over the place."

Then Cherry saw Orr practice in person one day.

"I was mesmerized by the things he was doing. I had never seen anything like it, and he was just jerking around. Nobody ever skated like him or handled the puck like him."

Orr, who never wore socks when playing, was magic on his skates. The opposition would chase him like farm boys in pursuit of the family chicken. The puck seemed glued to his stick, and his vision made it seem as though his eyes were on the side—and the front—of his head. And there was no way to match up with him because he would hardly take a shift off. Orr's defense partner was the rest of the Bruins' defense corps.

Orr impressed New York Rangers defenseman Harry Howell right off the bat. Upon winning the Norris Trophy in 1966–1967, the year Orr won the Calder Trophy as Rookie of the Year, Howell declared, "I might as well enjoy it now. It's going to be Bobby Orr's for the next 10 years. I'm going to be the last guy to win it before they change it to the Bobby Orr Trophy."

A Bobby Orr Trophy has been considered over the years—maybe to the best offensive defenseman—but to date the Norris is still the ultimate prize for blueliners. Orr proved Howell's words prophetic by winning the Norris the next eight years. Instead of an award in his honor, Orr set a standard with his play that has never been matched and a legacy that kids for generations have and will aspire to emulate. Well, at least they can try.

69 "Jumbo Joe" Just Couldn't Measure Up to History

Drafted No. 1 overall in 1997, Joe Thornton was obviously expected to be better than your "Average Joe."

Unfortunately, the Bruins as an organization seemingly wanted him to also be more than just "Jumbo Joe" and play like some of their most fearless legends—namely Cam Neely, Phil Esposito, or Terry O'Reilly. Whether that desire was ever fair, we'll never know. All we do know is that after seven springs with just one playoff-series victory and a slow start to the 2005–2006 season, Thornton was dealt to San Jose. Instead of earning a place in franchise history alongside those who eventually were enshrined in Toronto, Thornton will always be most known for being the export in one of the worst trades in franchise history.

"We based the decision on what we saw over Joe's years here," since-fired general manager Mike O'Connell told the *Boston Globe*

Often criticized while with the Bruins, center Joe Thornton was traded to the San Jose Sharks in 2005, where he went on to win the Hart Trophy as league MVP and the Art Ross Trophy as top scorer, while becoming a perennial All-Star.

four years after the Thornton trade. "Right or wrong, we didn't think he could lead our team to where we wanted to be.

"Days before we made the deal, I went through the entire organization, and that was unanimous. I asked [executive vice president] Charlie [Jacobs], the chairman [owner Jeremy Jacobs], and [president] Harry [Sinden], 'Is this the guy?' None of us thought he could do it, and there was no pushback.

"Once I had that answer, then it became, 'Well, we have to move him.'"

No one could've imagined it would come to that back in the summer of '97 on that day in Pittsburgh, where Boston used the top pick and the eighth pick overall to select Thornton and speedy winger Sergei Samsonov, respectively. Both players made the NHL squad out of their first training camp, and the Bruins' sales pitch was, "The future's so bright, you've gotta wear shades." While Samsonov won the Calder Trophy that season, Thornton took a little longer to develop.

In 2002–2003 Thornton blew up with a 101-point campaign. The next season his production dropped to 73 points, but he was the No. 1 center on a team that finished second in the Eastern Conference and carried large expectations into the '04 playoffs. However, Thornton was held scoreless in a seven-game playoff flop against Montreal. At one point in the series, Hall of Fame *Boston Globe* columnist Kevin Paul Dupont called for Thornton to be stripped of his captain's "C." When the series ended, it was revealed that Thornton had played through torn rib cartilage.

Criticism of Thornton's style of play and quiet leadership had already been simmering from anonymous corners of the organization. If there was going to be a rift, the franchise's inactivity in defending Thornton during that series was going to start it. The fan base, meanwhile, was always split. There were those who wanted Thornton to become the next Neely and those who were content with his propensity for dishing from behind the net or along the wall as long as he put points on the board.

While the Bruins pre-lockout business plan led to the departure of a number of key players, Thornton still re-signed after the work stoppage ended. The elder Jacobs proclaimed the Bruins would be Stanley Cup contenders in the new-look league, but Boston sat with an 8–13–5 record after a loss to New Jersey on November 29, 2005. The next night O'Connell and San Jose general manager Doug Wilson consummated a deal in a hurry that would put Thornton with the Sharks, and Marco Sturm, Brad Stuart, and Wayne Primeau with the Bruins.

"It's definitely a shock," Thornton said at the time. "I signed a three-year deal with Boston, hoping to stay another three years. I came back just because I love the guys here, and I really thought this was a good, contending team. But obviously when you don't win games, things are going to happen, and that's what happened here. I came here to win, and we haven't been winning. Whose fault that is, I'm not really sure. But I'm out of here, so it must be mine."

"I'm just excited," he continued. "You know, I'm going to a team that the management, they've already told me how excited they are to have me on their team. So it's going to be a nice change."

Thornton's veiled shots at Boston management paled in comparison to the heat the Bruins took from their fans and media over the trade. The club still missed the playoffs, while Thornton went on to win the league scoring title and the Hart Trophy. Although the Sharks have suffered playoff failure similar to Thornton's Bruins teams, they've always been among the upper-echelon clubs, and Thornton has always contended for the Art Ross Trophy.

Indirectly, the Bruins were able to make the Thornton trade work in their favor. The salary-cap space the deal opened up allowed Boston to sign free agents Zdeno Chara and Marc Savard. Sturm became a solid-scoring top-six winger, and new general manager Peter Chiarelli was able to flip Stuart and Primeau for Andrew Ference and Chuck Kobasew, who were key members of the resurgent Bruins at the end of the decade.

A month after the trade, Thornton was still answering questions about where things went wrong in Boston. "I played my heart out for the Bruins every shift, and that's all you can ask for," he said.

However, there was more asked of him. An organization yearning to resurrect the "Big, Bad Bruins" couldn't be satisfied by just "big" and "skilled."

"It was part of what hastened Joe Thornton's departure from town. Joe Thornton, I don't think I've seen a player as big as he was with better hands and passing ability.... But everyone wanted him to be Cam Neely, too," said New England Sports Museum curator Richard Johnson. "They wanted him to have good hands, but they wanted him to play big. He played smaller but he played skilled."

In an ironic moment, Thornton's return to Boston with the Sharks ended just 5:13 into the game when he checked Bruins defenseman Hal Gill from behind and was assessed a game misconduct. Maybe that finally satisfied those who demanded Thornton add physicality to his résumé. If it didn't, it didn't matter. Thornton and the Sharks proved a less volatile marriage. And the Bruins took a few years to recover from his departure.

Boston's vaunted past might've cost the Bruins the services of an all-time great.

70 Horton Hears the "Woos!"

It was unfortunate for the Florida Panthers that in their six seasons with Nathan Horton in their lineup after they drafted him third overall in 2003, they never once made the playoffs.

In an effort to right their course, the Panthers decided to part ways with Horton in June 2010 in a multiplayer trade that landed Horton in Boston and defenseman Dennis Wideman and a couple draft picks in Florida.

Twelve months later, Horton showed the Panthers just what they had been missing by not providing him with a postseason stage to perform on.

In the 2011 Stanley Cup playoffs, Horton scored the game-winning goal in both Games 5 and 7 of the Bruins' first-round playoff series victory—both in overtime—over Montreal, and in Game 7 of the Bruins' Eastern Conference Finals victory over Tampa Bay. Horton's third-period goal was the lone score in the Bruins' 1–0 win over the Lightning that clinched their first Stanley Cup Finals berth in 21 years.

Horton became the first player in NHL history to score game-winners in two Game 7 situations.

"Yeah, I mean, I really didn't know that was anything," Horton said. "But I mean it's definitely special for me to be able to do that and help my team win. There's nothing like scoring in overtime or a game-winner to move on to the next round, and it's like I've said all along, it's definitely hard to describe how good of a feeling that feels."

Seven hard-fought games later, the Bruins had defeated Vancouver for their first Cup championship in 39 years. Although a concussion suffered as a result of a high hit from the Canucks' Aaron Rome in Game 3 kept Horton from playing the rest of the Finals, his presence around the team served as a rallying point. And he famously dumped a bottle of Boston water on the Vancouver ice hours prior to Game 7.

Horton finished the postseason with eight goals in 21 games after he scored 26 goals in 80 regular-season games. Not only had he never skated in the NHL playoffs before, but Horton had never played in a hockey hotbed before. There was no telling how he would handle the heat, especially considering his goal total had declined every season from a career-high 31 in 2006–07 to just 20 in his last season in Florida.

Initially, he struggled after scoring three goals in his first two games with the Bruins. He scored just seven goals from November through January. But then he matched that total in February with not just a nose for the net but a physicality he hadn't shown in his prior four months with the Bruins. Horton proved he could be a modern-day "big, bad Bruin" with seven fighting majors (he'd recorded just seven in his entire NHL career with the Panthers).

Doubts about Horton's passion for the game followed him from Florida to Boston. From February through the Cup victory, he disproved every last one of them.

"I think it would motivate anyone," said Horton. "A lot of things were said. And just coming into here, I wanted to prove people wrong and to really show what I can do. There's been some tough times. It's not easy all the time. But the big thing is you just keep working at it and know that in the end it's going to pay off. I think that's all I've been trying to do."

Bruins head coach Claude Julien witnessed a transformation by Horton over the course of their first season together.

"When you bring someone like that in and as the season goes on you see how he changed. To me he became more and more of a consistent player in the second half, and physical, and emotionally engaged," said Julien. "And I thought he really grew as a player this year with us, and that just carried over into the playoffs. And that's why there was no way you were going to keep him out of the lineup, even with that shoulder separation."

The shoulder separation Horton suffered early in the playoffs didn't keep him from scoring those clutch goals and contributing to Boston's magical run. The three game-winning goals didn't just earn him a spot among the greatest players in Bruins history, but also among the most clutch Boston sports performers—like Red Sox slugger David Ortiz and Patriots kicker Adam Vinatieri—in the city's lengthy history.

Horton more than made up for six years of sitting and watching the playoffs.

71 Punching Their Way into Fans' Hearts

Almost from the inception of the franchise, long before the actual formation of the teams that were known as the "Big, Bad Bruins," Boston fans have embraced those who fit the mold as the meanest, toughest players in the land.

A special place in their hearts is reserved for those whose No. 1 skill is pounding an opponent with fists rather than beating the other team with scoring or skating.

"Lyndon Byers, he's still a folk hero," explained New England Sports Museum curator Richard Johnson. "Jay Miller's a folk hero. If Jay Miller went into a bar somewhere here, and a couple guys [recognize him], he's not buying a beer or a meal. He's still a folk hero. That's what Bruins fans appreciate."

Miller, a Wellesley, Massachusetts, native who has run The Courtyard restaurant in North Falmouth almost since he retired as a player, said that today his extra pounds might make him less recognizable and prevent him from getting that free drink or meal. But there's no doubt he, Byers, Chris Nilan, and players of their ilk have been and always will be held in higher regard by Bostonians than those rooters in other cities.

"But I think at times we had more camaraderie with the fans than even Ray [Bourque] or Cam [Neely]," said Miller. "I think it was because we were folk heroes. We were the 'Big, Bad Bruins' carrying on the tradition, and everybody appreciated it back then."

Fighting was part of hockey almost from the time it was created. It didn't take long for the Bruins, led by the combination of skill and nastiness known as Eddie Shore, to find out after they joined the NHL that they would have to defend themselves.

226

Throughout the '30s, '40s, and '50s, even in years they didn't match up with the best teams in the league, the Bruins weren't pushed around. One famous brawl on Christmas Day 1930 required seven policemen to break it up.

During some of their darkest days in the '60s, they could lean on the likes of "Terrible" Ted Green to pulverize another player to entertain the fandom, even if Boston was on its way to another loss.

The hiring of Harry Sinden as coach, the signing of Bobby Orr, and the trade for Phil Esposito, Ken Hodge, and Fred Stanfield gave birth to the "Big, Bad Bruins" in the late '60s. Team toughness—with or without gloves on—solidified itself as the No. 1 hallmark of the Boston Bruins.

"We almost expected it from everybody," Sinden said. "Of course, you don't get it from everybody, because it's not their makeup. But you almost expect it from everybody. If not the actual fight, the last shove—you shove me, I shove you, I get the last one."

Some guys, of course, fought more than others. But from the "Big, Bad" days to Don Cherry's "Lunch Pail A.C.," Boston was not to be messed with. John Wensink personified that notion on December 1, 1977, when after a fight against Minnesota, he skated to the front of the North Stars' bench. Wensink stuck out both his arms and beckoned anyone to emerge and meet his challenge. When no one took him up on his offer, Wensink skated toward the penalty box and turned back and gave a wave of disgust on his way off the ice.

"They never said a word to me," Wensink said.

For 14 seasons Terry O'Reilly earned his piece of Bruins history—and eventually the retirement of his sweater number—not only with goals and assists but some vicious fights that satisfied Boston's blood lust like no other. Wensink, Stan Jonathan, Mike Milbury, and basically anyone who laced up skates for Cherry's teams could make a player in a non-black-and-gold sweater pay for stepping out of line or taking liberties with another Bruins player.

Nilan Sends a Historic Message

If Bruins enforcer Chris Nilan wanted to set the tone for Boston's upcoming opening-round playoff series with Hartford during the 1991 regular-season finale against the Whalers, he found a monumental way to do it. Nilan accumulated 42 penalty minutes on a still-record 10 penalties in a 7–3 Bruins win.

"If those guys are going to play tough, then we're going to respond," said Nilan after the game. "I don't know if any messages were sent, but the game was chippy. If they want to be chippy, we can be chippy, too."

Nilan gave "chippiness" a whole new meaning that night. Whether it had anything to do with the Bruins' intimidation, Boston downed the Whalers in six games.

They could also change the course of a game with their fists. Jonathan's one-punch knockout of Pierre Bouchard in Game 4 of the Stanley Cup Finals in 1978—a YouTube sensation these days—was a major turning point in Boston winning that game (although the Bruins lost the series).

In the '80s the emergence of the enforcers—one or two guys who do the bulk of the fighting—began, and the likes of Miller and Byers were thrown into the spotlight. Big and small, they've all fought for their teammates, for respect, and for the fans.

All the way through the P.J. Stock years and in recent times with Shawn Thornton, fighters get their due from the Boston faithful after they answer the bell.

"That went into the thought process of coming here, to tell you the truth," said Thornton, who joined Boston as a free agent in the summer of 2007. "There were a few factors, and that was one of them. Talking to other guys who had played here, I knew that fans respect the job here more so than maybe in some other cities.... It's definitely appreciated when the fans appreciate it. It's been a perfect fit. I appreciate it; every time I fight, I don't see anybody sitting down, so it's definitely been a good fit."

Once a fighter has earned the adulation of the Boston fans, he never loses it. It's that relationship that turned Byers into a transplanted Bostonian for life. Once ticketed to return home to Vancouver Island and run a pub with his parents (including his mom, who's a world-class darts player), Byers is now in his second decade as a host on the *Hill Man Morning Show* on WAAF.

"Being a Bruins fan favorite is a gift, and I've always appreciated it," he said. "I appreciate that Bruins fans are AAF fans now. I'm fortunate that I've been able to have two careers now here in Boston, and both careers have allowed me to try to give back to the community as much as I can. Because without the Boston Bruins, without the Boston Bruins fans, my life wouldn't be as incredible as it is today."

And without the fighters, Bruins history wouldn't be as incredible, either.

Thomas Terrific

Wherever he's gone, Tim Thomas has had to battle.

So it shouldn't have been any surprise that when it came time to carry the Bruins to the 2011 Stanley Cup championship and end a 39-year drought, Thomas had to fight his way through three Game 7 victories over the course of the four rounds while outdueling his two fellow Vezina Trophy finalists—Montreal's Carey Price and Vancouver's Roberto Luongo—along the way.

Just as Thomas reaped the rewards of all his hard work to emerge as a perennial All-Star and two-time Vezina winner later in life than most, he also was able to savor the Cup title more because of how difficult it was to obtain.

"It's probably a good thing that you don't anticipate how difficult it's going to be because…it could seem overwhelming if you knew exactly how hard it's going to be," said Thomas, who at 37 years old and in just his fourth full season as an NHL starting goal-tender also won the Conn Smythe Trophy as playoff MVP. "It's very difficult, I think. I've heard everyone's always said it's one of the most difficult trophies to win and my experience backs that up 100 percent."

Winning the Cup was a lot easier with Thomas at the top of his game during almost the entire playoff run. He set the NHL record for saves in a Cup Finals (238) and in a playoff season (798) to follow up on his second Vezina Trophy–winning regular season, which featured him setting a new single-season record for save percentage (.938) and leading the league with a 2.00 GAA.

All this after he sat as Tuukka Rask's backup in 2009–10 and then went through off-season hip surgery.

"I don't think I've ever seen anything like that from the first exhibition game to the last game tonight, I don't think I've seen goaltending like that ever," said teammate Mark Recchi after the Bruins won Game 7 against Vancouver. "I don't know if we'll ever see something like that again. It's that special."

Carrying the Bruins to the Cup was just the biggest and latest addition to Thomas' amazing life story. A former ninth-round pick, Thomas' pro career had taken him from the University of Vermont to Birmingham; Houston; Helsinki; Detroit; Solna, Sweden; Karpat, Finland; and finally Providence before the Bruins tried to put him through re-entry waivers to join the parent club and save a sinking season in January 2006.

It took then-Bruins general manager Mike O'Connell crossing every one of his limbs and extremities—and the presence of plenty of non-believers among other NHL teams' management groups—to get Thomas to Boston. From there Thomas threw his body into so many contortionist positions to stop pucks that he eventually established himself as an NHL goaltender.

Thomas had won a Finnish Elite League title in 1998–99 and produced an MVP season in that circuit in 2004–2005 (he posted

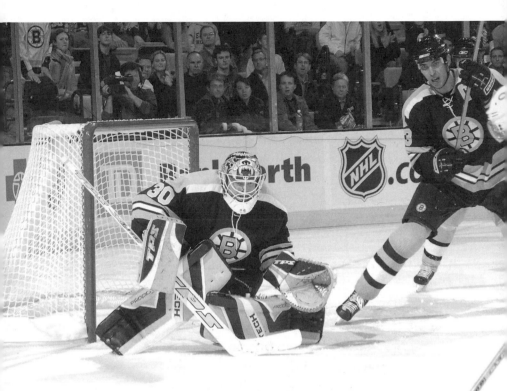

*Though it took him a while to make it in the NHL, once he became the Bruins'
No. 1 goalie in 2005, Tim Thomas has been among the best in the league. Here
he makes a save against the Montreal Canadiens during an October 2006 game
at TD Garden in Boston.*

a 1.58 goals-against average and 15 shutouts that season), but he
knew there was no guarantee the NHL would ever give him a legit-
imate shot.

"I made peace with the fact that I wasn't going to play in the
NHL," Thomas said in '06. "I was happy to end out my career in
Finland. Signing this year, getting sent down [to Providence] wasn't
in my plans, but getting called back up, it was like awakening an
old dream that you'd forgotten about.

"It's actually even better that way. I know how much luck it
actually takes to get here. I needed two goalies to get hurt, but [I

know] also how much hard work you put in over the years, so you appreciate it more."

You learn that sort of appreciation growing up in a working-class neighborhood of Michigan with a father who sells cars. Thomas helped support his family by delivering pizzas, working in a grocery store, and selling apples door to door. That work ethic never left Thomas once he entered the pro ranks. His mother once hawked her wedding ring to collect enough cash to help send him to a hockey tournament.

After a solid 2006–07 season individually, Thomas improved as much as the Bruins team the next season with a 2.44 GAA and .921 save percentage. The Bruins made the playoffs for the first time in four years that spring.

Thomas, however, didn't get satisfied. Not only did he work hard on the ice to refine his goaltending style, he also rededicated himself to an off-ice regimen that put him in the best shape of his life. That program included yoga.

"The more you go on in your career, the better it is to open up yourself to different ways of working out and becoming a better athlete," he said. "My whole career has been about proving to people that I can play in the NHL and that I can be very success-ful in the NHL. So yoga is just part of the journey."

Thomas won his first Vezina in 2009 after he finished atop the NHL in GAA (2.10) and save percentage (.933). Amazingly, Thomas wasn't done accumulating personal accolades. Moments after he beat the Philadelphia Flyers on New Year's Day 2010 at the Winter Classic at Fenway Park, he learned he was one of three goal-tenders selected to the U.S. Men's National Team for the 2010 Winter Olympics in Vancouver. He emerged from the Red Sox's dugout to a rousing ovation from the hometown crowd adorned in his red, white, and blue sweater.

"I think I had pretty much given up on [the Olympics] knowing, realistically, if you're playing the rest of your career in Europe—which is what I thought at one point I was going to be doing—you're probably not going to make the Olympic team," said Thomas. "Because there are goalies in the NHL who are going to get first dibs because they are playing in the highest league in the world."

Thomas returned from Vancouver with a silver medal. He logged just 11:31 of ice time in relief of Buffalo star Ryan Miller in the semifinal win over Finland.

"Obviously being able to actually get in the game and get playing time was special, especially against Finland, because I know so many of those guys and have so many friends in Finland who were watching on TV. But in the long run, winning the silver medal is going to be the biggest memory," he said. "It was going to be one of the best experiences of my life, regardless."

Since returning to North America, Thomas hasn't let an opportunity—or many pucks—slip by him. All the battling has paid off.

'53 B's Slew Goliath-Like Wings

Everyone loves a David-and-Goliath story featuring the "little guy" winning. While the 1953 Bruins weren't able to finish off their underdog journey through that spring's postseason—those hated Montreal Canadiens were always in the way—knocking off the Detroit Red Wings in the semifinals changed a bit of history.

The Wings were the defending Stanley Cup champion in '53 and won the Cup the next two seasons, as well. But a feisty band of Bruins made sure that there wouldn't be a shot at four in a row by putting the clamps on Detroit in a fantastic five-game upset.

To measure Detroit's powerhouse status that season, all you have to do is look at the goals-for column in the final standings. The Wings scored 222 goals, while no other club in the six-team league scored more than 169. The Bruins finished in a third-place tie in the standings, with Chicago with 69 points, 21 behind the first-place Wings. The Bruins, by virtue of one more win in the regular season, earned the unenviable opportunity to face Detroit in the first round of the playoffs.

Bruins coach Lynn Patrick knew the only chance Boston had to challenge Detroit was to slow down future Hall of Famers Gordie Howe and Ted Lindsay—who finished 1-2 in the scoring race with 95 and 71 points, respectively. The Bruins had found that out while going 2–10–2 against Detroit in the regular season, including a pair of defeats by scores of 10–1 and 10–2.

Patrick decided the line of former Kraut Line mates Milt Schmidt and Woody Dumart (Boston's best defensive forward), joined by Joe Klukay, would shadow the Howe-Lindsay line. The plan failed miserably in Game 1, a 7–0 Detroit shellacking. Howe didn't score, but Lindsay scored twice, and Marty Pavelich added two goals.

"Lynn Patrick, I must give him credit," former Bruins forward Ed Sandford recalled one night before tending to his duties as an off-ice official at Bruins games. "He was coaching at the time, and he kept harping that they've got to win four. The series isn't over until they win four. So if we could prevent them from winning four…"

Patrick was also determined to keep Dumart all over Howe. In Game 2 Howe scored his first goal of the series. However, he only found the back of the net once more in the series. Somehow the Bruins solved Detroit Vezina Trophy–winning goaltender Terry Sawchuk for five scores, including two by Dave Creighton (he had only scored eight in the regular season), in a 5–3 series-tying victory.

Boston returned home with momentum, and Jack McIntyre made sure the Bruins didn't relinquish their surge. Despite getting outshot 44–32, the Bruins won Game 3 2–1 in overtime on McIntyre's score 12:29 into the extra session.

"He hurled over the Detroit blue line and flicked his wrists," longtime hockey writer Stan Fischler wrote. "The puck took off like a jet leaving the runway and eluded the transfixed Sawchuk at 12:29. The goal sent the Bruins' fans into wild transports of joy."

Boston's other goal in that pivotal win came off Sandford's stick. It was the first of six goals he scored in the series after notching just 14 in 61 regular-season games. In fact, Sandford's entire line, along with Johnny Peirson and Fleming MacKell, took over the series with a combined 19 points.

Sandford had played with MacKell at St. Michael's of the old OHA, and that contributed to the great chemistry the trio had.

"I thought it was the best thing in the world that I had heard [when the Bruins acquired MacKell the year before]. He was an offensive centerman. He'd get the puck and fly up the ice and get it to them quickly. The defense didn't have a chance to set up. I could back-check and I could cover for him and dig the pucks out of the corners," Sandford recalled. "Johnny Peirson was a good goal-scoring forward. He had a good shot and he played his position well. So we kind of meshed pretty well in that series."

In Game 4 Sandford scored twice in a 6–2 win, which gave Boston a commanding 3–1 lead in the series. The Bruins lost a wild one in Game 5 back in Detroit, 6–4, but then they didn't waste the home-ice advantage in Game 6.

Sandford scored 3:41 into the game and set up Peirson's goal at 11:36 of the second. From there, Boston didn't look back en route to earning a spot in the Finals. The Bruins, who hadn't won a playoff series since 1946 and were facing staggering odds, had knocked out the defending champs.

Unfortunately for Boston, after grabbing a split in the first two games in the Finals in Montreal, the Bruins dropped three straight. The Habs won their first Cup in seven years, while the Bruins didn't return to the Finals again until 1957.

Nonetheless, attendance in Boston had been down, and interest in the team had waned since the Cup-winning year of '41. Fischler credits that Game 3 win over Detroit with "starting the hockey revival in Boston." The series upset of the Wings was certainly a turning point in franchise history, as even when things went really south in the early '60s, the Bruins maintained a spot in fans' hearts.

The eventual arrival of Bobby Orr in the late '60s would turn the Bruins into Goliaths, but in '53 they proved that they could fill the David role well enough.

Kluzak Over Bellows

If only Harry Sinden had listened to his wife, Eleanor.

The Bruins' general manager had a multitude of options at his disposal as the 1982 NHL Entry Draft approached, and his long-time spouse made it quite clear what she hoped Sinden would do with the No. 1 pick.

"For once I wanted him to take the easy way out," Eleanor said after Sinden decided to pick defenseman Gord Kluzak over forward Brian Bellows that June day. "I wanted everything to be rosy so that we could have a nice, quiet summer."

Eleanor had nothing against Kluzak personally. It was just that had Sinden made the Bellows pick, he would've avoided the tons of scrutiny that followed. Instead, Sinden agreed to a trade with Minnesota that involved left winger Brad Palmer and prospect

Dave Donnelly (who combined to play just 135 games for Boston) moving from the North Stars to the Bruins in exchange for Boston not selecting Bellows. Sinden then selected Kluzak.

Were it not for injuries, Sinden's choice might've proved ingenious. But Kluzak racked up more knee surgeries (11) than full seasons played (4) in his NHL career until his retirement on November 11, 1990. Kluzak, just 26, had played his final NHL game just six days earlier at New York. For his career, he skated in just 299 of a possible 658 games.

"We won the game in overtime, I think I was second star of the game, and I played really well," recalled Kluzak one night before fulfilling his role as a studio analyst for NESN. "We won the game in overtime, I remember not feeling anything, I was totally numb. And at that point I was just like, 'You know what? I'm not going to be able to walk if I keep doing this.' That's why I had to decide that my life came first. And as much as I love hockey, I just wasn't going to be able to keep doing it without risking my long-term health."

The Bruins, who had acquired the No. 1 pick in '82 from Colorado in a trade that landed free agent Dwight Foster's rights in the Mile High City, might've taken an early hint about Kluzak's future during the player's final year of junior hockey. Kluzak missed time with a left knee ligament injury. However, Sinden and his staff selected Kluzak, and even claimed that had they possessed the option, they would've taken Kluzak over Bellows even without the Minnesota trade.

Kluzak was solid in 70 games as a rookie the following winter—with one goal and six assists—and then took the next step toward stardom with 10 goals and 27 assists in 80 games as an NHL sophomore. Bellows was on his way to a career that would feature more than 1,100 NHL games and 400 goals, but Kluzak was emerging as a star. The draft-day deal had also allowed the Bruins to acquire goaltender Pete Peeters from Philadelphia for defenseman Brad McCrimmon. Peeters won the Vezina his first year in a Bruins sweater.

One play in the last game of the 1984 exhibition schedule, however, turned the Kluzak pick into a disaster. A collision with New Jersey defenseman Dave Lewis left Kluzak with a torn ACL, torn MCL, and torn medial meniscus. Kluzak missed the entire next season, and after a full year back—scoring a career-high 39 points in 1985–1986—he missed the 1986–1987 campaign with complications caused by blocking a Larry Robinson shot in the Bruins' last game the previous spring. Three more surgeries allowed Kluzak to return to full-time duty for the 1987–1988 season—a year which provided Kluzak with his best career memories because he was healthy and effective, and because Boston reached the Stanley Cup Finals.

He played a regular shift with the legendary Ray Bourque and produced 37 points.

"We played against the best lines on every team and really dominated. We had a great year," he said. "And I really am thankful that I had that. That was as close to fulfilling my potential as I came, and that's something I look back on and cherish, and I had a lot of fun."

By the following September, Kluzak had to undergo another procedure to determine the cause of fluid build-up in the knee. Complications with his knee limited him to just 11 more games over the next two seasons before his final comeback. After skating in just two games in the fall of '90, Kluzak called it quits.

"But it wasn't to be," Sinden said during a press conference at the Bruins' ninth-floor offices on Causeway Street. "No one in the history of the sport could say they've tried harder to get back on track."

"If we'd only known that night," Sinden said referring to the Lewis hit, "we could have said, 'Kid, forget it, we'll fix you up and you can forget about hockey.' That would have been impossible, of course. But instead, for five years he drives himself crazy, and the end result is he can't play. The work he's done—that's where the admiration comes from me."

During his rehabilitation, Kluzak had started to take some courses at Salem State College. Although he never expected to retire so young, he was preparing for life after hockey. In 1994 he graduated from Harvard with highest honors in economics, a degree that allowed him to have a successful career in the private sector. And his decision to stop playing hockey when he did paved the way for success in life.

"I see a lot of guys who have knee replacements, hip replacements. And I—knock on wood—I'm in very good health," said Kluzak. "I can golf, can walk, can bike, can play with my kids without any problems. That means a lot, and it's not always something you're really thinking about when you're 24, 25 [years old]."

On the ice, the Bruins obviously would've benefitted more had Sinden tabbed Bellows over Kluzak. But no one—not even Eleanor Sinden—could have predicted what wound up costing Kluzak a chance to be a Bruins superstar.

75 Julien Joins Champions Club

The Boston triumvirate wanted to become a quartet, and Bruins head coach Claude Julien was willing to do whatever it took to be that fourth man in.

When the Bruins downed Vancouver to win their third Game 7 of the 2011 postseason and their first Stanley Cup championship in 39 years, Julien finally joined New England Patriots head coach Bill Belichick, Boston Celtics head coach Doc Rivers, and Boston Red Sox manager Terry Francona as title-winning Boston leaders.

"All three coaches at one point have reached out to me, even before I won," explained the Bruins head coach. "They really wanted me to succeed like they did. To me that meant a lot."

Bruins general manager Peter Chiarelli hired Julien after the team's disastrous 2006–07 season. By bringing structure and a devotion to defense, Julien was able to get Boston back into the playoffs in his first season.

Boston lost in the first round that year, but won a playoff series for the first time in 10 years the next season. After winning again in the first round in 2010, however, the second round brought the ultimate collapse. The Bruins lost all of a 3–0 series lead to Philadelphia in the second round to become just the third team in NHL history to squander such a commanding lead. Many were calling for Julien's head, but Chiarelli refused to heap all the blame for the historic loss on the coach's shoulders.

Throughout the 2010–11 season, the Bruins went through more ups and downs, and the call for a change behind the bench was often heard. Chiarelli stuck it out with Julien, just as the coach stuck with his streaky players through thick and thin.

Bruins head coach Claude Julien raises the Stanley Cup after Boston defeated Vancouver in Game 7 of the 2010–11 Finals.

In the postseason, the Bruins fell behind 2–0 against Montreal in the first round and Vancouver in the Stanley Cup Finals. Julien, however, stuck with the lineup that had gotten the Bruins so far in the first place. He tweaked alignments here and there, including pairing Zdeno Chara and Dennis Seidenberg against the Canadiens to make sure Boston had a shutdown defense duo, but mostly kept the faith that his players would come through.

In the end, Julien took over as the Bruins' all-time leader in playoff coaching wins.

"I think we all believed in his system and in him and we all knew we could do it," said center Patrice Bergeron. "That's why we responded every time that he was asking us to step up or to come back from adversity. I thought he deserved a lot more credit than he's going to get."

He doesn't need credit. Julien became a Cup champion and a member of Boston's "championship coaches' club." There's nothing else he could ask for.

76 Orr Ends Up in Chicago

To sum up what it was like around the Bruins and the city of Boston on June 9, 1976, the day Bobby Orr signed a free-agent contract with the Chicago Blackhawks, all you have to do is ask the man in charge of damage control that day—longtime public relations guru and assistant to the president Nate Greenberg.

"I started in 1973. That happened in 1976. And I said to myself, whatever this franchise faces, and I as an employee face, and however many years I have left with this team, nothing will compare with this. It's impossible to think of any greater PR calamity than that," said Greenberg some 30-plus years later and well into his retirement.

Injuries that limited Orr to just 10 games played in his last season in black and gold in 1975–1976 also kept him on the sideline for all but 26 games over his last two seasons in the NHL with Chicago. However, Orr's injuries did little to soften the blow to Boston and the Bruins.

"Our waiting list—in fact they stopped it—we had at least 10,000, 15,000 names on our season-ticket waiting list.... The day the whole thing fell apart, when Orr left, the waiting list was non-existent," remembered Greenberg.

Many a tear was shed the day Orr left the Bruins. It becomes more painful to think about in retrospect, because Orr never should have left. The Bruins had made Orr an offer no one would've refused. But he was never told about Boston's offer of an 18.6 percent stake in the club.

That revelation didn't really come out for some 15 years. In summer 1976 negotiations on what would've been Orr's last contract with the Bruins continued from in-season talks. He underwent his fourth career knee surgery in late September 1975 and then a fifth surgery in November. All the while, Orr's agent, Alan Eagleson, and the Bruins' new owners, Sportsystems, were talking about how to keep Orr in the Hub. The owners were obviously getting some cold feet in relation to Orr's damaged knees, and they had turned the negotiations over to their lawyers (removing general manager Harry Sinden, a close friend of Orr's), who might not have quite understood the legacy of Orr in Boston.

Eagleson started getting other teams involved, even though Orr was still under contract to the Bruins. And Orr was open and honest about the fact that any team might be "purchasing damaged goods." That was Orr. Even when trying to cash in, he couldn't be anything but honest.

Of course, he proved too honest, too trusting when it came to Eagleson. It was Eagleson who negotiated Orr's record-breaking first contract to join the Bruins and then two subsequent deals after that. Over the years, Eagleson had managed Orr's affairs, landed him major endorsements, and sold the "Orr brand" throughout New England.

Not everyone trusted Eagleson as Orr did. Phil Esposito wanted nothing to do with him, Gregg Sheppard so despised him he would walk out of any room the lawyer was in, and Mike Milbury was among the first to question Eagleson's conflict of interest as a player's agent and the head of the NHL Players' Association. Years later, through lawsuits and criminal charges, revelations upon revelations would become public about Eagleson's illegal dealings, his thefts, and the Orr offer he hid. Eventually he served six months in prison after pleading guilty to fraud and embezzlement and was disbarred.

But in the summer of '76 all anyone knew was that Orr was on his way out of Boston, and it seemed as though the Bruins' brass was to blame. Boston made one last offer to the game's greatest player—a five-year deal with the first year guaranteed, a total of $600,000 due to Orr. All the defenseman had to do was pass a physical before the 1976 opening of training camp.

Instead, Eagleson let Orr hit the open market after June 1. While there were other teams involved in the bidding, it should be no surprise that Orr landed with Chicago. Eagleson was close with Blackhawks owner Bill Wirtz and was often seen lounging on the owner's boat.

Obviously, Bruins fans and ownership felt like they'd been punched in the gut. But no one felt the departure more than Orr's teammates.

"I think it was [a shock] in the beginning. It's hard to understand all the things that go on behind the scenes," said fellow defenseman Gary Doak.

Boston was not only denied the best player in the game, but also the chance to see what the top two defensemen in the league would've looked like together.

"That was really heartbreaking, and I'll tell you why," said then–Bruins coach Don Cherry. "When we had Brad Park and him on the points, I think they scored—in 10 games between the two of them—10 goals. I'm almost positive we won nine out of 10. It was almost like having two cannons back there. It was really going to be something. I told everybody, 'It's a guaranteed Stanley Cup with these two guys.' And to lose him, it broke my heart, I'll tell you that."

While hearts were broken, the Bruins' spirits were not. And helped by some shrewd dealings by Sinden, the Bruins thrived in the post-Orr era with trips to the Stanley Cup Finals in 1977 and 1978, and a berth in the semifinals in '79.

Even though the Bruins made the most of the disastrous situation, Orr followed Eddie Shore and preceded Ray Bourque as legendary Bruins defensemen who didn't get to finish up in Boston—a mark on the franchise's history that can't be erased.

"It's a shame," said Doak, "that Bobby Orr didn't finish his career in a Boston uniform."

77 Bourque Finished atop the Mountain

A storied career as a Bruins defenseman wasn't the only thing Ray Bourque had in common with Eddie Shore and Bobby Orr. All three ended their respective careers in another club's sweater.

However, Bourque's departure from the Bruins—while highly emotional—wasn't nearly as acrimonious as those of his legendary predecessors. And, of course, Bourque's exit finished triumphantly in his new city.

A combination of free-agent defections, season-altering contract holdouts, and injuries had set the Bruins back during the 1999–2000 season. They were going nowhere fast and were winless in seven of eight games when Bourque finally decided to do something on February 28, 2000, that few expected the loyal blueliner would ever do: he called general manager Harry Sinden and asked for a trade.

"That 'but' really got to me. They talk about Ray Bourque as a great player, a great Bruin, *but* he never won the Cup," Bourque said years later. "I wanted to challenge myself and kind of remove that 'but.' That was the one thing I need to go out and try to win. As fun as it was, that whole experience, the toughest thing was leaving and asking for the trade. That was the hardest thing I ever did was calling Harry Sinden and asking him to trade me to another team."

There had been rumors about the Bruins giving Bourque a chance to win elsewhere. But the limited number of teams Bourque would be willing to report to and the PR hit the club would inevitably take by trading its all-time leading scorer stood in the way. After the trade demand, however, Sinden got to work on the deal. Bourque favored a trade to Philadelphia because he was building a new home in the Bay State and didn't want to go too far away. The Flyers were one of a number of teams in the mix as the next week unfolded.

The reality of the situation solidified after a 3–0 loss to Philadelphia on March 4. After the Bruins dropped to 19–25–17 on the season, en route to a second non-playoff season in four years, Bourque grabbed the game puck on his way off the ice. It later was revealed that Bourque made a heartfelt good-bye speech to his teammates in the locker room after the contest.

Bourque didn't practice the next day nor did he suit up for the March 6 game with Ottawa. The FleetCenter crowd already missed its team's captain. Signs supporting Bourque and skewering owner-ship, as well as some choice chants about what the fans thought of owner Jeremy Jacobs, were the only excitement during a 5–1 defeat to Ottawa.

And then the news broke: Bourque and forward Dave Andreychuk were dealt to Colorado for Brian Rolston, Martin Grenier, Samuel Pahlsson, and a first-round draft pick.

"The best deal that we thought at the time was with Colorado. So he didn't want to go there. That was not his first choice," Sinden said. "When I called him, he said, 'Oh no, not Colorado.' And his wife was in the background, and he called the name of the team to her with a French accent—Color-a-doh. I heard that. And I don't know what she said. But it ended up, because they were very good friends with Patrick Roy, it ended up being a very good situation for him.

"The only thing you regret was that you weren't able to do it here for him."

The next morning Bourque held a teary press conference at the airport. He had reached two Cup Finals in '88 and '90 with the Bruins, but knew he needed to go elsewhere to have a chance of winning a championship before his retirement. Although the Avalanche came up short that spring, the next year Bourque kept on trucking. A seven-game triumph over New Jersey in the Stanley Cup Finals permitted him to finally raise the most famous trophy in sports. He retired shortly thereafter.

The Bruins, meanwhile, trudged along. Shell-shocked at first, and leaderless without their captain, to a man the Bruins understood why Bourque wanted to leave.

"He could have left numerous years and then attacked in free agency and been like a merchant marine, for crying out loud, a gun for hire, if he was just chasing that," said longtime teammate Don Sweeney, explaining why and he and most Bruins didn't begrudge Bourque's decision.

On the ice, the Bruins wouldn't turn things around for some time. They missed the playoffs again in '01 and didn't win a playoff series until 2009. Dealing a future Hall of Famer for negligible return rarely aids a franchise turnaround. And it's almost impossible to replace a player and person like Bourque within a generation.

"The thing I always remember is, because he never really got hurt much, to go into those first couple games and realize he's never going to play here again," recalled longtime *Quincy Patriot Ledger* beat writer Mike Loftus. "That might not have been his best year, but he was still their best player. He was playing 30 minutes a game, and to have to fill all those holes. It didn't even feel like an NHL team anymore."

78 Bruins Slip on Couple Oil Slicks

After losing the 1988 Stanley Cup Finals to Edmonton in four straight games, the Bruins, led by future Hall of Famers Ray Bourque and Cam Neely, were probably wondering what it would be like to get a shot at the Oilers without Wayne Gretzky.

Two years later a similarly constructed Bruins team got that opportunity, as some 21 months after the sale/trade of the Great One to Los Angeles, the Oilers again served as Boston's opposition in the Cup Finals. However, except for one Boston win, the result was the same in 1990.

Without a doubt, the '90 team had a better chance to end the franchise's Cup drought. Boston won the President's Trophy as the only team in the regular season to surpass 100 points in the standings (just the second time since '67 only one club did so). Instead, the Bruins' regular-season success proved of little use against an Oilers team that still featured future Hall of Famers Mark Messier, Jari Kurri, and Glenn Anderson. For a fifth time since winning the Cup in 1972, Boston failed to win hockey's ultimate prize.

"When you look at it on paper, which I have, it wasn't really meant to be," Mike Milbury, who was a rookie head coach in 1989–1990, said. "But the triple-overtime game really sealed our fate."

Most people today just refer to that contest as the "Petr Klima game." After all, it was the seldom-used Oilers forward who stepped off the bench, fresher than anyone else who had competed that night, and scored the game-winner after 115 minutes, 13 seconds of game action (5 hours, 32 minutes after puck drop) in Game 1 at Boston Garden. The Bruins had outshot the Oilers 52–31, but lost on Klima's lone attempt of the game.

Real curmudgeons could call that classic the "Glen Wesley game." After all, it was the Bruins' defenseman who had the victory on his stick two minutes into the second overtime, but instead of scoring, he "air-lifted the potential game-winning shot into the ozone," as the *Boston Globe* described Wesley's failed backhand shot.

"When I watch the amount of time Wesley had to put it on his forehand and put it in, it might've changed everything," said Milbury.

Weeks after that game, in the aftermath of the Bruins losing the series, Wesley was quoted as saying, "It was a great chance, and I blew it." His frustration was felt throughout the region. Longtime ESPN columnist Bill Simmons once wrote that his father never forgave Wesley for the miss. When Wesley was traded to Hartford in 1994, Simmons wrote, his father laughed and said, "I would've given the guy away."

Of course, there was more to the series than Klima and Wesley. There was Craig Janney, who couldn't return to Game 1 after the second overtime because of dehydration, failing to score a point in the series. There was Cam Neely managing just four assists and no goals after burying 55 pucks in the net during the regular season and 12 in the previous three postseason series. And there was the goaltending duel that went to former Bruins puck-stopper Bill

Ranford, filling in for injured future Hall of Famer Grant Fuhr, over Bruins goaltender Andy Moog, who had been acquired by Boston for Ranford and Geoff Courtnall just two years earlier.

Milbury recalls that Moog, who shared the Jennings Trophy for lowest goals-against average in the regular season by a goaltending duo with Reggie Lemelin that season, never recovered physically from the triple-overtime thriller in the heat of the Garden. In Game 2 Milbury pulled Moog after Edmonton scored three goals on eight shots. Lemelin didn't fare much better, but Boston's scorers were as much to blame in the 7–2 Edmonton win. Boston, which lost forward Dave Poulin to a knee injury for the rest of the series in that second game, outshot Edmonton 27–22 over the 60 minutes, but at different points held edges of 16–4 and 22–6 on the shot clock even while the Oilers held the lead on the scoreboard.

Boston earned a split of the next two games in Edmonton, but Anderson's goal 1:17 into Game 5 sent the Oilers well on their way to the clinching triumph.

"It's the absolutely worst feeling," Neely said of losing in the Finals. "It's worse than getting beat in the first round. You battle that hard and that long, you're four wins away from winning it. But having said that, that ride to the Finals is pretty special."

The '88 journey to the Finals was glorious, as Boston vanquished the ghosts of decades past with a five-game win over archrival Montreal in the division finals and then ended Cinderella New Jersey's hopes of a Cup berth in seven games in the conference finals. But Edmonton outplayed the Bruins in every facet of the game en route to a four-game sweep. A defense led by Kevin Lowe and Steve Smith (two first-game assists) and Fuhr in net made sure that the offensive efforts of Gretzky, Messier, and company wouldn't go to waste.

Like the Canadiens of the '70s and the New York Islanders of the early '80s, the Oilers dynasty put up a road block on the Bruins' attempt to stage a Causeway Street parade. Don't for a second think that still doesn't sting.

"Just in general," said Neely, who never played in the Finals again after '90, "anytime I see some of those classic games of the Bruins-Edmonton Finals on, I choose not to watch it."

Uniform Timeline

The beloved spoked "B" has a long-held place in every Bruins fans' heart.

But did you know that the spoked "B" didn't make its first appearance on a Bruins uniform until the 25th anniversary of the franchise in 1948–1949. That year the "B" was sandwiched by the numbers 24 and 49 to represent the current year and the year the Bruins were born. After that, the Bruins dropped the numbers, but the spoked "B" stuck around.

It wasn't until the mid '90s, when Boston began wearing the gold "Pooh Bear" jerseys, that they ever wore another uniform that didn't feature a spoked "B." Those jerseys featured the word "Bruins" on the shoulders.

The adoption of the "B" was one major change to the Bruins' uniform over their 85-plus years in the NHL. It's believed that the Bruins, more than any other Original Six team (or any NHL club ever for that matter), have made the most uniform changes.

Boston's original uniform was in the team's inaugural colors of brown and yellow. The crest of the sweater featured gold block letters that spelled "Boston" arched over a bear with block letters spelling "Bruins" underneath on a brown background. The pants were brown, and the barbershop-pole-style socks covered players' shins. From then on, there were slight alterations—and some major changes—made every few years along the way.

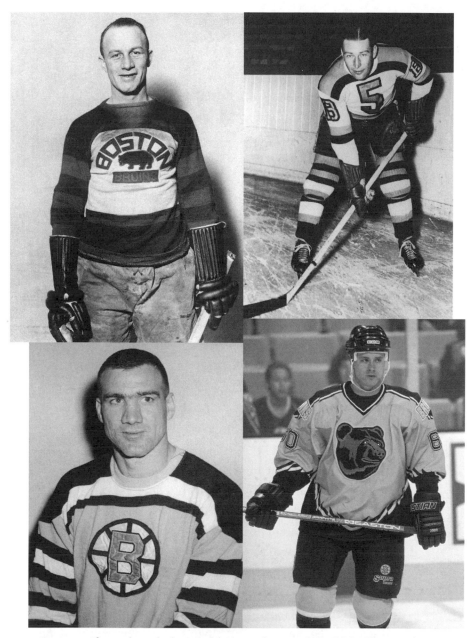

Bruins uniforms through the ages (clockwise from top left): Eddie Shore in the original brown-and-yellow uniform in 1929; Dit Clapper in a revised look circa 1930s; Kirk Nielsen models the "Pooh Bear" jersey in 1997; and Jerry Toppazzini sports the classic spoked "B" with stripes in the mid-1950s.

In the mid-'30s, the Bruins changed their colors to black and gold. It's difficult to determine why the club changed from the colors that were adopted from owner Charles Adams' First National Stores chain. Some believe it might've had something to do with Weston Adams wanting to change the club's fortunes, or it could've been a way to differentiate from the minor league Boston Cubs.

The mid-'50s brought separate home and road jerseys, usually based in black and white. In the 1956–1957 season the Bruins also introduced a gold-based jersey with black shoulder yokes trimmed in white. This particular jersey might've been jinxed. Or at least that's what we can take from general manager Milt Schmidt's move to phase it out—and then discontinue it—in the late '60s prior to the reign of the "Big, Bad Bruins" as one of the league's power-houses. The gold uniform had become too closely associated with the awful teams of the early and mid-'60s. The 1966–1967 team is also the last to wear barbershop-pole-style socks.

When the third "Pooh Bear" jersey was introduced (using a bear-head logo inspired by the 1990–1991 press guide), there was a slight gaffe. Boston skated with white helmets for the first period, but once they realized that that color combination didn't work, they switched to black helmets.

The third jerseys became even more of a rage after the lockout. And then the 2009–2010 season saw the birth of the Winter Classic sweater in the old-school brown and yellow. Bruins Hall of Fame player and vice president Cam Neely consulted with Reebok to design the uniform, which featured the club's original spoked "B" that debuted during the Bruins' 25th anniversary season of 1948. The laces of the sweater were reminiscent of the teams in the '70s, including the 1970 and 1972 Cup winners. The gold socks were first worn in the '30s, including by the team that won the Cup in 1938. And the gold sweater was similar to the one introduced in 1940 and worn by the 1941 championship club.

It's difficult to say why the Bruins have changed their uniforms so often, especially when their main logo is such a historic icon, but they might keep transforming their look until they find another championship ensemble.

80 Pluses and Minuses to O'Connell's Stints

He was known as the "guy who was traded for Al Secord." Later he left the Bruins as "the guy who traded Joe Thornton."

Mike O'Connell might've earned some dubious tags during his stints in Boston as a player and then as management, but they shouldn't cancel out the positive contributions he made to his hometown franchise.

The Cohasset, Massachusetts, native was part of the crop of American-born players who started to make an impact in the Canadian-dominated NHL in the late '70s and early '80s. In his fourth NHL season, he was swapped for Secord, who similarly was having a hard time getting a legit opportunity to be an NHL regular in Boston in his third season.

Sure Secord went on to be a productive forward with three seasons of 75-plus points (including 86 points in the 1982–1983 campaign). But O'Connell more than held his own in black and gold. After slumping from 53 points to 39 in his first Bruins season, O'Connell followed up with seasons of 53, 60, and 55 points. In 1982–1983 he posted a remarkable plus-44 rating. During the 1983–1984 campaign 60 of his points were recorded on 18 goals, including a streak of seven straight games with a goal (a record by a defenseman that stood for more than 20 years).

"A good modern day comparable for O'Connell would be Brian Rafalski," wrote Joe Pelletier. "Not only are they similar sized defensemen, but both were strong offensive contributors thanks to their skating, passing, and offensive reads and pinches. O'Connell relied on his heavy shot perhaps more than Rafalski, but both were really crafty."

O'Connell obviously didn't let the pressure of playing in front of his family and friends, or the magnitude of wearing the sweater of the team his family owned season tickets for, slow him down. He finished up his playing career in Detroit. After retirement, he went right into coaching with San Diego of the International Hockey League. In 1991–1992 he returned to the Bruins as assistant coach and then coached the Providence farm club in the American League for two seasons before ascending to the assistant general manager's post that was vacated by Mike Milbury.

Although there was a change in "Mikes," general manager Harry Sinden predicted he would pass the reins on to his heir apparent within three or four years. Well, it took a little longer, but in 2000 Sinden relinquished the GM title, stayed on as president, and anointed O'Connell as the new GM of the Bruins.

O'Connell was hampered from the outset, as Sinden had already hired the volatile Mike Keenan as Boston's coach. But under O'Connell, the Bruins won two Northeast Division titles and won the Eastern Conference in the 2001–2002 regular season. In 2004 O'Connell was even able to swing a couple trade-deadline deals to add Sergei Gonchar and Michael Nylander to the Bruins' cause. However, first-round playoff exits—both to Montreal—in those two seasons ruined the regular-season success.

Under his watch (and aided by the forward-thinking assistant GM Jeff Gorton), the scouting operation was revamped. By the end of his reign, O'Connell's staff had claimed future stars Patrice Bergeron and David Krejci in the second round of their drafts.

"Mike O'Connell, I know he takes his hits, but there's not too many people who are brighter and carry themselves the way Mike did," said Gorton.

O'Connell's track record as far as trades was pretty even pre-lockout, despite having to operate under the same business model that Sinden had worked (budget and profit above all). But he maintained the reputation he developed being a meddler when he was the assistant GM (he briefly feuded with head coach Pat Burns) and once even took over the Boston bench himself. His reputation with agents was also sour because of his franchise-mandated philosophy to barely budge in negotiations, especially with restricted free agents. There were almost more holdouts than there were playoff wins in those days.

After the Bruins as an ownership/management team misjudged what the result of the lockout would be—and let all but a handful of players leave or go into the work stoppage without a contract—O'Connell was behind the 8-ball. He re-signed Joe Thornton and Glen Murray, but had to fill in around them with a B-list supporting cast. A slow start to the 2005–2006 season convinced O'Connell that he had to trade Thornton, who was dealt to San Jose for Marco Sturm, Brad Stuart, and Wayne Primeau—not an All-Star in the group—in late November.

"And we based the decision on what we saw over Joe's years here," said O'Connell years later. "Right or wrong, we didn't think he could lead our team to where we wanted to be."

The Bruins' plan was to remove Thornton—and his $6-million-plus salary—and build the team around Bergeron and whoever they could land in free agency the following summer. O'Connell never got to enact that strategy; he was fired in March 2006. Of course, his farewell moves—so to speak—were long-term extensions for goaltender Tim Thomas and forward P.J. Axelsson. Thomas went on to win the Vezina Trophy twice in three years and was a key cog in the Bruins' 2011 Stanley Cup championship team.

Both as a player and general manager, O'Connell deserved a lot of the flak he took. However, a final grade on his contributions to the organization won't be in until the current Bruins are done making their run.

81 Chiarelli's Five-Year Plan

Robert Burns once wrote about the best-laid schemes of mice and men going awry.

In the case of Bruins general manager Peter Chiarelli, the plan didn't always go as he had predicted. But when the dust settled on his scheme, the Bruins had conquered all the mice, men, and other critters of the NHL to win the first Stanley Cup for the franchise in 39 years.

Through some shrewd dealings and then a lot of patience with the personnel he assembled, Chiarelli built the 2011 Cup championship club over the course of his first five seasons at the helm. After a seven-game Cup Finals victory over Vancouver, everything he'd plotted along the way was validated.

"Well, it feels really good," said Chiarelli just days after the Bruins' championship drought ended. "And you know, everyone talks about a plan. Whenever a manager takes a job, they always have a plan or else they wouldn't be doing their job. And I've talked to other managers and managers-to-be, and talked about certain plans. And ours…pretty much everyone has a five-year plan and so did we. And it's not like it fell exactly into place but we were adding certain elements, certain elements to get to that point.

"And it's happened, so I'm a genius."

Chiarelli's joke elicited laughs before he went on to explain more about the plan.

"So I guess the common theme in the plan was character. I remember talking about being hard to play against, closing gaps. It's character, and at the end of the day that's what I wanted for us. My father was at Games 3 and 4 [of the Cup Finals] and after Game 4

I said to him, 'We're going to win the Cup,' and he said, 'I think you will, too, but why?' I said, 'Because there's too much resolve in the locker room.' You could just feel it, and at the end of the day that's what happened."

The Bruins' character showed through in their overcoming 2–0 series deficits in the first round and the Finals. It showed through in winning a do-or-die Game 7 three times, becoming the first team to ever accomplish that. And it showed when the Bruins staved off elimination against Vancouver in Game 6 and then won Game 7 on the road.

Owner Jeremy Jacobs knew exactly how the Bruins had accomplished their goals.

"I think that Peter has put together a dream team, his dream, and as he saw it within the parameters that they have to work," said Jacobs.

The Bruins didn't take off right at the outset of Chiarelli's stint as the team's GM. The Bruins needed a change of culture after their ill-fated first season after the NHL lockout. So Jeremy Jacobs and his son Charlie decided to replace Harry Sinden's hand-picked successor Mike O'Connell with an outsider—the first to hold the title of GM since Sinden returned to the franchise some 30-plus years earlier.

Chiarelli's only previous ties to Boston were the four years he spent at Harvard before going on to a career as a player agent and then an assistant general manager with the Ottawa Senators.

"We want to create a culture where players want to come here to play and fans want to watch exciting hockey in one of the best arenas in the world," said the elder Jacobs the day Chiarelli was introduced. "I found Peter to have the strategic approach to hockey operations, a deep appreciation for the way the game is played, a solid reputation as one of hockey's top emerging leaders, and a passion and energy toward building a strong, transparent team."

Chiarelli echoed his owner's sentiments.

"I want to introduce a new, fresh culture to this organization," he said. "I want players to want to play here. I want players to want to stay here. I want players to move their families here."

The Chiarelli era got off to an inauspicious start, as his first hire as head coach, Dave Lewis, was an epic failure and the Bruins failed to qualify for the playoffs for a second straight year. But with ingredients like Zdeno Chara and Marc Savard—two players who had signed with Boston partly because of their prior ties to Chiarelli—and Patrice Bergeron and Tim Thomas—two players left over from the prior regime—already in place, ownership realized Chiarelli had shown enough improvement to earn a mulligan on his coaching hire. Chiarelli's second selection, Claude Julien, not only led the team to the playoffs the next season, he then won the Jack Adams Trophy as Coach of the Year in 2008–09 when Boston finished atop the Eastern Conference and then won a playoff series for the first time in a decade.

The structure Julien brought to the team and the winning the coach's philosophies and players' talent created made Boston the target destination Chiarelli wanted it to be. Over the course of a few seasons he was able to supplement his core by acquiring and retaining veteran players like Mark Recchi, Dennis Seidenberg, and Andrew Ference. Young stars like Bergeron, David Krejci, and Milan Lucic made commitments to remain in Boston long-term. And when Phil Kessel didn't want to stay, Chiarelli was able to package him to Toronto for three high draft picks that had the potential to set up the Bruins for another five-year run of success.

When the ultimate goal of a plan looks elusive because of unpredictable occurrences, the easy thing to do is change course. Chiarelli, however, never wavered. He was adamant about not blaming Julien for the Bruins historically losing a 3–0 series lead to Philadelphia in the spring of 2010. He had complete faith in the leadership hierarchy of that club to bounce back the next season.

In dramatic fashion, the Bruins proved him right. The best-laid scheme in recent Bruins history worked out as well as possible.

82 Savard's Star Dimmed by Concussions

Pittsburgh forward Matt Cooke was not penalized, nor was he dealt any supplemental discipline, for his blindside hit on Bruins center Marc Savard on March 7, 2010.

Not that any punishment for the repeat offender Cooke would've done anything to get Boston's star playmaker's career back on track. It just might have made Bruins fans feel a little better to know that Cooke didn't get away with potentially ending the career of one of the sport's best players.

Well, Cooke did get away with it because the league's disciplinarians couldn't find official grounds to suspend him. Although weeks later the league temporarily adopted—and then before the next season made permanent—Rule 48, which outlawed blindside or lateral hits to the head, that did little to improve Savard's outlook.

The Bruins center was able to make it back for the team's ill-fated seven-game playoff series with Philadelphia two months after the hit. But the summertime brought on new post-concussion syndrome symptoms and a delayed start to Savard's season. When Savard returned to action, he was a shadow of his former self. And then he suffered a second concussion in January after a routine, clean hit from Colorado's Matt Hunwick.

By the time the Bruins won the Stanley Cup championship five months later, Savard had seen only slight improvement in his condition and a little reduction in the effects of his symptoms. He was able to attend a few playoff games and take part in the celebratory "Rolling Rally" parade. As far as continuing his playing career, though, there were many doubts about Savard's future.

No one could've predicted the tragic turn things would take for Savard when he signed his salary-cap-friendly seven-year contract extension worth a little more than $4 million per season in the fall of 2009 or when he signed his initial contract with the Bruins on July 1, 2006, for four years and $20 million.

The Bruins imported Savard in 2006 to replace the point production that was shipped away when star pivot Joe Thornton was sent to San Jose the previous fall. Savard lived up to expectations with 96 points that first season in black and gold, but he wasn't satisfied. In his final season with Atlanta, Savard had made a salary run with both 97 points and a plus-7 rating—his first plus season in the NHL. With Boston, he had dropped back to minus-19.

It would've been easy for Savard to just cash his checks and count his points. However, he wanted more. So he refocused his efforts, accepted the tutelage of new head coach Claude Julien, and suddenly found himself as a two-way force worthy of two All-Star Game selections.

"Coming in here [in 2007–2008] with Claude, and him stressing defense so much, now I get more benefit going home at night, knowing I was a plus player that night and I helped my team win," Savard said during that first season under Julien, which finished with the player owning a plus-3 rating. "I don't want to be a minus, I don't like getting scored on, and I think it's helped me out."

Savard became defensive-minded without losing his nose for offense. The ability to find open players never left him, even when he began to polish his defensive play. His 78 and 88 points in his next two seasons in Boston were still tops on the Bruins' scoring charts. In that third Boston season, he posted a remarkable plus-25 rating.

Savard's transformation impressed Hall of Famer Cam Neely, who took over as the Bruins' president after the 2009–10 season.

"It's been a learning process for Marc," said Neely. "I credit the coaching staff for helping him understand that. He's obviously a very gifted player and for Marc, it's become not just about his points, it's become about how to win as a team. He's certainly an integral part of our hockey club.

"He's counted on to do a lot of offensive things for our team. But aside from that, he's been counted on to play a role defensively…and I think he's taken pride in that."

Savard's success in Boston convinced him there was no place better to play, so he re-signed with the club in 2009.

"I think I've achieved what I thought I could. But there's more there," he said after inking the new deal. "There's more to give. I'm surfacing right now and I'm going to try to do that going forward."

Unfortunately for Savard, Cooke—one of Boston's biggest modern-day villains—postponed that opportunity to strive for more, possibly forever. While Savard was expected to get his name etched on the Cup, he wasn't able to participate in Boston's championship run. In a long line of Bruins players whose careers were shortened by injury, Savard seemed destined to be the newest name on the list.

For that, Savard, the Bruins organization, and its fans were punished, while Cooke got off scot-free.

83 Gorton's Great Climb

When it comes to climbing the corporate ladder, you'd be hard-pressed to find someone in the history of the Bruins who did a better job of pulling himself up to a prominent position than Jeff Gorton.

Remarkably, the Melrose, Massachusetts, native started as an intern in the public relations department in 1992. By the end of his 14th season of his stint in Boston, he had earned the title of interim general manager. He played a huge part in the revitalization of the franchise in the late 2000s with the signings of Zdeno Chara and

Marc Savard as unrestricted free agents on July 1, 2006. And he helped with the trade for Tuukka Rask at the '06 NHL Entry Draft while newly hired general manager Peter Chiarelli was still obligated to finish his job as assistant GM in Ottawa.

"He deserved every part of it," said former GM Mike O'Connell, who was with the Bruins for almost all of Gorton's ascension. "He's just a smart guy who works extremely hard. He knows the game, and he works at it."

Gorton, a former goaltender in his high school playing days, graduated from Bridgewater State College in 1991 and then earned his master's degree in sports management from Springfield College in 1993. While in graduate school, Gorton tried to stay as close to hockey as he could. He took a job pouring beer at minor league games at the Springfield Civic Center, but more important began an internship with the Bruins in public relations.

Although it was a road less traveled, Gorton was hoping he'd be able to make the move from PR to hockey operations someday.

"That was my plan, just to get in the door," said Gorton, who was thrilled to be doing any work for the team he grew up rooting for. "I had talked to some other people along the way, in other sports, other professions, who'd taken the intern route, and they said, 'Just go in there with an open mind, and I know you want to be in hockey, but you're opportunity is to get in the door whichever way they let you in. And then you'll have to show them you know what you're doing.' That's what I did."

After his internship ended, a full-time PR job opened up. It was a no-brainer for Gorton to take it. In addition to his PR duties, Gorton was doing stats and video work for Mike Milbury and then continued to do that for O'Connell. In 1994 he earned the title of Director of Scouting Information. In addition to traveling the continent scouting, Gorton helped O'Connell revamp the Bruins' scouting department by creating a computer database, along with a local company, that became the prototype for the database almost every NHL team uses today.

With role models like O'Connell and Hall of Famer Harry Sinden, Gorton kept honing his natural ability to identify talent and work with the club's scouts. In 2000 he became O'Connell's assistant, and when O'Connell was fired in spring 2006, Gorton took over as interim GM.

"The feeling was he knew players. He worked at it, he knew players, had the right personality.... He's a very smart hockey guy," said longtime Bruins PR guru and senior assistant to the president Nate Greenberg. "He had that ingredient that Harry liked to talk about that he could tell who could play and who couldn't. And the timing was right."

A dispute over compensation when the Bruins hired Chiarelli away from the Senators in May 2006 left Gorton in charge until mid-July, when Chiarelli was finally released. On draft day '06 Gorton swung a major deal with Toronto that shipped former Calder Trophy–winning goaltender Andrew Raycroft for prospect Tuukka Rask, who the Maple Leafs had chosen one spot before Boston in the previous year's draft. The Leafs had made a couple offers to the Bruins, but Gorton and his staff knew what they wanted.

"We were pretty excited about Rask because...he was a guy we wanted the prior draft," recalled Gorton, whose staff also drafted Phil Kessel and Milan Lucic that day. "We watched him in the World Junior right after that. Just to get the opportunity to get him, we were like, 'Oh, man, we're going to get a guy who's going to set us up for a long time.' Right around their pick, we made the deal."

The Bruins then needed to make an impact in free agency, coming off a last-place finish that was made worse by the trade of star center Joe Thornton to San Jose. By the end of the first day the market opened, Gorton, then–director of player development Don Sweeney, and even Hall of Fame player Cam Neely, who had yet to take a job in the Bruins' front office, saw the fruits of their tireless labors with the signings of Chara and Savard.

"Everybody knew that once we let Thornton go, we needed a No. 1 center. And then a lynchpin of the organization that had been missing obviously since Ray [Bourque] left was a No. 1 defenseman," Gorton said. "So those were two things we knew we needed. Those were the best players. To be able to land those guys on that day, and have it go the way it went, I feel proud for a lot of people who are no longer there that that...came through."

The work Gorton did to speed the Bruins' rebuilding process didn't earn him a spot in Chiarelli's regime to enjoy the fruits of those labors. After one season, Gorton was not re-signed. However, his ascension through the Bruins' ranks earned him a spot in Bruins history, and his accomplishments continue to benefit his hometown organization.

84 McNab Made Esposito's Area His Own

Much the same way Bruins general manager Harry Sinden covered himself for the eventual end of Bobby Orr's career—be it with Boston or another team—by acquiring Brad Park from the New York Rangers in November 1975, Sinden made sure Boston didn't go long without a Phil Esposito-like net-front presence.

Just seven months after striking the Esposito-Park deal, Sinden brought in Peter McNab in a swap with Buffalo. All the 6'3", 210-pound McNab did after that deal was average close to 80 points per season over seven full campaigns in black and gold. While not quite as prolific as Esposito, McNab made it easier for the Bruins to get by without their former star center.

Three decades later, McNab is still one of the most underrated players the Bruins have suited up.

"He never got the credit he deserved," said McNab's former teammate Rick Middleton. "But Peter, they kind of expected it out of him. It was right around the time in the '80s of getting people with more conditioning and less body fat, so they were always on him. He was a big guy, and maybe not the fleetest of skaters. So they were always picking on him for something. And they were never satisfied with his game. Here's a guy, he scored 40, you should be pretty happy with him. I don't think we had another 40-goal scorer until I came up in the '80s and got them."

If his size and point totals weren't enough to draw comparisons to Esposito, the way McNab scored his goals were Espo-esque. Whether he was on a line with Terry O'Reilly and Don Marcotte, or John Wensink or Middleton were part of his trio, McNab set up shop in the area in front of the goal that Esposito once called home.

"People would always say to me, 'Why do you stand in the slot and shoot shot after shot in practice?' Because these guys are in the corners getting the crap kicked out of them, and they're going to pass the puck to me, I better be ready to shoot it," said McNab on a day off from his current job as Colorado Avalanche color commentator. "That's all they're asking me to do is shoot."

McNab scored 99 points over two full seasons with the Sabres before his rights were traded to the Bruins on June 11, 1976. Sinden said he liked McNab's accurate shot, and over time the player's skating improved. He impressed with 38 goals in his first season in Boston and then tallied 40 twice. He did it all despite some tough love from coach Don Cherry and Sinden. Famously, Sinden once criticized McNab loud enough to hear: "Your checking, McNab, has not improved by one iota." While the criticism sometimes sent McNab into a funk, that particular remark allowed Cherry to use a new nickname for McNab: "One Iota." McNab managed to shake off the verbal assault enough to be as productive a center as there was in his day.

"It's one of those things in life and it's a lesson that I've taught my kids. When you're criticized, you have to weigh it for what it's worth," he said. "And if it's valid and you can honestly learn, 'You know what? I'm not playing very well; I'm not playing with the kind of spirit that the Bruins played with, I deserve to be sat at the end of this bench.'"

O'Reilly remembers that nothing could stop McNab from getting his points.

"They would get mad at him for not being physical enough, because he was a big guy," said the former Bruins captain. "They'd bench him for a while. He'd sit there and ride the stationary bike between periods and keep himself ready. And the next time he stepped on the ice, he'd score a couple goals."

The exciting victories and the many times he lit the lamp outweighed the tough times for McNab, who remembers the years he played for Cherry's "Lunch Pail A.C." as the best of his career. At home or on the road, McNab loved the camaraderie of those clubs and playing alongside Bruins legends like O'Reilly and Wayne Cashman. A pat on the back from one of those guys was as satisfying as scoring, McNab said.

There were times that McNab shed his label for not playing physically. In December 1979 he famously followed his teammates into the stands at Madison Square Garden in New York to battle with some fans. And during the years he played between O'Reilly and Wensink—the "safest place in hockey" it was called—he obviously had to tussle now and then. In those days every scrum led to players pairing off, and McNab's popularity soared.

"Guys would argue about who had me first," he recalled. "One guy was holding on so tight, he ripped the skin off my chest. The last thing I saw, he was with O'Reilly getting the shit kicked out of him."

McNab might not have followed Esposito to the Hall of Fame, but he filled his predecessor's role perfectly for only one less season. That's something that should earn him tons of credit in Bruins history.

Bruins Just Missed Getting Jack

It's hard to imagine anyone but Jack Parker behind the Boston University bench.

The Terriers have earned three national championships—including the 2010 title—21 Beanpot trophies, seven Hockey East titles, and 23 NCAA tournament appearances with Parker at the helm for almost 40 years.

However, twice Parker had an opportunity to leave his alma mater and become head coach of the Bruins. Both times, in 1991 and 1997, he decided to stay on campus.

"On two different occasions I made the decision," Parker said months after winning that third NCAA crown. "And I stuck with it both times.... I guess in one way it would've been nice if little Jackie Parker from Somerville became the Bruins coach, but one of the reasons I didn't take the Bruins job is I kept telling myself, *Think about this after the press conference. Don't let your ego get in the way here.* The press conference would've been cool, the first check would've been nice, but it's a different lifestyle."

The lifestyle wouldn't have been the only different thing had Parker moved up to the game's highest level. He admits that he would've had to alter his collegiate tactics in order to succeed on Causeway Street.

"I would have had to change a lot, I think. It's a completely different way to coach," he said. "Rick Pitino [with the Celtics] learned that.... You don't run the show like you do in college. In college, you're the coach and general manager. Players are more concerned with what the general manager thinks than what the coach thinks nowadays."

Parker removed his name from consideration before the Bruins made their final decision for a replacement for Mike Milbury, who moved upstairs as assistant general manager, in 1991. The team wound up hiring Rick Bowness to be its new bench boss.

In 1997, however, the Bruins' pursuit was much more serious. In May of that year, after several interviews with several prospects, the Bruins offered Parker the job on a Wednesday and gave him until the following Monday to mull it over.

"The issue is, do I want the Boston Bruins or BU?" he said at a press conference at Walter Brown Arena when he chose a 10-year deal to remain at the college level over the Bruins' offer. "I've chosen to stay with a place that has treated me extremely well."

No one could argue with that decision in retrospect. Parker went on to run his win total on Commonwealth Avenue well past 800. The rink at state-of-the-art Agganis Arena, which he was a driving force behind the construction of, bears his name—Jack Parker Rink.

The Bruins, who have averaged a new coach every other year since that spring, hired Pat Burns instead of Parker. He won the Jack Adams Trophy as coach of the year in the NHL after leading the Bruins to a second-place finish in the Northeast Division that season. Burns won 105 games in three-plus seasons behind the Boston bench.

The question, however, still persists. Would the Bruins' fortunes have improved with Parker at the helm, and would Parker have been able to coach millionaires rather than scholarship athletes? Ted Donato, who in his post-playing days took over as head coach of his alma mater Harvard, would have been one of Parker's pupils on that 1997–1998 Bruins team, which finished second in the Northeast Division.

"I think he's a great coach, and great coaches find ways to fit into the situation. I think he would have been successful," said Donato. "There's no question that there are a great many differences. The same style might have had to been augmented a little bit. Because there are more powerful people in the organization, and some of them are wearing uniforms. But I'd like to think that he would've found a way to have success."

Parker, instead, found the best way for him to succeed, which was to stay where he could work his magic best. And the Bruins will never know if Parker's championship acumen would have translated to the NHL.

86 Fantastic Finish at Fenway

It sounded like something a mad scientist and Boston sports fan would cook up in his laboratory when it was first rumored during the winter of 2009 and even when it was officially announced that summer. What were the ingredients? A hockey rink, the Fenway Park infield, the Bruins, the Flyers, and more than 30,000 hockey fans packing the hallowed ballpark on New Year's Day.

When January 1, 2010, arrived, it was obvious that the 2010 Winter Classic—the third edition in the annals of the NHL—was in fact not the product of a madman but a magical life experience for lovers of baseball and hockey alike in Boston. And the fact that the Bruins rallied late for a dramatic 2–1 overtime win didn't hurt, either.

"You could tell our fans were just waiting for something. When we tied the game, you could just feel the whole stadium, the whole vibe was there, and you could feel it," said winger Mark Recchi, whose tying goal with less than three minutes left helped catapult the Bruins to victory. "You could feel our whole emotions on our bench go up another level, and it was a great thing to be a part of. We are glad to give them something to cheer about."

Win or lose, this Bruins performance would have made history just for taking place on a rink in the shadow of the Green Monster. While they were making history by battling the Flyers at the home of the Red Sox, the Bruins were also honoring history. They took the ice decorated in the brown-and-gold uniforms team vice president Cam Neely designed with Reebok months earlier. Different elements of the uniform represented different eras in Bruins history. The color scheme was the Bruins' original combination—what they wore during their first Stanley Cup–winning year of 1929. The crest was the club's original spoked "B" that debuted during the Bruins' 25th anniversary season of 1948–1949. The laces of the sweater were reminiscent of the teams in the '70s, including the 1970 and 1972 Cup winners. The gold socks were first worn in the '30s, including by the team that won the Cup in 1939. And the gold sweater was similar to the one introduced in 1940 and worn by the 1941 championship club.

Neely liked the way his designs looked in person and on the tube.

"They did [look good], and then I TiVo'd the game so I was able to see it on TV, too. And they looked great on TV, too. I was happy. At first there was so much history, and we wore so many different uniforms, so many different styles. But it came together very nicely, and I think everybody was happy with it," he said. "The players liked them, and I heard a lot of great comments, which is nice."

The Bruins goaltenders took their tributes to the past and the circumstances a step further. Starting and winning netminder Tim Thomas had a special mask painted to honor the late Fred Cusick, Boston's television play-by-play man for four decades. And backup goaltender Tuukka Rask's Winter Classic mask featured a mean Bruin eating a New York Yankees jersey.

The only thing that could've ruined the party was the weather. A steady snow had fallen the day before, making the teams' practices

The Bruins' David Krejci battles for a loose puck with the Philadelphia Flyers' Arron Asham during Boston's 2–1 overtime victory at the NHL Winter Classic at Fenway Park on January 1, 2010.

fun but unproductive. Game day, however, featured no precipitation, overcast skies, and temperatures in the 30s. NHL facilities operations manager Dan Craig kicked off the day by updating the media about the ice and weather conditions.

"Awesome. The Good Lord couldn't have done better for us right now," he said.

The Bruins might've thought they were seeing God as they headed to the ice for warm-ups led by Boston's living deity Bobby Orr, who patted the players on the back as they stepped through the boards onto the pristine outdoor ice. When the puck dropped, the Bruins had to then strike a balance between enjoying the pomp and circumstance of the situation and winning an important game in the standings.

"I think for the most part, once it got going, I think we realized it was just a game," Recchi said. "The weather was incredible. I mean, the atmosphere and the weather, it couldn't have been better for a hockey game. It wasn't too cold; it was nice. The ice was good. It was a little bouncy, but it was fast, and we were able to play hockey. I think the guys did a really good job of realizing that two points were at stake, and this wasn't just a game that we were going to go out there and throw our sticks and play around."

Recchi's late power-play score caused an eruption usually reserved for late October baseball at Fenway. The announced crowd of 38,112, minus the healthy showing of Flyers fans, got worked up into a frenzy. And then in overtime Marco Sturm made sure the memories of the Winter Classic would be sweet in the Hub.

"It's probably going to be my most memorable goal ever, and I'm going to enjoy it," said the German forward.

The night didn't end with Sturm's goal. A traditional hand-shake between the teams—usually only witnessed after playoff series—capped the evening for all but one player. After everyone left the ice, Thomas was announced as a member of the U.S. Olympic team. He took the ice to a rousing ovation with a Team USA jersey over his Bruins gear.

"This will go down as one of the most memorable days of my life and my career," said Thomas.

No doubt Thomas was speaking for legions of Bruins fans and fans of hockey throughout the world.

87 Gretzky's Shadow

"I half expected to see Kasper standing at the altar in a tux."
—Wayne Gretzky, who was married months after being shadowed
by Bruins forward Steve Kasper in the '88 Stanley Cup Finals

If you're still wondering, Steve Kasper did not attend Wayne Gretzky's wedding.

The Great One's quip about the longtime Bruins defensive stopper was one of many about Kasper over the years, whether he was shutting down Gretzky, Mario Lemieux, or any other of the league's best scorers. There was the night Kasper held Gretzky to no points in a game in Edmonton, and after the game the answer to the question, "Where's Stevie?" elicited the response, "He went home with Gretzky." When Kasper showed up in Montreal in 1982 to collect his Selke Trophy as the best defensive forward in the NHL, the joke went that he would follow Gretzky up to the stage when hockey's eventual all-time leading scorer accepted his Hart Trophy as league MVP.

Kasper even still owns a poster produced by the *Hockey News* featuring caricatures of Gretzky and his wife, Janet, on a beach. It's titled "The Honeymoon," and Kasper is seen in the background keeping an eye on the couple.

But for all the focus on Kasper as an individual stopper of the most prolific scorer in history, the Montreal native is more than eager to share the credit.

"Certainly, I'm proud of it and grateful for the recognition," said Kasper one night in Boston before working as an NHL scout for Toronto. "But I'm the first to tell you that it wasn't just an individual thing, it was a very team-oriented thing.... A player like

Kasper Showed Quick-Strike Ability

Known throughout his career for his defense, Steve Kasper still had a knack for scoring goals, including a career-high 26 in 1987–1988. In one game against Toronto in 1985 Kasper combined his defensive and offensive abilities during a 50-second span of a 5–3 win over the Leafs, as the veteran center recorded two short-handed goals during one Leafs penalty.

Two short-handed goals in one *game*, never mind one shift, tied an NHL record, which has since been broken. But Kasper could've broken that record had he been thinking about it during the win over the Leafs.

"The thing I remember about that game is later in the third period, I had another short-handed opportunity on a two-on-one, and I passed," Kasper recalled one night in Boston more than 20 years later. "And I remember the linesman yelling at me down the ice, going, 'Why didn't you shoot? You already had two.' But when you're playing, it's the farthest thing from your mind."

Gretzky was great at beating the double team…. And when the Bruins had me shadow him, it was critical that other players stay disciplined and didn't go to him also. So I've got to give my teammates a heck of a lot of credit, because he was a type of guy who, if two of us went to him, he was going to find the open man. So our team was disciplined enough that if he was open for a while and had time, no one panicked and went to him because they knew I was on my way."

With all due respect to Kasper's cohorts, the strategy never would've worked without Kasper's ability to stick like glue to a man hardly anyone else could catch up to. Kasper might've cost Gretzky a 100-goal season in that 1981–1982 campaign, as Gretzky scored just one goal in three Oilers-Bruins contests that season. In one of those games Gretzky managed just one shot on net.

Of course, "the Shadow" didn't always hold down Gretzky. In the Oilers' sweep of the Bruins in the '88 Finals, Gretzky tallied three goals and 11 points in the four games. That didn't ruin Kasper's reputation, however, as a master checker in Gretzky's eyes. A trade in January 1989 actually turned Kasper from Gretzky's nemesis to teammate.

"There's no question. He's the most effective checker I've had to play against," Gretzky said upon his Los Angeles Kings acquiring Kasper. "He played me hard. I like to get to the blue line, and he wouldn't let me. He made it hard for me to hit the angles. He made it tough for me to pick the holes and made it tough for me to go to the net."

Kasper was more than just a solid checker and penalty-killer and more than justified the Bruins selecting him with a fourth-round pick in 1980 over his eight-plus seasons in black and gold. In his last full season with the Bruins he totaled 70 points and helped Boston reach the Finals with 13 playoff points. In the historic Game 5 win over Montreal in the divisional finals Kasper scored twice against his hometown team.

When Gretzky was inducted into the Hockey Hall of Fame in 1999, Kasper didn't follow him. But Kasper's reputation as the superstar's shadow will always hold a lofty place in Bruins history.

88 Sweet Success for Sweeney

The NHL came back from the season-obliterating lockout in the fall of 2006 with rules designed to increase offense by strictly enforcing interference, holding, and hooking penalties.

This made it more difficult to battle guys in front of the net, but also opened the door for more diminutive defensemen to carry the puck up the ice and also use their speed and positional abilities to defend.

While the NHL returned, Don Sweeney did not. At 38, and with a year off because of the labor dispute, Sweeney decided to deny hockey fans the chance to watch him work his magic for one season under the new guidelines. Content with his decision at the time, Sweeney, now serving as one of the Bruins' assistant general managers, admitted years later that he wonders what it might have been like to throw his 5'10", 185-pound frame into the fire of the "new" NHL.

"Not that it's easier to play defense in this league by any means. Understanding that pucks are going to be chipped in, you can't hook and hold or whatever. But from the 'escapability' aspect of it, when you go to get a pass and someone's not locking you down and doing things, I think those sorts of things, I would have benefitted from these changes," he said. "But, every new era provides different challenges in different ways."

The challenge for opposing players during Sweeney's 16 NHL seasons, 15 of which were spent in black and gold, was to keep their heads up when crossing into the Bruins' zone and into Sweeney's crosshairs. His ability to level the largest of puck carriers, skate stride for stride with the game's best burners, and, for the bulk of his career, prove a perfect shutdown partner for Hall of Famer Ray Bourque, made is possible for Sweeney to overcome his size disadvantage and actually compete in 1,115 regular-season NHL games.

"I needed to use my skating ability and competitiveness from the defensive aspect of it, and embrace playing against the Mogilny, LaFontaine, Bure type of guys, the Gartners, the players who would beat you at full speed," he said. "I struggled against the Jagrs of the world. I guess everybody did. The guys who have that size, skill, and strength that are able to beat you a couple different ways. Those were real challenges."

Sweeney played alongside Bourque more than any other Bruins blueliner. The Harvard grad remembers apprenticing at Bourque's side when he first broke into the NHL and then in later years, as a more experienced and improved player, becoming a formidable sidekick. Hall of Fame *Boston Globe* writer Kevin Paul Dupont once described Sweeney as the "bow to Ray Bourque's Stradivarius."

Bourque held his longtime partner in high regard.

"He's a true professional in how he approaches everything: the game, his life, and his dedication to whatever he does," Bourque once said. "He's a hard-working guy, on and off the ice. He prepares really well, and he's a smart kid."

Sweeney wasn't just about defense. His 52 goals, 210 assists, and 262 points all rank among the top 10 all-time for Bruins defensemen. He was also as clean as a player with his grit could be; even if he doesn't want to own up to it—"I don't know about the cleanly aspect of it. I had my moments," he admitted. He never exceeded 74 penalty minutes in a season. And he was durable enough to skate in 1,115 regular-season NHL games. A lot of that had to do with Sweeney's dedication to a reported 52-week workout regiment, similar to that of his partner Bourque.

"Obviously, you're blessed with health, overall. I had my nicks and surgeries and stuff along the way, but most of them were during the off-seasons," Sweeney said. "I had to work awfully hard, physically to maintain a certain weight level and strength level, ratio-wise, to be able to play and be able to compete. And I was diligent about it."

Many an unsuspecting, dangling forward probably wishes Sweeney had been on the ice less. But they didn't get their wish until the lockout short-circuited Sweeney's run. But what a sweet run it was for Sweeney.

89 Ulf Leads List of Who to Hate

You don't have to be a Bruins fan long to know who Public Enemy No. 1 is when it comes to villains, active or retired.

Ulf Samuelsson's cheap shots against Bruins superstar winger Cam Neely in the 1991 Wales Conference Finals did more than just help Pittsburgh win the series. They hurried the arrival of the Hall of Fame forward's retirement, as Neely battled knee, thigh, and hip problems that could be traced to those hits for the next few years. Samuelsson, who accumulated close to 2,500 PIM in his NHL career, was a pest of the highest order. And his tendency to hit from the blind side and then not answer the bell when challenged prevented Neely from ever burying the hatchet with Samuelsson.

"I've said it a million times, I didn't respect the way he played. And I don't mind guys playing hard and physical, but respect needs to be there," said Neely more than a decade removed from his retirement and serving as the Bruins' vice president.

When thumbing through Bruins history, there are several names that have to inspire hatred in your heart. Whether you're talking about Pat Quinn, Dave "the Hammer" Schultz, Ted Lindsay, Wayne Maki, Mario Tremblay, Claude Lemieux, or Dale Hunter, the levels of disdain might vary, but there's no way you could do anything but boo if you saw any of them take the ice.

Quinn earned his place in infamy with his brain-rocking hit on an unsuspecting Bobby Orr during a 1969 playoff series against Toronto. Orr suffered whiplash and a concussion, which were diagnosed after a trip to a nearby hospital. Quinn, meanwhile, endured a difficult stay in the penalty box and then the Leafs dressing room with seemingly everyone present in Boston Garden wanting a piece of the Leafs player who had injured Boston's biggest hero. Orr held a grudge against Quinn for years, and the Garden faithful never forgave him.

Lindsay was a menace to the Bruins in the 1950s. In 1957 his high hit on Jerry Toppazzini caused season-ending facial cuts and fractures to the Boston player. While Lindsay denied it, Bruins coach Milt Schmidt accused Lindsay of intently leaping at Toppazzini. Lindsay also had a feud with Bill Ezinicki that dated back to their days in junior hockey. One particular NHL incident involved both players exchanging stick slashes to the head before duking it out. After Lindsay headed to the penalty box, he had to stop and fight again after Ezinicki broke free of the linesman.

"He was real easy to dislike," longtime Bruins fan Harvey McKenney said of Lindsay.

When physical play, and sometimes fighting, becomes a hallmark of your franchise's brand of hockey, you're players are bound to have their share to run-ins with the opposition. Sometimes tempers will flair and someone will step over the line. In the decades ahead there should be plenty more Bruins villains to add to the list.

90 Kasper Kept Cam on the Bench

As an opposing player, if you had the audacity to get under Cam Neely's skin, you always wound up paying a price. Things haven't changed much since Neely traded in his skates for a business suit as the Bruins' president.

One topic that still stokes Neely's ire, makes his eyes grow to the size of saucers and his voice become tinged with anger is the night of January 3, 1996. The site was Toronto, and the Bruins were coming off a 5–2 home loss to Chicago the night before. Despite dressing for the game and joining his teammates on the bench, Neely, along with fellow former All-Star forward Kevin Stevens, finished the night with the same amount of minutes played as he started it.

While that night was just a notorious part of Stevens' forgettable stint in the Hub and his rapid decline as a player post-Pittsburgh, for Neely that evening might've represented the lowest point of a Hall of Fame career.

"I certainly would never expect a free pass if I'm not pulling my weight," Neely explained one day in his TD Garden office. "My hip was bothering me all year, I had knee problems. I just felt that what I had done for this organization, I didn't deserve to sit on the bench in full uniform for 65 minutes."

It's still difficult to fathom that the Bruins would treat a player headed toward close to 400 career goals, who just two seasons earlier potted 50 goals in a near miraculous comeback from serious injury, as though he were some sort of scrub. Neely admitted after that game that he hadn't "played as well as I would have liked this year." But at the time he had scored 19 goals in 35 games. Days later, the same afternoon Neely and his agent Jay Free met with then–general manager Harry Sinden to clear the air, Neely was named to the Eastern Conference All-Star squad.

It seems that game the previous night against the Blackhawks was the last straw for rookie head coach Steve Kasper, who in a previous incarnation with the Bruins was a Selke Trophy–winning forward and a onetime linemate of Neely's. Neither Neely nor Stevens played well at the FleetCenter, or as then–assistant general manager Mike O'Connell put it, they "didn't play worth a damn against Chicago."

Sinden recalls Kasper calling with the idea to play Neely just on the power play in the Toronto game. Sinden admits it might've been best to just give Neely a seat in the press box. However, with injuries hitting the roster and a snowstorm preventing a player from being flown in from the Providence (AHL) farm club, Boston would've had to play the Maple Leafs with less than a full roster. The Bruins decided to dress Neely.

An Original Six matchup in the self-proclaimed "hockey capital of the world" at Maple Leaf Gardens was always a festive affair, regardless of the teams' records. On this night, however, hardly anyone paid attention to what was going on on the ice.

"There was like a murmur throughout the crowd," longtime *Quincy Patriot Ledger* beat write Mike Loftus recalls about that night. "All anybody was paying attention to was that. They'd go off between periods, and everyone would be wondering, 'Would they come out again?'"

The two benched players returned to their seats after the first and second intermissions. Loftus remembers that while Stevens rocked back and forth and shook his legs on the bench to stay loose, Neely hardly moved the whole night. He was obviously seething.

Boston was en route to just a second-place finish in its division and a first-round playoff exit. If earning a point in the standings on the road was worth embarrassing a future Hall of Famer over, then the Bruins accomplished their goal. After outshooting the Leafs 51–33, Boston came away with a 4–4 tie. Dave Reid scored twice, and Rick Zombo notched the equalizer 8:13 into the third period.

"I certainly don't want to create any controversy because I'm going on the record as telling you that I think the world of Cam. He was a great hockey player. But I was a young coach trying to win hockey games, and we were struggling as a team," Kasper explained one night before fulfilling his duties as a scout for Toronto. "I gave some other people an opportunity at the start of the hockey game, and my team excelled, and I stuck with it. I'm not going to sit here and tell you I regret doing that. If anything, I regret maybe the fallout from the media. There was no animosity of saying, 'I'm doing this for Cam.' I did it trying to win a hockey game. And I stand by that."

Neely missed just two of the next 13 games with injury—scoring seven goals in those 11 contests—before his ailing hip made it impossible for him to go on. On February 21, 1996, he played his last game in the NHL. As if having a career ended by health issues wasn't bad enough, dressing and not playing that night in Toronto made Neely's final season on Causeway Street a more bitter one.

"That's been tough because it was the last year that I played," said Neely, looking back. "The other reason it's tough is, I think of all the players I played with over the years and the types of players and the type of effort that some of these players put forth—never in a million years would I think I'd be a player who sat on the bench for a whole game. The lack of communication was disappointing. I thought I'd at least earned something more from that just based on what had happened throughout either my personal life or professional life while playing here. I just felt like I had done everything I could do—worked hard and came back."

Kasper outlasted Neely in Boston by just one more season. The Bruins sunk to sixth in their division the next season with him behind the bench, and Kasper got the axe. Over the next couple seasons some players and potential free agents pointed to the night Neely was benched as one of the tarnishing factors that made the Bruins a less-than-ideal destination.

In 2005 Neely was back in Toronto for his induction into the Hockey Hall of Fame, that night in '96 a mere blip on his impressive résumé. No one can bench him now as president of the franchise he made his name with.

91 Hear Rene Rancourt Sing Both Anthems

There are two types of Bruins games with two distinct feels.

The ones that are preceded by a generic anthem singer belting out "The Star-Spangled Banner," and the ones that feature Rene Rancourt, decked out in his black tuxedo, rocking the Garden with the U.S. national anthem and—when necessary—"O Canada." Rancourt's appearances bring with them an extra air of importance.

"Rene Rancourt has the ability to make any game look like a big game," said Bob Snow, who has followed the Bruins for more than 40 years as a season-ticket holder and sports writer. "But when he came out to do the big games, especially against the Canadian teams, there's something about singing both anthems that makes the game a little more special. But when he belted it out, you knew it was a big game."

The year 1976 was big in the U.S. because of the country's bicentennial celebration. It was huge for the Bruins because that was the year, on the recommendation of longtime organist John Kiley, that they hired Rancourt to sing the anthem before their games. For the next three decades Rancourt sang before every home game, and it was only in recent seasons that he scaled back his schedule with the Bruins.

"When I saw the intensity of the fans, the pounding on the Plexiglas, I said, 'This is my kind of scene. These are my people.' And I've been showing up there ever since without a contract," said Rancourt, who's not afraid to admit that he wasn't much of a hockey fan until he became a regular at Bruins games.

A student of opera and, along with his wife, Maria, a leader of a dance band that entertains at weddings and other family functions, Rancourt has in recent years matched Kiley's record of "playing for" Boston's sports teams. The trivia question was always, "Who has played for the Bruins, Red Sox, and Celtics?" And the answer was always Kiley, who has since passed away. Rancourt has done his old friend Kiley—the two met when Rancourt was a frequent anthem singer at Fenway Park—one better by "playing for" the Bruins, Red Sox, Celtics, *and* Patriots.

But it's with the Bruins that Rancourt is most closely associated. Whether hated-rival Montreal or less-thrilling Columbus is the opposition, the Garden crowd begins to buzz when Rancourt steps out to the end of the rug to kick off the night's festivities. And the Bruins' players take notice the way the fans do.

"He's such a legend over here that everybody knows who he is, and people really enjoy him singing the national anthems," Bruins captain Zdeno Chara explained. "He gets the crowd really ready.

Every time he sings, it's not too short, it's not too long. It's just perfect. I don't know how many times I've actually stopped to watch the anthem, but I would say it's in the span of two, three seconds every time."

There's more to Rancourt's pregame performances than just his powerful voice. Of course, there's the tuxedo, which became a staple when he once wore white tie and tails to a season-opener. After that, he kept getting asked where his tux was, so he started wearing one for every game. Now he can't do any public appearances without being decked out.

"If I ever leave the house without my tux, my wife scolds me," he said.

Then there are his performance-closing gestures. When the last notes of the songs are out of his throat, he gives a military-style salute, a point toward the camera, and a fist pump. The fist pump is a tribute to a player Rancourt really enjoyed watching, former Bruins forward Randy Burridge, who used to do the same gesture after scoring a goal. It's funny then that without knowing the story, Chara explained about witnessing Rancourt's fist pump: "That just tells you that for him, when he sings, that's for him like scoring a goal. So he's happy, that's good."

The salute and point at the camera require a little more explanation. Rancourt once got a call from what he figures was a "sweet, little old lady."

"She said, 'I pay for cable television, and I always tune in to the Bruins to hear you sing the national anthem. And after you sing, I change the channel.' I thought, *My God, that's the best compliment I ever got from anyone*," he recalled.

Rancourt told her that he would salute her after every performance from then on.

"So from now on I salute and I point—as far as I know, she's probably deceased," he said.

Rancourt salutes his fans, the Garden crowd lavishes him with cheers, and the Bruins get an extra pregame jolt of energy. There's no better singer-team combination in the Hub.

92 Read about Plimpton in Goal

"There was one major sport I thought I would never find myself involved in as a participatory journalist. Ice hockey. I had what seemed a logical excuse: I am very poor on skates."
—George Plimpton's opening words in Open Net

Fortunately for George Plimpton and every hockey fan who ever wondered what it would be like to man the crease and stare down enemy fire, *Sports Illustrated* editor Mark Mulvoy saw no reason why America's foremost "participatory journalist" should let his inability to do much with a pair of skates on stop him from joining the Boston Bruins for training camp in 1977.

Previously, Plimpton's book *Out of My League* detailed his attempt to pitch to the National League lineup before the second MLB All-Star Game in 1960. He also sparred with championship fighters Archie Moore and Sugar Ray Robinson and went through the rigors of training camp as a backup quarterback with the Detroit Lions of the NFL for what became the bestseller *Paper Lion*. He went on to detail his experiences with the Bruins in a series of *SI* articles and another book, *Open Net*.

While Plimpton's experiences could've taken place in any NHL sweater, it was the Bruins that approved of the writer's presence and even agreed to let him play in an exhibition game against the hated Philadelphia Flyers. Boston, just emerging from the "Big, Bad Bruins" days and about to start the "Lunch Pail A.C." era, probably provided an atmosphere for Plimpton's play and writing that no other club could. Along for the ride were Terry O'Reilly, Wayne Cashman, Rick Middleton, and Gerry Cheevers. And, of course, the bunch was coached by the irascible Don Cherry. You'd have been hard-pressed at the time to find a team featuring as much talent and personality as the Bruins, who would reach the Stanley Cup Finals the following spring.

Even the lesser-known players present at that '77 camp brought with them plenty of quirks and idiosyncrasies. Rookie goaltender Jim "Seaweed" Pettie made that quite clear upon meeting his room-mate Plimpton for the first time at the Holiday Inn in Fitchburg, Massachusetts. Pettie "appeared at the window, wrenched it open, and clambered in over the windowsill from the parking lot outside."

"Welcome to the Union," was Pettie's greeting for Plimpton, as both the professional and the amateur were now bonded by one thing—their position as goaltenders.

So armed with slightly improved skating skills from weeks of practicing on his own in New York, a wire-cage model mask issued by the Bruins, and a protective cup filled with an "entire front section of the *Fitchburg Sentinel* and *Leominster Enterprise*" (not to mention all the other goaltending equipment), Plimpton started his apprenticeship in the inglorious world of puck-stopping at the sport's highest level. His trials and tribulations weren't confined to the rink, as he got to see what life was like for the Bruins off the ice, in the taverns of suburban Massachusetts, and found out about rookie initiations (although he was spared).

When the night finally arrived to take on the Flyers at the historic Spectrum, Cheevers gave Plimpton a pep talk, and a few other Bruins helped the still weak-ankled skater rough up the ice around the crease the way netminders like it. For the first two minutes, it looked like Plimpton would be spared, as the Bruins dictated play in the Philadelphia end. Then the deluge arrived, as the Flyers scored on their first shot attempt. But during a Flyers power play,

Plimpton accounted for himself well with five saves (and help from the crossbar on a sixth shot). The writer/goaltender capped his performance with a remarkable stop of Reggie Leach, who had once scored 61 goals in a single season, on a penalty shot after defenseman Mike Milbury threw his stick at an attacking winger.

Plimpton famously moved out of the crease and then flung himself sideways before Leach's shot.

"He lifted the puck, and it hit the edge of one of my skates and skidded away, wide of the goal behind me," Plimpton wrote.

He was then carried off the ice by his temporary Bruins teammates in celebration of his performance.

No Bruins fan, or fan of hockey for that matter, could read Plimpton's account without a little daydreaming about being in the author's place. Of course, most would've also wanted to be part of the game-delaying mêlée between the Bruins and Flyers after Plimpton's stint on the ice, but the writer actually missed it while addressing some executives about his experience.

After sweating and working alongside Bruins players for so long, Plimpton, who passed away in 2003, admitted he found himself pulling for the Black and Gold from there on out. They had made him into a fan, just as his writing had made fans feel more a part of the NHL club. Sitting down with Plimpton's book is a great way for Bruins fans to pass a few hours and feel like they're behind the scenes with some legends of the organization's past.

Photos by Babineau

If you've laid your eyes on an action photo from a Bruins home game in the last 40 years, you're already familiar with Steve Babineau.

And if you've attended a game over that time at the old Boston Garden or the Bruins' current home rink, you've probably crossed paths with the club's official photographer. Never one to just sit in one spot and snap away, Babineau has been known to show up at different times in all kinds of different locations of the arena in pursuit of the ultimate shot.

That creativity is somewhat inspired by the Ray Lussier photo of Bobby Orr's Stanley Cup–winning goal in 1970. Babineau was a teenaged jock and big-time Bruins fan when Orr scored and went "flying" through the air in front of Lussier's lens.

"To see that picture as a fan, which I was, I was ecstatic," Babineau explained one day hours before game time while taking a break from his pregame preparations. "And later on when I became a photographer, it was like, *Wow, how did that guy do that?* And then to find out that the guy, in the long run, really wasn't one of the sport's number-one guys, it all really comes down to being in the right place, at the right time, at the right angle—location is key."

Babineau took over as the Bruins' color photographer in 1977 and has been the man behind the lens ever since. That means that he has captured more than one-third of the franchise's history with his camera. From the end of Bobby Orr's reign on Causeway Street through the years of Ray Bourque and Cam Neely all the way through Zdeno Chara and Marc Savard, Babineau has not only photographed them but done it with a unique touch.

In many ways, Babineau's photography style is a lot like the playing style of one of his favorite players to photograph from the days of Don Cherry's "Lunch Pail A.C." clubs.

"Every time Terry O'Reilly stepped on the ice, you didn't know what to expect," Babineau said. "He was either going to run over somebody, he was going to fall down three times, he was going to fight somebody, or he was just going to make this unbelievable play in the corner, come out and dipsy-doodle on the way falling down

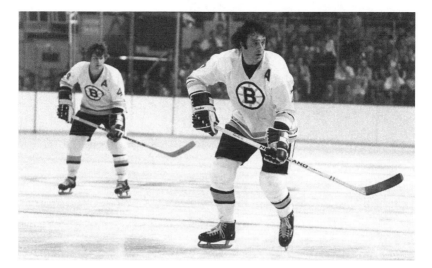

Phil Esposito (foreground) and Bobby Orr of the "Big, Bad Bruins" watch the action during one of the thousands of games Steve Babineau has captured with his lens since the 1970s.

and take a shot on goal. You knew every time he stepped on the ice, something was going to happen."

Babineau has also shot some of the best non-game moments in Bruins history, including the night Ray Bourque gave up wearing No. 7 and switched to No. 77 so Phil Esposito could have his number retired and never have to share a banner.

"To get Ray taking the jersey off when nobody else knew that there was another jersey. And then he's giving the jersey and the three jerseys are in the photo—he's wearing 77, he's handing him 7 Bourque, and he's already given him 7 Esposito, that picture right there to me is pretty spectacular," Babineau said.

The Babineau legacy will continue even after Steve calls it a career. He has been grooming his son, Brian, to take over the post—and the same post with the Celtics and Red Sox—since Brian was a teenager. As this century unfolds, Bruins photos at the Garden and in fans' homes will all have a Babineau behind them.

94 Boston Guys Have Basked in the Spotlight

As if playing hockey at the sport's highest level in front of tens of thousands of people every night isn't pressure enough.

Imagine doing it with tons of family and legions of childhood friends in the stands half the time.

Numerous Boston-area natives have had to deal with the extra distractions in a Bruins uniform over the last three decades since Americans became more prominent in the NHL. Winger Bill Guerin, a native of Wilbraham, Massachusetts, didn't have any problems playing at home.

Guerin finished off an 85-point season by racking up 63 points in 64 games after he was acquired from Edmonton in the 2000–2001 season. He followed up with 66 points in 78 games the next season. For his efforts, the fans voted him the Seventh Player Award (the player who most exceeds expectations) both years.

"I guess I nipped it in the bud right when I got here," said Guerin, who admitted he was a bit scared to play for Boston because failing under the home microscope could've been a disaster. "I just kind of said, 'This isn't just a homecoming for me. This isn't just Billy coming home to hang out with all his old friends and, oh, by the way, also play for the Bruins. This is coming to play for the Bruins first. This is my job.' And then everything else came second. That just kind of helped me.

"And my family and my friends did help a lot, too," he continued. "They didn't bother me with a lot of ticket requests or a lot of things like that. So that definitely helps, it takes a burden off of you."

The "Big, Bad Bruins" of the early '70s and then the success of the 1980 U.S. Men's Olympic Team in Lake Placid, New York, sparked a major influx of Americans into the Canadian-dominated NHL. Among the first to really break through was Walpole, Massachusetts, native Mike Milbury. Despite not being drafted and playing for some awful college squads at Colgate, Milbury battled his way to a 12-season NHL career—all with Boston.

"I don't think I felt the pressures right away," he said. "As time went on, we had some sorry years, and it was painful to hear booing at the team or in my direction. But it was a thrill for me.... I was still star-gazing when I got to the locker room. I'd only been to one Bruins game in my entire life before I played for them."

Unlike Milbury, who hadn't attended games at the Boston Garden, Mike O'Connell's family actually had season tickets for the Bruins for years. So when the Cohasset, Massachusetts, native was traded to Boston in 1980, he was suddenly living the career he'd imagined for years growing up and glaring over the Garden balcony.

"I was ecstatic. It was a dream come true," said O'Connell. "But I'll say that when it happens, now you've got to do it, now you've got

Picking the All-Bostonian Team

You can put together a solid couple lines and defense pairs with just Boston-native Bruins.

Up front, you could line up Ted Donato, Steve Leach, and Bob Sweeney. Bill Guerin, who only played two seasons in black and gold, can't start, but he could be on the second line along with Steve Heinze and Tim Sweeney. Every Bruins team needs enforcers, so Jay Miller and Chris Nilan could add some depth at forward.

On the back end, Mike O'Connell could provide offensive flair, and Mike Milbury would be your stay-at-home guy. While Hal Gill was never appreciated by the hometown fans, his size would be an important ingredient as a third defenseman. Dan McGillis enjoyed one solid year on Boston's blue line.

And then you look at the crease and have to make a decision. The 1980 "Miracle on Ice" hero, Jim Craig, would get the nod, although he played just 23 games for the Bruins and posted a 3.68 goals-against average. The only competition would be from Jim Carey, who won the Vezina Trophy the year before he was traded to the Bruins. In black and gold, Carey won just eight of his 29 appearances.

to show it. And it worked out tremendously. All I did was come to play hockey, and that's really what I did. All I thought about was the game of hockey, and I had the experience to get through that."

The hometown pressures didn't stop O'Connell from posting three seasons of more than 50 points, including a 60-point season in 1983–1984. Later on, in his time as assistant general manager and eventually GM, O'Connell took a different sort of heat for his personnel decisions—most notably the trade of star center Joe Thornton. But that had nothing to do with where he was from.

Some Hub-area natives, like goaltender Jim Carey (Dorchester), have failed along the way. And some, such as Shawn McEachern (Waltham) and Tom Fitzgerald (Billerica), were only in black and gold briefly. But for the most part, Boston has embraced its native sons, and they've returned the favor with solid performances. Ted Donato climbed the ladder from the Dedham youth programs to Catholic Memorial High School to Harvard before spending all or part of nine of his 13 NHL seasons with his beloved Bruins. His hard-nosed play and willingness to sacrifice his body for the good of the team made him a hero just like his idols, Terry O'Reilly and Rick Middleton.

"For me, personally, the experience was incredibly positive. I loved every second of it," said Donato, who stuck around to become Harvard's head coach. "I think I started out a Bruins fan, I ended a Bruins fan. So I think, for me, it was extra special."

Attend a Providence Bruins Game

You love the Bruins, whether you're at TD Garden or watching on television.

But the problem is, the Bruins go on road trips, they get nights off—so how can you get your daily hockey fix and still root for the Black and Gold? Well, a short jaunt down I-95 takes you from Boston to the Dunkin' Donuts Center—formerly the Providence Civic Center—in downtown Providence, Rhode Island. That's where Boston's American League farm club, the Providence Bruins, resides and nurtures the future stars of the parent club.

Every Boston Bruins fan has to make at least one pilgrimage a year to see the P-Bruins, as they're affectionately called. Whether you want to see recent draft picks who are on the cusp of stardom or veteran journeymen who are battling to keep their careers alive, a Providence regular-season game can actually exceed the action of an NHL game.

"It's exciting hockey," said Ken DiRaimo, a Rhode Island native and longtime Providence season-ticket holder. "These people, the players, they're fighting for positions so they can make it up in Boston. They play hard, no matter what."

DiRaimo, a self-described diehard Boston Bruins fan, as well, actually started attending games when the Providence franchise was known as the Reds. The Reds had a storied tradition, which included time as the farm club for the New York Rangers, Colorado Rockies, and the Bruins. In the 1930s Bruins greats like Milt Schmidt, Bobby Bauer, and Frank Brimsek went through Providence on their way to the NHL.

The Reds folded after the 1976–1977 season. Then in time for the 1992–1993 season, the Bruins' Maine Mariners farm club moved down to become the Providence Bruins. That first season, the P-Bruins won their division and led the league in attendance.

"People in Rhode Island and New England, they love the Bruins," said DiRaimo. "So just to be affiliated with Boston was phenomenal. That's what got this place so excited when they came here."

Providence fans could now root for players affiliated with their favorite NHL team, wearing uniforms with a spoked "P" instead of "B" with colors similar to Boston's, and then easily follow those skaters' careers in the NHL. Providence's ability to ice a championship-caliber team has fluctuated over the years, but in 1999 the P-Bruins—coached by future Stanley Cup–winning bench boss Peter Laviolette—captured the Calder Cup. Dave Goucher, the longtime radio voice of the Bruins, was honing his pipes in the AHL that season. He got a first-hand look at how much hockey fans in New England embraced having Boston's farm club so close to the Hub.

"I think Providence Bruins fans liked the fact that they could see a guy play on a Friday and then the next night you might see them play in Boston," said Goucher. "Let's face it, in New England, Rhode Island, Massachusetts, the culture of hockey runs pretty deep."

There are more perks to going to Providence for a game than just the chance to see a great game and future stars. There's ample, affordable parking, and the tickets are priced to encourage family attendance, as well. In-game promotions and giveaways keep the kids' attention during breaks in the action. And the smaller building means you're always closer to the action than you'd be in most seating in Boston.

But, of course, the hockey junky in you is going to enjoy the trip even more because there's a chance to catch a glimpse of the next Patrice Bergeron, David Krejci, or Glen Murray. It's just 50 miles door to door from the Garden to the Dunk, and it's well worth the trip.

96 Meet Me at Bobby Orr

First there was "The Goal." Then there was "The Photo."

As of May 10, 2010, there was also "The Statue," which serves as the perfect place to meet up with your friends and family before heading into TD Garden for a Bruins game.

Bobby Orr's Stanley Cup–clinching goal in Game 4 of the 1970 Finals against St. Louis ended the Bruins' 29-year championship drought and became an iconic image around New England thanks to the famous photo by Ray Lussier.

So there wasn't really any better pose to use than the one of Orr "flying through the air" after scoring that goal when the time came to build a statue in Orr's honor. The 800-pound bronze statue now stands at the west end of the TD Garden, some 20 yards off of Causeway Street at the head of the pathway to the building's entrance.

"When I arrived here from Parry Sound, Ontario, I really didn't understand what the Bruins meant to the citizens of Boston and all of New England," Orr said after the unveiling of his statue. "Neither did I realize how completely our fans would embrace us once we became part of the Bruins' family. And that reaction from all of our wonderful fans, their loyalty and support, made playing for the Bruins very, very special.

"The specific moment in time that we celebrate with the statue is something that we can all now nostalgically remember with fondness together each time we enter TD Garden."

Always a team-first type of guy, Orr was grateful that sculptor Harry Weber, ironically a St. Louis resident, created the base of the statue to include a replica of the portion of the Cup that bears all the names from the '70 Cup-winning team. Many of Orr's former teammates were on hand for the unveiling.

"There is nothing more valuable in life than the love and support from friends and family," Orr said. "That makes me the richest man in the world."

The idea for the statue first came from businessman Dan Flynn, who recommended it to Garden president John Wentzell and Bruins principal Charlie Jacobs. The process took off from there.

Weber had in the past created statues of Boston College star Doug Flutie and other sports icons. But he called the commission to sculpt Orr his biggest honor.

"I've had many commissions to honor sports and historical figures and this one is unique. It was meant to represent a hero whose stature in his sport is unmatched," said Weber. "But it also had to capture a specific moment in hockey history, a moment that won the Stanley Cup and defined the pinnacle of the entire sport of hockey. I had the help of Ray Lussier's famous photo, films, stills of Bobby, and the advice of hockey historian Bob Vitt to get all the details right. You can check them. Even the laces are placed the way he did, from the skates all the way to the blade of the stick and the way Bobby taped it that night.

"The process of making a bronze statue hasn't changed much in 2,000 years. It's one thing to make a metal figure stand up. It's another thing to make it fly through the air. This statue required cantilevering about 1,000 pounds of Bobby out on the toe of his right foot."

Orr's statue instantly perked up the area where it stands and became a hotbed of tourist and fan activity on game and non-game days. Taking a picture with Orr soaring up above is a must.

Next time you head to the Garden, make sure you meet up at Bobby Orr.

97 Visit Matthews Arena

The beloved Boston Garden is long gone, paved over, and is now a parking lot.

The TD Garden, not quite as enchanting but modern and temperature-regulated, is going strong.

However, neither of the Bruins' two most recent homes can match the combination of history and modernity of the franchise's original home rink—Matthews Arena on St. Botolph Street on the campus of Northeastern University.

Matthews Arena, known as Boston Arena until 1982, hosted legions of prize fights over the decades, and the greats in all weight classes—John L. Sullivan, Marvin Hagler, Sugar Ray Robinson—graced its ring. The Boston Celtics used the arena as their first home. Convocations and graduations have brought some of the country's most famous citizens as speakers. Hockey-wise, all the major area colleges used it as their home rink at one point, and tons of area high school athletes skated at Matthews Arena.

And in 1924–1925, the brand-new Boston Bruins—the original U.S.-based NHL franchise—called it home until the opening of Boston Garden in 1928.

The oldest multiuse athletic and special events facility in the world and the first indoor hockey arena, Matthews celebrated its 100th anniversary in 2010. Part of the celebration was a major renovation (the latest of many) that built a permanent snack bar, moved the press box from the balcony to a cozy booth just a few rows from the ice, and modernized the seats, locker rooms, and weight/trainers rooms. But there are still sights to behold that bring back memories of Eddie Shore and the original Bruins.

If you want to head down to Matthews, plan to go on a night the Northeastern men's or women's team is in action. Students and local fans alike will fill the seats to mimic what it must've been like when the original Bruins fans were first building a voice.

When you stand just outside the main entrance and look at the brick façade, those bricks cover what used to be an art-deco marquis out front. When you walk through the doors and look up and around, most of the Victorian lobby is still the same—even though a few coats of paint have been added over the century.

The rink, as it is today, looks almost exactly as it did when the Bruins first took the ice in 1924. If you look up, where a banner honoring the Bruins' residence in the arena for four seasons hangs, you'll also notice two different-colored boards in the ceiling. Some are covering where there used to be glass to let sunlight in and provide light when electricity was in its infancy. There also used to be windows around the sides, which could hinder the games with sun glare.

However, the balconies weren't added to the building until 1926, when the Bruins were so popular, they needed to make more space. Consider that the precursor to the Bruins moving to the Boston Garden. Now you can sit in the balcony, which hangs over the ice surface, and imagine what it would be like to see Shore flying down the ice or Hal Winkler make a save. The overhanging balcony might be as close to replicating what it was like to sit up above in Boston Garden as still exists anywhere.

There's no rush to get down and check out Matthews because the venerable old building isn't going anywhere. Over the years it survived two attempts to demolish it long after the Bruins left. In 1953 Garden Arena Corporation sold the arena to be developed as factories. An outcry from the colleges and high schools forced the state government to purchase the arena and keep it going.

In 1977 Northeastern took over management of the building and bought it in 1979 to make sure it would be preserved. With Northeastern giving the place its recent makeover, Matthews seems ready to last another 100 years. That's fortunate, because now Bruins fans can still experience it.

98 Watch "Rescue Me"

How can a one-hour basic cable "dramedy" about a post-9/11 New York firehouse grab a place in Bruins history?

Well, with creator/writer Denis Leary, a Bay State native who got his start in the comedy clubs of Boston at the helm, hockey and the Bruins inevitably were going to enter the mix. The combination came together with hilarious results in one episode in particular, titled "Sanctuary"—the series' season one finale.

Lyndon Byers, playing Leary's character Tommy Gavin's fire department teammate Ryan, recommends a new player for the FDNY to grab an edge on the NYPD for an upcoming game. That player is Mungo Monahan, who we soon find out is played by Bruins Hall of Famer Cam Neely.

"He's out on a leave of absence. He beat up three cops at a St. Paddy's dance. They couldn't even put the cuffs on him. He can score at will, he's as big as a goddamn triple-decker, and he loves to fight," Ryan tells Gavin about Mungo.

When the scene opens with a shot of the pregame locker room activity, we see a jumpy Mungo getting himself ready with smelling salts. During a pregame speech, Gavin warns his teammates not to fight until after the FDNY has a comfortable lead and he can "release the hounds." Then, before heading out to the rink, he pauses for the following exchange with Mungo:

Gavin: "Hey, Mungo, aren't you going to wear pads?"
Mungo: "Pads are for pussies."
Gavin: "What about a helmet there, pal?"
Mungo: "Helmets are for pussies."

As the game's ready to start, a cop player tells the ref to ask Mungo to put on a helmet.

"Just drop the goddamn puck and let's go!" yells Mungo.

If you haven't had your fill of Neely by that point, the on-ice part of the scene ends with Neely, Leary, and Byers duking it out with three cops. And the scene doesn't end until there's an all-out brawl between cops and firefighters just outside of the locker rooms.

The Bruins' appearances in *Rescue Me* don't end there. Byers and Neely made a return in the second season. A gentler Gavin, who has been taking some "happy pills" to improve his marriage, doesn't want there to be any rough stuff in the FDNY-NYPD match-up. When Mungo tries to fight, Gavin breaks it up and tells him to go sit on the bench for three shifts and "ruminate about what you just did."

"I would, but I don't know what 'ruminate' means," says Mungo.

It's pretty obvious that Neely's knack for timing isn't limited to clutch goals and momentum-changing body checks.

"That's always fun. Denis is a great writer. And Peter Tolan, his partner there, is a great writer," said Neely one day at his TD Garden office while taking a break from his duties as team vice president. "It's a fun show. It's a fun group of guys."

Later episodes featured Bruins legend Phil Esposito as a fire chief/hockey coach. So is there any irony behind Leary's decision to include some of Boston's most famous hockey players in his show about the Big Apple?

Not really.

"I need guys who could play hockey and act," Leary said after participating in the Legends Classic at Fenway Park. "And I'm obviously aware that Cam can not only play, but he can act. So he was easy. And

Bruins Show Up on Screens of All Sizes

Whether you dig up some footage of Derek Sanderson's talk show from the early '70s or catch Marc Savard on *The Price is Right*, it's not difficult to find Bruins players of all skill levels on the big and small screen. Cam Neely's appearances on *Rescue Me* were his most recent dabbles into comedy following his appearances in Farrelly Brothers flicks *Dumb and Dumber* and *Stuck on You*.

Of course, fictional Bruins also take center stage. Adam Sandler dons a Bruins sweater for much of his movie *Happy Gilmore*, and Jay Thomas played made-up Bruins goaltender Eddie LeBec for nine episodes of the Boston-based smash hit *Cheers*. Alas, LeBec, retired from hockey, met his demise while pushing an ice show castmate out of the way of an oncoming Zamboni.

You don't have to look too far to get find a Bruins player on screen—real or fake—trying to get a laugh.

L.B. has never had any fear as an actor. So it was easier for me to just cast those guys than try to get other hockey players. That's always the first requirement for me is—if they can come in and we don't have to use stuntmen for their action scenes, and they can handle the acting part of it. Phil Esposito was the same thing. They were looking for a coach who could improvise because we wanted to play with those scenes—who could look like a chief and act like a chief."

Getting a chance to watch a top-notch dark comedy featuring a few of your favorite Bruins heroes could be some great alternative programming during the off-season and All-Star break.

99 Go Green Like Ference

You can lace up your skates, grab a stick, and try to emulate some of your favorite Bruins players, from Zdeno Chara to Marc Savard to Patrice Bergeron. However, you're not likely to get the same results those high-end talents do when they're shooting, passing a puck, or throwing a body check.

Although he has been a less-heralded player on every team he has played for, including the Bruins, defenseman Andrew Ference has gained a measure of notoriety for the type of hard-nosed play that helped him overcome his size deficiency and earn respect from observers. He has also been a vocal proponent of something everyone can do with the same proficiency of an NHL player—preserve the environment and reduce the threat of global warming.

Ference was out in front when the NHL Players' Association Carbon Neutral Challenge started a couple seasons after his arrival. As part of the program, players purchased carbon credits to offset all the polluting that goes on during in-season travel. In 2008–2009 the entire Bruins team went carbon-neutral.

Bruins defenseman and environmental activist Andrew Ference skates with his daughter, Ava, during practice on New Year's Eve 2009, prior to the 2010 NHL Winter Classic at Fenway Park.

In big ways—like the Carbon Neutral Challenge—and small, Ference influenced his teammates during his tenure in black and gold.

"As far as players go, I'd be kidding myself if I said that everybody is all gung ho," Ference said. "But I know there's definitely been a few guys who it definitely impacted and definitely introduced to the carbon-neutral stuff. Just talking about it and not being ashamed about driving a Zipcar or riding a bike. So it's just about making guys think about it, and at the end of the day you change a few guys and get people to think about it, and that's half the battle right there."

Ference, always an environmentally conscious person, first became actively involved in the fight against global warming when he met Dr. David Suzuki of the Suzuki Foundation. It was Suzuki who empowered Ference to make a difference with more than just his stick and skates.

"He said, 'Look, you're going to stand for something. As a player you have an opportunity to talk and be intelligent or unintelligent. You make those decisions based on what you stand for. Whether you like it or not, you're a role model to a lot of kids. And when a kid thinks of you, what's he going to think about?'" recalled Ference.

Ference decided to be a positive role model. Using his notoriety as an NHL player, Ference has spoken at numerous schools and even made a speech at the New Democratic Party convention in Canada in the summer of 2009. Although he tries to get out the word as much as he can about positive steps people can take, Ference also tries to remain in the shadows a bit because he "detests" celebrity endorsements. He doesn't want anyone to do something just because he, or any other hockey player, does it.

Right to Play Gets Right into Spotlight

Andrew Ference did more off the ice when he joined the Bruins than promote green initiatives. He also brought Right to Play into the consciousness of his teammates, fans, and the media in the Hub. Right to Play is a humanitarian organization that works "to improve the lives of children in some of the most disadvantaged areas of the world by using the power of sport and play for development, health, and peace."

In the summer of 2007 Ference and fellow NHL defenseman Steve Montador made a field visit to Tanzania, where they interacted with the children who the charity benefits.

"It was pretty special to see how Andrew and Steve jumped in and got involved, playing games with the children," Right to Play deputy director Mark Brender told the *Boston Globe*. "We use games to teach children about malaria, HIV, cooperation, and how to use sport and play as tools to open up discussions on so many other topics. They allow children to express themselves and gain confidence. When he was there, he just jumped in with all his passion and gave it everything he had."

Back in North America, Ference influenced some of his teammates, including captain Zdeno Chara, to take an interest in Right to Play. In the summer of 2008 Chara made a field visit to Africa—a trip that famously included Chara and a camera crew climbing Mount Kilimanjaro to raise money for Right to Play.

Nonetheless, when he does make a presentation or chat with friends, opponents, and teammates, he gives them a major piece of advice.

"Whether it's me or somebody else recycling or going carbon-neutral or anything like that, I think it's a nice thing, it's a nice gesture, and it does a lot of good for your conscience. But the thing now that I realize is the best thing you can do is to vote, write letters, or call your representatives—get it out in the media," he said. "Luckily, I've been fortunate enough to do it. Personally, we can all do whatever we want at home, but it's not going to mean anything on a grander scale if government and industry don't take action....

"I just tell people now, 'Vote with your wallet, vote politically, and don't be afraid to demand action.'"

Ference wouldn't want you to do anything just because he does it, but know that if you do anything with the environment in mind—riding your bike to work or voting for a candidate with a green-friendly agenda—you're at least accomplishing something that some of your Boston Bruins heroes can do that's easier than scoring a big goal or making a big save.

100 Bruins Benefit from Camping Kids

The Collective Bargaining Agreement signed in 2005 to end the season-killing lockout of 2004–2005 brought the NHL a salary cap, rules for earlier free agency for players, and a limit to how much an entry-level player could make on his first contract.

Those factors added extra incentive for teams to develop their own prospects into NHL players, and do it fast. So in the summer of 2007 the Bruins decided to follow an example set by numerous other clubs and run a development camp shortly after the draft.

The camp would be a way for the team's most recent draft picks and several prospects already in the organization to get acquainted with the team's staff and give the front office and coaches a chance to assess the players in all aspects of their games.

That first camp featured such key components of the Bruins revitalization in the late 2000s as Milan Lucic, David Krejci, Tuukka Rask, Matt Hunwick, Byron Bitz, and Vladimir Sobotka.

"I think you can ask anyone who came to the first one that I came to, it was kind of a 'hell camp.' We almost had six-, seven-hour days. We did a workout in the morning and always a skate in the afternoon," Lucic said. "I think as young guys, it's great because it puts in your mind how hard you have to work to maintain at this level and be good at this level. Obviously, conditioning is a big part of it, and that's what we all took from it."

The camp was such a success—Lucic even used the momentum from it to earn a NHL job at this first training camp—the Bruins have continued to hold them every July since.

"I think in a lot of ways, maybe we were behind the curve just a slight bit not having implemented that prior," said Don Sweeney, who as director of player personnel and later as assistant general manager has been instrumental in the machinations and success of the development camps. "But that being said, I think you are seeing younger players coming into the league at a younger age now more and more readily. And so for us, the jumping-in point of running one of those, and having Looch, Krejci, and certain guys, and the next year [Blake] Wheeler, I think the timing was actually good.

"We wanted to make sure that these guys understood from day one, as they were joining this organization, what the expectations were going to be. We wanted to learn about them, let them learn about us and maybe learn a little bit about themselves and what they had to do to fill in the gaps to have a chance to play. I think it's gone well."

The Bruins always wanted to make the players feel as though they had already attended an NHL camp before they actually arrived for their first training camp.

"One of the biggest things, for me, was to watch those guys come back for training camp the very first time and feel, I don't want to say comfortable, but walk through the door—as I've described before—not staring at their toes, not being intimidated of the process of attending a training camp, some for the first time. Or better yet, challenging for a job," said Sweeney.

The development camps have been altered and improved on the ice by the Bruins to better assist in the maturation of the players. Off the ice, however, the camp continues to be a chance to foster camaraderie between guys who could be NHL teammates for years to come. A trip to Fenway Park is always a staple, as well as trips to other Boston landmarks.

"It's always fun to hang out with the guys," Hunwick said. "We have quite a few guys here now who were in that camp.... I think it's been good for everyone, to start those bonds and friendships a little bit earlier, and obviously it translated well that first year in Providence [with the Bruins' AHL farm club]. We had the camp, and then we ended up having a really good season."

That very first camp included a tour of Boston on one of the city's famed duck boats. That put the teenaged Lucic into a position even more different than that of a potential NHL forward.

"It's a group of guys, most likely, who you're going to be with in this organization, so it's nice to get things started off with something more casual with that," he explained. "They asked if anybody wanted to drive the boat, so [I said], 'Why not, man?' It's an experience, so why not make the most of it?"

The Bruins' future stars have made the most of development camps, and the front-office staff has done the same. That's why for the foreseeable future the camps will provide a summer dose of hockey for the Hub.

Acknowledgments

First off, anytime you embark on a giant endeavor like writing a book, you can't get through it without the support of those closest to you. For me, that means my wife, Amy, who kept me motivated through all the research and pursuit of interviews, and understood when the dishwasher didn't get emptied and other chores got neglected while I was immersed in tales of the Kraut Line and "Lunch Pail A.C."

Some longtime beat writers might shun a guy with just five years on the job in pursuit of details that didn't make it into print over the years, but Mike Loftus of the *Quincy Patriot Ledger* and Mick Colageo of the *New Bedford Standard Times* answered all my questions as both great resources and great friends. Sitting next to them and sharing in their running commentaries of the games on the ninth floor of TD Garden were also great stress-relievers. Their written work was also a great aid, as well as that of many others from the *Boston Globe*, *Boston Herald*, and other publications I was able to access through the Boston Public Library.

I jumped into this project with a very general idea of the highlights and lowlights of Bruins history. Getting specific was a daunting task that was made much easier, however, by those who know it better than I know my own life story. That starts with Kevin Vautour, an invaluable resource, a wealth of information, and a good friend. Access to his archives added to my enjoyment of the work, and his stories made me feel like I had actually lived through some of the great events he can recall without hesitation. Thanks also to Kevin for introducing me to Harvey McKenney, and to Harvey for sharing with me his tales and archives.

I couldn't have even gotten started with my research without Heidi Holland of the Boston Bruins' media relations staff, who helped point me in the right direction and allowed me access to her archives and contacts. Nate Greenberg's enthusiasm for his beloved Bruins and his cordiality toward me provided me with a huge boost and some great insights. I have to also thank Matt Chmura, Eric Tosi, John Bishop, and the rest of the Bruins' media relations staff for arranging interviews with current team members.

Interviews with some of the former Bruins players were a bit tougher to track down, and I couldn't have done it without Brian Zechello and Naoko Funayama of NESN, James Lamont of CBC, Jean Martineau of the Colorado Avalanche, Richard Johnson of the New England Sports Museum, Courtney Megliola, Cleon Daskalakis of Celebrity Marketing Inc., Steve Cardillo of gerrycheevers.com, and the Bruins' alumni office. Adam Kaufman and Chris Drapala of the Providence Bruins, and Jack Grinold and John Gruppo of Northeastern University were also very helpful providing me with interviews and information.

Tons of thanks go to Mike Milbury, a person whose opinions carry so much weight and I respect so much, for writing my foreword. I also appreciate all the current and former Bruins players, coaches, and front-office personnel who took the time to speak with me and answer my questions as best they could—regardless of how tough it was to relive some of the bitter moments in team history.

The moral support of my PR aficionado Bethany Tripp and TheBruinsBlog.net staff photographer Sharon Bradley were invaluable throughout this process.

Finally, to Michael Emmerich and Adam Motin of Triumph Books, I can't express enough my gratitude and appreciation for giving me a chance to be a first-time author. Your confidence in me before, and your patience with me during the process made this experience as rewarding as any I have had in my life.

Sources

Books

Babineau, Steve & Rob Simpson. *Black and Gold: Four Decades of the Boston Bruins in Photographs.*

Brunt, Stephen. *Searching for Bobby Orr.*

Carey, Mike & Jamie Most. *High Above Courtside: The Lost Memoirs of Johnny Most.*

Cheevers, Gerry & Trent Frayne. *Goaltender.*

Cherry, Don & Stan Fischler. *Grapes: A Vintage View of Hockey.*

Cherry, Don & Al Strachan. *Don Cherry's Hockey Stories and Stuff.*

Cusick, Fred. *Fred Cusick: Voice of the Bruins.*

Dryden, Ken. *The Game: 20th Anniversary Edition.*

Esposito, Phil & Peter Golenbock. *Thunder and Lightning: A No-B.S. Hockey Memoir.*

Fischler, Stan. *Bobby Orr and the Big, Bad Bruins.*

Fischler, Stan. *Boston Bruins Greatest Moments and Players.*

Halligan, John. *New York Rangers Seventy-Five Years.*

Keene, Kerry. *Tales from the Boston Bruins.*

Mancuso, Jim. *Hockey in Providence.*

McFarlane, Brian. *Best of the Original Six.*

McFarlane, Brian. *MacFarlane's Original Six: The Bruins.*

Park, Brad & Stan Fischler. *Play the Man.*

Plimpton, George. *Open Net.*

Podnieks, Andrew. *The Goal.*

Sanderson, Derek & Stan Fischler. *I've Got to Be Me.*

Vautour, Kevin. *The Bruins Book.*

Willes, Ed. *The Rebel League.*

Newspapers

The Boston Globe
The Boston Herald
The New York Times
Quincy Patriot Ledger
USA Today

Magazines

The Hockey News
The Hockey News: Sixty Moments that Changed the Game
The Hockey News: The Top 50 Players of All-Time: The Definitive List
New England Hockey Journal
Sports Illustrated
2010 Winter Classic Official Program

TV/DVD/Film

The Best of Bobby Orr
CBS News: Eye to Eye
City of Champions: The Best of Boston Sports
CTV News
Frozen in Time: Joe Thornton 2005–06
The History of the Boston Bruins
Pioneers: Phil Esposito

Websites

BleacherReport.com
Boston.com
BostonBruins.com
ESPN.com
ESPNBoston.com
GreatestHockeyLegends.com
HabsEyesonthePrize.com
HHOF.com
Hockey-Reference.com
HockeyDB.com
HockeyGoalies.org
Hockey-Notes.com
LegendsofHockey.net
NHL.com
Vermonter.com
WEEI.com

Also used were the 2010 NHL Official Guide and Record Book *and the* 2009–10 Media Guide *for each club mentioned.*